JUGGALO

BOOKS BY STEVE MILLER

Author, *Murder in Grosse Pointe Park:
Privilege, Adultery, and the Killing of Jane Bashara*
PENGUIN/BERKLEY, DECEMBER 2015

Author, *Detroit Rock City: The Uncensored History
of Rock 'n' Roll in America's Loudest City*
DA CAPO, JUNE 2013

Author, *Nobody's Women:
The Crimes and Victims of Anthony Sowell,
the Cleveland Serial Killer*
PENGUIN/BERKLEY, OCTOBER 2012

Editor, *Commando:
The Autobiography of Johnny Ramone*
ABRAMS, APRIL 2012

Author, *Girl, Wanted:
The Chase for Sarah Pender*
PENGUIN/BERKLEY, JUNE 2011

Executive Editor, *Touch and Go:
The Complete Hardcore Punk Zine '79-'83*
BAZILLION POINTS, JUNE 2010

Author, *A Slaying in the Suburbs:
The Tara Grant Murder*
PENGUIN/BERKLEY, JANUARY 2009

JUGGALO

Insane Clown Posse
and the World They Made

STEVE MILLER

DA CAPO PRESS

Printed in the United States of America.

For information, address
Da Capo Press, 44 Farnsworth Street,
Third Floor, Boston, MA 02210.

Editorial production by Lori Hobkirk at the Book Factory
Set in 11.5 pt Cambria

Cataloging-in-Publication data for this book is
available from the Library of Congress.
LCCN: 2016010174
ISBN: 978-0-306-82377-0 (paperback)
ISBN: 978-0-306-82378-7 (e-book)

Published by Da Capo Press, an imprint of Perseus Books,
a division of PBG Publishing, LLC, a subsidiary of Hachette Book Group, Inc.
www.dacapopress.com

Da Capo Press books are available at special discounts for bulk
purchases in the U.S. by corporations, institutions, and other organizations.
For more information, please contact the Special Markets Department at
2300 Chestnut Street, Suite 200, Philadelphia, PA 19103,
or call (800) 810-4145, ext. 5000,
or e-mail special.markets@perseusbooks.com.

10 9 8 7 6 5 4 3 2 1

CONTENTS

PART III

Unruly Ascent of the Clown 163

Introduction

There was in 1997 a moment when a good friend whose musical taste I respected greatly played for me *The Great Milenko*. He and I grew up together, trading obscure music tips from Atomic Rooster to Cockney Rebel while buying the Stooges LPs from the cutout bins. It was like that before Internet: you learned about good music from your trusted friends. One errant referral could sink one's credibility, and you'd be listening to your Jobriath LPs by yourself.

The first spin of *Milenko* was enlightening, a heady carnival ride with big production, wiseass insolence, and a Detroit-rock aesthetic. The photos on the CD sleeve delivered a graphic mesh of glam and Stephen King imagery—two open-mouthed dreadlocked clowns shouting into the camera. It was a welcome addition to the musical family.

What I did not know at the time was that Insane Clown Posse, the creators of *Milenko*, were greatly reviled by people who considered themselves serious music fans. The only thing I knew is that it sounded good to me, possessed of the "fuck you" that made rock 'n' roll the resistance it needed to be from the start and continued through the years.

✛ ✛ ✛

I dove into punk rock as a genre fully. I kept meeting people who were as into music as I was. They could tell you the history of the Velvet Underground, saw the New York Dolls more than once, and owned at least one Magma LP.

I was floundering in January 1979, taking a class at the local community college, although I couldn't tell you what it was about. College was hardly the place I wanted to end up, but someone told me they gave you money to attend. Sign me up. I got a $3,000 student loan. I bought a cheap Cutlass and a Gibson Melody Maker and dropped all my classes except this one.

A guy in the class had classic rock hair, a whisper of facial fuzz, and a notebook with a sticker that said, "The Controllers." The name got me interested, so we started talking about music. His pals from a little country town called Vermontville had formed a band and moved to Los Angeles a couple of years before. A week later he brought me in what turned out to be a great seven-inch, "Neutron Bomb" by the Killer Queers.

"Los Angeles is where all the punk rock in the US is," he told me. One day he proclaimed that "punk rock is great because it turns everyone into their dads"—words I have repeated numerous times over the years. This was one smart guy.

Insane Clown Posse has more punk rock in them than any of the sold-out fare hitting charts today. The connection for me came quickly: I realized that everyone, indeed, turned into their dads as soon as you brought up Insane Clown Posse.

✛ ✛ ✛

Not long after the introduction to *Milenko*, the Insane Clown Posse trucks pulled up to Trees, a nightclub and institution in the Deep Ellum section of Dallas. Along with the regular gear, the crew started to offload some crates packed with two-liter bottles of Faygo, a cut-rate soda popular in the Midwest.

"So what's with the Faygo?" the Trees manager, Kris, asked Shaggy, as they stood at the side of the stage.

"Oh, we just like to throw a little around at our shows," Shaggy told him.

The next day my pal Kris, the manager, called me. "We had this band from Detroit in last night, Insane Clown Posse, and everyone's pissed off about it," he told me. He knew I was from Michigan and enjoyed a good caper. "They threw Faygo all over the place. It got into the monitors and even some of the fronts."

"Okay," I said. "That's fucked up. But funny."

That same week I scored a promo copy of *The Amazing Jeckel Brothers*, ICP's follow-up to *Milenko*, from a promo pile of music at the *Dallas Morning News*, where I was a metro reporter. No one missed it.

A few years later I was in Miami on a sunny summer afternoon, temps around 87 and 95 percent humidity. I was walking near the University Metro stop near the University of Miami, and three Juggalos—two guys, one girl—came walking out from the stop and through the parking lot in full makeup. It was like seeing a walking cartoon, this blaze of bright white and black clown paint in the glaring sunlight.

I'm no fashion maven, but I thought it was a pretty cool thing to be sporting that look in a major city in bright daylight. I knew what they were and why, but no one else did, and people were freaking, staring, laughing, pointing.

They did this and endured the ridicule and made the statement because they believed in a music that made them feel part of something. Isn't that what rebellious music was at some point? A call to bring people together. The fifties greasers, sixties hippies, the seventies punks and underground ravers all came together with like-minded enjoyment of sounds and the culture around them.

But Juggalos are scorned and ridiculed, if they're acknowledged at all. Juggalos enjoy the outsider status, and that pisses off their critics even more. Juggalos are easily lampooned and don't seem to take themselves too seriously to enjoy the joke. Which results in even more angry foes. That finger in the eye of the music cognoscenti and culture elitists is a cool thing to watch.

The experiences were adding up for me. Although they may not end here, they certainly come to a head with this book.

When I began reporting this book, people who were interested in my previous reporting journeys were uninterested and unamused. When someone would ask me what my next project was and I told them it would be about Juggalos and the Insane Clown Posse, the conversation would go something like this:

Other person: "Those guys are terrible."

Me: "Have you ever heard them?"

OP: [hedging a bit] "No."

There was more than one conversation like this with people I had before thought of as open-minded if not enlightened.

"You're going to the Gathering?" one friend said over lunch one day. This guy was at one time a burly punk who had given many a beat-down. But to attend the Gathering? "Those people are crazy," he said. "You'd better be careful."

As it turns out, yes, they can be. The dude who cut off his nipples, which you will read about, made an interesting choice, for example.

Watch any number of video clips from the Gathering—some call them documentaries, but that's overly generous—and you can see intoxicated Juggalos flying their idiot flag.

But for everyone I ran into who made some dubious moves in their life, I also met some generous folks who were socially and culturally adventurous. They didn't have to wallow in the dirt for four days in July—they wanted to.

✝ ✝ ✝

Juggalos have committed some crimes. Too many to name. Really dumb ones too.

One of my favorites went down in 2014, when two Juggalos in Maryland tried to cut a Juggalo tattoo off the arm of their buddy because they felt he hadn't earned it. The arm had to be amputated. Both of the assaulters were sent to prison.

The real reason the two suspects gave for the assault, according to a police report, was that the victim had been smacking around his girlfriend, and the two didn't dig it. The tattoo burning was an afterthought, if "thought" can be applied in any manner here. But most of the news accounts focused on the tattoo burning and the word *Juggalo*.

A media group bent on sensationalizing crime will run with Juggalos, ideally in the lede and/or headline. It's all so unseemly, these clowns, and the perception that most Juggalos take up the lower ranks of society ensures that there will be little pushback or support for them.

So when an ex-con named Josh Durcho, who had an IQ of around seventy-two, strangled his family in their home outside Oklahoma City in 2009, the local newspaper reported it like this:

> The ex-convict accused of strangling his girlfriend and her four children is a fan of Insane Clown Posse, a rap/hip-hop duo known for profane lyrics about murder fantasies, necrophilia and violent acts.
>
> They perform in concert as "wicked clowns," wearing black and white clown makeup.
>
> A line in one song, "Murda Cloak," goes "I'm killing today to take this feeling away."
>
> The lyrics of another song, "Sleep Walker," include the lines "Choke 'em. Kill 'em. And sleep right through the night."

There are a million ways to report this crime, but putting ICP in the lede is a particularly craven stretch, journalistically speaking. And this kind of thing is rampant.

Many Juggalos have lived on the margins, which is one of the elements that makes them so interesting. That faction of them is, perhaps, more prone to committing crimes, just as anyone with limited means might be.

✝ ✝ ✝

"They are mistaken, that all law enforcement is lumping all Juggalos into the gang thing," Bernard Plaskett tells me, sitting in an interview room at the headquarters of the Las Vegas Metropolitan Police Department.

Plaskett is a gang squad detective, and he insists that some Juggalos are gang members.

"It's not us or the FBI doing this. The FBI is only going on the criminal statistics, which are of people who have admitted to being Juggalos that are committing violent crimes."

Plaskett slaps his right hand into his left palm to emphasize his point.

People who have admitted to being Juggalos . . . committing violent crimes.

He adds that the percentage of Juggalos that are gang members is low: "There are three thousand Juggalos in Las Vegas and I have five hundred in the [gang] database. That's a fraction."

I ask if I can see the gang data, the reports, anything that would confirm what he says.

No, he says, that's not public information.

Although Plaskett strikes me as a good guy whom I disagree with, his word isn't enough to convict an entire population of music fans.

I heard a lot of the same hedging when I asked police departments to show me their records regarding Juggalos during the time when the FBI was contacting them for their information on Juggalos for its biannual gang report, the study that, in 2011, included Juggalos.

The FBI gang assessment report in 2011 saw no nuance, as Plaskett does. No one ever thought a gang would push things as it has, but when the Juggalos and ICP filed their suit against the FBI over the gang designation, it was a moment. Even if they're the most hated band in the world, they are willing to fight back against a government that wants access to our iPhones and provides military weapons to local police departments.

There's a story there.

Steve
March 2016

PART I

The Hybrid Gang

1

The Most Hated Band in the World

First they ignore you, then they ridicule you, then they
fight you, and then you win.
—MOHANDAS GANDHI

ICP "an utter lack of talent or vision. Welcome to the
Terrordorks."
—USA TODAY, JUNE 1, 1999

Something big's gonna happen. We're so sure of it that if
my nuts were in a guillotine right now, I'd bet we
haven't seen our best days.
—VIOLENT J, 2010

At six o'clock on any given fall
evening, the Sunset Strip is hardly the kingdom of blow and babes
that it had been for decades. It looks more like the mall parking lot

in places and too much like Beverly Hills in others, all high-end sobriety and douchiness, people carefully walking and talking and eat-
ing $100 plates of whatever as long as it's noted on the menu that it
comes from "only the freshest local ingredients."

But tucked behind the now-shuttered House of Blues at the corner of Olive and Sunset is a market that's fresher than anything Michael Voltaggio can rustle. The Insane Clown Posse is in town, a
Friday night show by the rap duo that spawned the Juggalos, an un-
derworld that has stumped both the average and the hipsters.

The show starts early in the afternoon with a merchandise booth in
the parking lot where Juggalos can buy anything imaginable connected
to ICP and the roster of its homegrown label, Psychopathic Records.

Juggalos scoop up Hatchetgear to the tune of hundreds of thousands of dollars every year. Owning three hundred T-shirts pimping
the Psychopathic roster is nothing for a single Juggalo. The couples—
you could triple that. When the kids get old enough, be sure to clean
out the basement because you'll need some room. So setting up a
couple hundred square feet of selling space eight hours before show-
time is a solid move for the force that is Psychopathic.

At around seven o'clock, with the sun fading and the cool
sweeping down off the Hollywood Hills, a woman, let's call her
Jacki, crosses Sunset two blocks east of the venue, headed to the
Starbucks.

She's light skinned, black, in her late twenties, and sporting pig-
tails and black framed glasses. Jacki has been an ICP fan since she
was fourteen, and tonight she is seeing the band for the fifteenth
time. Her outfit is a tribute to the band's 1999 release, *The Amazing
Jeckel Brothers*. She's sporting a hatchetman jersey with the number
five on the back—*Jeckel Brothers* is the fifth ICP album—and her pig-
tails are tied in red and gold string in keeping with the colors of *Jeckel
Brothers*. She's wearing white ICP-branded athletic socks pulled up
to just below her knees with her high-top sneakers and black slim-
cut sweats.

"Hey number five, what's the score?"

Two white, preppy guys, maybe her age, maybe younger, sit in a red late-model Chevy Malibu at the stoplight as she crosses in front of them. They giggle to each other. *A weirdo*, they think, *perfect for some harassing*. Something outside their world is always safe to make fun of.

Jacki's heard this shit before and usually from more intelligent foes. She never wavers, moves on, ignores. Cool.

The light turns, her weakling tormentors move on to whatever meaningless, vapid fun such people move on to. And almost immediately a Ford pickup truck with two face-painted Juggalos drives by, headed toward the venue. They beep at Jacki.

They wave and utter the traditional Juggalo greeting: "Whoop, whoop!"

Jacki smiles.

In a sea of supposed weirdness on the fabled Sunset Strip they still have to stick together.

Later that night I meet Violent J and Shaggy 2 Dope in their dressing room at House of Blues. They are ICP, the platinum-selling duo and "the most hated band in the world" according to that most reliable arbiter of taste, *Salon*.

"'The Most Hated Band in the World' gave birth to the most obnoxious fans in the world, the Juggalos, who are virtually a gang at this point," the website wrote in 2013. The band liked the title so much it made a—wait for it—T-shirt commemorating the moniker.

J and Shaggy—aka Joe Bruce and Joey Utsler in their day-to-day—have been tight friends since they met in junior high. Imagine taking that roller-coaster ride to fame—and make no mistake, they are famous—and staying pals all this time. They live ten miles from each other back home in Detroit and see each other several times a week. And when they tour, they share a bus and a dressing room.

"Yes, it's a cape," Shaggy says to me as an assistant dresses him in his stage gear. I looked twice, remembering his Superman costume at Woodstock '99. "You know, there are few people who can wear a cape," he continues. "A vampire, superman. I'm neither."

J and Shaggy are both squeezing into black back braces. Both are older now, and neither cares a whit for fitness, and they've also endured injuries from a life of recklessness both onstage and off.

J spouts an endless stream of jokes poking fun at his three hundred pounds and ever-expanding girth. Then he gets serious. "I go to the gym a couple of times, and then I just say 'fuck it' and don't go back for a year," J says.

So for now it's some supporting—and slimming—elastic bands.

The backstage is empty. Oh, sure, Kevin Gill is wandering around, a tall amiable guy who's always in a good mood and manages to appear at virtually every ICP show. And Chop, J's right-hand man, tall like Gill, with tattooed eyebrows and a smattering of facial piercings, is always nearby. There's no booze and not a hint of rock-biz excess. Catering is Styrofoam containers with the remains of some fried chicken, and an array of iced Cokes and Diet Cokes.

After getting dressed, J looks around the room. "It's weird that we're playing here," he says to no one. "Usually we play Orange County. "

"They say this place is getting torn down," someone mentions. "Ah, no wonder they let us in here again. They have to wreck it anyway."

J thinks back, his mind rewinding to the first rock-biz ICP tour in 1997. The bus arrived early in the day and parked on Sunset, just as it did a few hours ago.

A guy about their age and half their size named Matt Zane approached the bus with a small retinue of video crew and some strippers. Zane was a twenty-three-year-old porn mogul obsessed with merging rock 'n' roll and skin flicks. "Can we do a shoot on your bus?" he asked. Zane was a "wolf," the ICP crew's term for a long-haired rocker type.

"I guess so," was the consensus, and before they knew it, there was some mad fucking going on. Welcome to the jungle, indeed.

Now, though, J and Shaggy are married fathers with no interest in such vices. "My family just went home a couple of days ago," J says a little wistfully.

He looks at the tapestries on the walls, all gauzy maroon wrapped around plaques of bluesmen like John Lee Hooker and Fred McDowell.

"I hope they preserve some of the cool parts of this place," he says.

Chop walks in and announces, "It's time," and hands both of them their cordless mics and opens a door leading to another door that . . . wait a second, Joe and Joey aren't moving. Both have their heads bowed as we prepare to move out.

"I say a prayer before every show," J tells me later. "I ask God to bless my family and the people that have allowed me to do this."

We walk through the doors, down some stairs, and into a darkened, narrow hallway, and then up some more stairs. We arrive at the side of the stage, and everyone stops. Fist bumps all around, smiles. The lights go out. Shaggy stands with his head down, waiting, as the first song, "Night of the Chainsaw," begins. He barks his first line while still standing beside the stage, then walks into the light.

The show never slows, song after song, as the backing tapes don't allow much of a break. The Faygo sitting in huge round buckets is quickly cracked by J and Shaggy—for this is who they are for these seventy-five minutes—and the crowd is baptized, Juggalo style.

I stand at the side, just out of eyeshot of most of the crowd and out of the way of the stage hands dressed as clowns who hustle constantly to replenish the Faygo and help soak the crowd during "Faygo breaks" in which a half-dozen clowns shake and open the two-liters of diet root beer and douse anyone within fifty feet of the stage.

At the front of the house, stage right, is Jacki.

She's singing every word to every song, and when the rain of Faygo gets to be too much, she takes off her glasses, wipes them on her jersey, and puts them back on without missing a word.

This is Jacki's night, her sixteenth ICP show. She can be ridiculed by kids taking the safe route through life, kids who refuse to take a stand or love anything outside the mainstream, but Jacki is happy to be basking in the love of her clan, the Juggalos.

2

Devils Descend on Small-Town America

Juggalos are ICP's insanely devoted, mostly poor and working-class white fans who gather annually at a farmyard somewhere in the Rust Belt for four days of drinking, drugging, tattooing, fighting and pelting newbies with balloons filled with grape Faygo (or worse liquids). The four-day festival, which also showcases a massive roster of horrorcore and past-their-prime mainstream rappers, culminates in the terrifying ICP taking to the main stage.

  —JAMES GRAINGER, CANADIAN NOVELIST

Think of it as a white-trash version of Burning Man, but with a much lower collective IQ, no good-looking people, pregnant drunk chicks with cigarettes, and empty two-liter bottles of Faygo orange soda littering the landscape.

  —RICHARD METZGER, AUTHOR, TELEVISION HOST,
   ON THE GATHERING OF THE JUGGALOS

By the time the sun crests the eastern horizon, a sea of Juggalos presses against a creaky wooden trailer set up on a stretch of Ohio prairie land. It's already 80 degrees on a late July morning, and that face paint looks like it would melt and take the face with it.

I mention as much to the tall, portly scrub standing behind me. "Doesn't matter to me," he says cheerfully. He's without makeup, and his round face and shaved head merge into what looks like a small balloon. His name is Shad Adamson, and back home in Salt Lake City, Utah, he's a bouncer. "This is our vacation. We wait all year to come to this, and whatever happens, it's all good."

The Gathering of the Juggalos is always good for the seven thousand people who manage to make it Christmas, Fourth of July, birthday, and New Year's Eve all rolled into one bitching blast. There are clouds of pot smoke drifting into the air above the crowd, and a few have already cracked the first of what will be a long day of Keystone, Old Milwaukee, or Natural Light beer.

The bedraggled trailer holds both will-call and walk-up tickets, as many of the Juggalos tend to leave things to the last minute. And the guys in the trailer trying to serve are frazzled—they aren't used to a few hundred people clamoring for entrance to their own little slice of Nirvana.

If this scene had a soundtrack, it would sound like the circus, all surging sideshow, like a Tom Waits calliope on fire. Confusion all around, from the muggled-out patrons to the three stressed-out thirtysomethings behind the two sliding-glass windows that are barely large enough to slide the demanded envelopes through.

"If you don't quit pushing against this trailer, we're going to shut it down," one of the handlers shouts out the window. He's sweating, and his glasses keep sliding down the bridge of his nose.

"Whoop, whoop," the crowd jeers back at him, a rallying cry with many meanings in the Juggalo world.

It doesn't take much to make this the place to be for the nation's five hundred thousand or so Juggalos—just a few hundred acres of reasonably secluded property that is, in this case, Legend Valley, an amphitheater about thirty-five miles east of Columbus, Ohio.

They come down Interstate 75 and US 23 from points north, jammed into Ford Tauruses, Chevy TrailBlazers, or pretty much any utilitarian rattletrap that could be used for the five-day weekend. Others, hailing from Tennessee, South Carolina, Virginia, Illinois, Washington, New York, and the rest of North America, use the Facebook ride board, offering to both help pay for fuel and provide some smoke.

A Juggalo from Peterborough, Ontario, wants a ride from either Canada or Columbus. "Seriously debating taking the Greyhound from Ontario (Canada) to Columbus and walking the ten hours to get to the gathering, but would prefer hitching a ride!" he posts.

Another Juggalo offers, "Any fan coming through Montana wanna pick a ninja up for his first gathering? I can help with gas and anything else."

Heath, Ohio, at ten thousand people, is the largest town in Legend Valley, and locals are checking out the arrival of the clowns.

A vanload of Juggalos from Iowa rolls in to the Burger King on the main street of Heath. Two girls, four guys, three of the six with Psychopathic T-shirts and tats, unfold into the empty lobby of the fast-food joint. One guy walks over to the garbage and drops two Faygo empties—twenty-four ounces, peach—and the rest ponder the menu and work the six-hundred-mile drive out of their bodies.

"I . . . feel . . . like . . . crap," one of them, a twentysomething female with dreadlocks in turquoise, red, and blue, says as she staggers out. Her upper chest is adorned with a hatchetman tattoo.

The Juggalos made the drive in one shot, stopping only for fuel and bathroom breaks. They will be among the 90 percent of attendees who camp on the site, sleeping in anything from an open-air sleeping bag to a full-on Luxe trailer hauled by an F-350 pickup.

Strangers going in and out of the BK regard the Juggalos. Anything passes for different in Heath, and these cartoon-colored characters have a Hanna-Barbera-gone-sinister impact that combines fun with a touch of danger.

The Holiday Inn Express and the Hampton Inn in Heath are sold out, two of three hotels that will be Juggalo central for a few days. The Hampton is where the Psychopathic crew stays. There's some considerable construction going on in the area, and tossing several thousand celebrating Juggalos into the mix makes the town look like a movie set.

"What is it?" the clerk at the Holiday Inn asks me. She's eyeballing a Gathering T-shirt on the back of a kid in the lobby.

"A music festival," she's told. That's putting it in its simplest terms, but more aptly, it's a festival that is significantly different from the corporate rape that is Fun Fun Fun or Electric Daisy Carnival. It's like a roller coaster for your eyes, ears, and nose, with free Skywalker OG. She's a pretty blonde about thirty years old and, as seems befitting for the carnival in town, has a claw-like left hand that she self-consciously tucks away whenever possible. It's called ectrodactyly, a cleft hand. There's no doubt she was the butt of jokes in her childhood.

Her smile is radiant, her manner charming and inviting. "Is this the thing that's being held out at Legend Valley?" she asks me. She's heard about this group of outlaws that would be descending on the town, but, she says, "I don't believe that stuff. The locals are always worried about something."

"Nothing will happen to Ma and Pa Kettle," she's told.

She smiles.

She would be accepted as a Juggalo, because if you have a quirk, be it physical or mental, you can still belong to one of the last true subcultures in America. You just have to be down with the clown as well. From there, it's a culture revolution for the ages.

✚ ✚ ✚

If there's a Juggalo around, there's some weed, and maybe more. The Gathering is a festival of drugs, although it's not as intense today as it was in the Cave-in-Rock days.

With the gang reports in the news, some of the more tight-assed cops seem ready and willing to nail someone firing up a blunt, but most law enforcement agents are willing to let it go.

At all of the Gatherings cops agree before the festival that the routine practice of smoking weed would not be policed.

"We understand there are a lot of drugs, but that's not our concern," says Licking County Sherriff's Captain Chris Slayman, who patrols the Gatherings at Legend Valley in Ohio, where Gatherings numbers fifteen and sixteen have been held. "Really, who cares if they have marijuana?"

So they smoke at will, wandering the grounds hitting joints, one hitters, toting bongs, and talking complete, baked shit.

"You know, they own the majority of Faygo shares. They just went in and bought them so they get all the Faygo they need," the kid said. He was sitting at a shaky, folding wooden table under a blue awning next to the ticket trailer at the Gathering entrance. It was a beautifully hot day, and the canvas of the awning baked as the trail of smoke curled up from the joint he was holding.

"Oh yeah?" I managed, mostly irritated at the inaccurate, stoned info. This is how incorrect information gets out there, with a dumb assertion from people who talked to a kid from a click-bait site like BuzzFeed, who puts it on a blog, and it travels from there.

He passed around the joint. A couple passed on the offer, afraid what he had was catching. Is stereotypical stupidity contagious?

At a tent encampment inside the grounds, a guy calling himself Ned sits in a quandary. In his right hand is a tabletop butane torch, the kind you can probably score at Home Depot. For most suburban homeowners it's a means to fuse rope ends or whatever.

Ned, though, is pondering another hit off the glass pipe in his left hand. He's dabbing. To drug alarmists, it's akin to freebasing but for potheads, and for most people it's just another way to smoke herb, although it does get you a little higher than smoking a bowl or joint. The torch synthesizes the pot into an oil, which is then smoked.

"Just a little bit really goes a long way," Ned says. He's wearing a hatchetman T-shirt, cutoff Dickies and shades. He's also baked at 2 p.m., and you have to wonder how that blowtorch mixes with the vast expanse of highly flammable canvas tent material around him.

Yes, Juggalos love them some smoke.

There is no more drug bridge at the annual Gathering of the Juggalos. The bridge was an open-air market where you could score anything from $20 baggies of Molly to $10 caps of junk, the former with a dubious molar mass—no, that *ain't* MDMA—and the latter undoubtedly stepped on with enough Noscapine to guarantee you a roller-coaster ride that makes a speedball feel like just another night on the couch in front of the TV.

The Gathering wrought the drug bridge. Pack a bunch of pot-loving music fans into a hundred-acre space, and you're going to attract serious action from the dealing contingent. These guys are like any good salesman, and they know a captive audience when they see one.

"I went to the Gathering three times, and I always sold out," one dealer from Oklahoma City says. "The kids were absolutely ravenous for whatever I brought—cocaine, acid, mushrooms. One time I had some Xanax, and one guy bought all five hundred. Ten milligrams too."

So sure, no surprise that these kids like to let it out when they hit the festival. It's a time-honored act of rock festival inebriation that pre-dates Woodstock. So in 2014, when the festival moved from Cave-in-Rock, Illinois, to Legend Valley, it seemed like a good time to end the bridge.

The last straw was the death in 2013 of twenty-four-year-old Cory Collins. He'd scored some heroin on the bridge around 4 a.m. on day three of the Gathering. Collins was an experienced user, but this stuff hit him pretty hard, and he asked some Oklahoma Juggalos who were lounging outside, watching the scene, if he could crash for a bit in their oversized tent, which could hold up to ten Juggalos comfortably. To refuse would be frowned upon in a place that stands for togetherness.

Twelve hours later someone went to check on Collins—the stranger, after all, had been out for a while—and he was cold and stiff. Collins was a junkie; his arms were covered with tracks. Some Juggalos disparaged him as an outsider who brought disgrace on the Gathering, but that notion was shot down quickly.

"We're a family, were not suppose [sic] to be hating or fighting each other," one Juggalo said on the Facebook frenzy that followed Collins's death. "Because we're supposed to be fighting together against haters."

Within an hour two semis pulled up on each end of the bridge, blocking passage and sending the drug dealers to the exits.

"They used that as an excuse to stop the bridge," says Sandra Rosko, an actress from Los Angeles. She's been to ten Gatherings, and as she stood outside the gates of Legend Valley, she puffed on a morning joint. "It was really time to do it. Some people were coming to the Gathering just for that, and it reflected pretty badly on the whole event."

So starting in 2014 the crowd included undercover officers from the local jurisdictions that made actual busts. It was easy pickings for any veteran narc. Imagine this: you see a topless woman with her boyfriend, proudly posing for a photo with "molly for sale" drawn across her chest in black marker (her name is not Molly). Then you watch her boyfriend, a skinny whelp who clearly doesn't belong in this place, sell something to approaching strangers. He was holding MDMA and acid. He's an easy target.

Another guy reported his backpack was stolen, and wow, he really needed that thing. At the same time, the cops were looking into an alleged assault, and what do you know, the backpack turned up in the same area. And in that backpack were 191 hits of LSD.

There's also a vetting at the gate. If you look like a drug dealer, you get sent packing. The guy with the new hatchetman sticker on his vehicle gets an extra look. One such guy came to this one in Ohio.

"Hey, you, stop. Pull over here for a second," yells Bill Dail, the CEO of Psychopathic Records.

Dail was watching a parade of traffic coming through the gates.

Two local cops stood with him and asked the driver to get out of the car. Coming onto the grounds gives them all they need to search, and sure enough, they found a sack of crystal, with the glass neatly divided into little bags. He wasn't arrested; he just had to turn around and head back to Columbus.

"Oh yeah, it's easy to tell who's coming there just to sell drugs," says Dail, a lifetime friend of J and Shaggy, who handles the overall coordination of the event. Dail is a solidly built, compact fellow who's been known to bust some heads, and when he asks you to leave, it's a good idea to do exactly that, as he's not going to ask twice. "They don't really have to be told twice once we tell them we know why they're there. They don't even try to lie their way out of it."

Cops are mostly helpful, but when the Gathering came to Cave-in-Rock, it was tough going almost the whole time, with an underlying vibe of tension between the Juggalos and the local law enforcement types. The sheriff's office wasn't allowed to have deputies on the grounds, so they took to waiting outside the gates and pulling people over as they left on a beer run, a drug buy, or whatever.

But when you get inside, the four-day music festival is a place, according to the Psychopathic promotional materials, full of "people with open-hearted kindness to one another."

"There was no reason to have [the drug bridge], and it had gotten out of hand," says Jason Webber, aka J-Webb, a rubber-faced, good-humored ex-journalist who serves as a media liaison for Psychopathic and all things ICP.

That didn't dissuade the Feds from trying some truly rookie shit.

Four men who represented themselves as agents from the Federal Bureau of Alcohol, Tobacco, Firearms and Explosives arrived at a back gate over by the wrestling ring near a small pond on the afternoon of the second day of the Gathering. Two yellow-shirted employees of the promoter were sitting back there, watching the production crew gate, making sure no one snuck in. The agents arrived on individual ATVs. No one knew which direction they came from; the nearest ATF office is thirty-two miles away, in downtown Columbus.

The men demanded to be allowed inside, claiming there were reports of minors drinking on the premises. Why the ATF cares about minors having a few beers is one of those mysteries rooted in a history of bullying and intimidation.

The guards were wise enough to know that having the ATF on the grounds, if that's who they were, would be a bad idea.

One of the guards got a Psychopathic honcho on the walkie-talkie. He came to the scene and had a brief conversation with the ATF agents, who were not used to being told they couldn't go anywhere, let alone a campground full of obvious dope fiends. The honcho called Farris Haddad, who in addition to being a Juggalo was one of Psychopathic's Detroit lawyers. He was on the grounds and reported to the scene as well just to tell the agents, "No, you can't come on this property—you don't have permission." The ATF bruisers sat in their vehicles, flummoxed at how quickly the Juggalos could legally defend themselves. Haddad asked to see their badges. The agents refused.

They then turned tail without a word, driving away to the east, the last one flipping the finger to Haddad or, more likely, the entire Juggalo culture.

✟ ✟ ✟

The evolution of the Gathering has moved it from what the uninformed public considered a cultural, low-rent free-for-all to a formidable music festival for everyone, but caters to the freedom-craving world of Juggalos.

"You know, there's girls walking about topless, and it gets everyone huffin' and puffin' and arresting her," Violent J says. "People pay good money to get in there, and if they want to walk around topless, please, let it go, man. She's partying at a rock concert. The only time we have problems is when there are people interacting with Juggalos. The Gathering is their time. There are no problems between Juggalos, and there's no reason to interfere."

Adds Shaggy: "Especially authorities. They don't need to control Juggalos, and that's been the problem in the past—putting their hands on them, trying to control them. No grown man wants someone to put their hands on them."

Finally they're getting their wish, at least in part. The cops are hands off at the fifteenth annual Gathering.

Meanwhile the classification of Juggalos as a gang in the FBI's 2011 *National Gang Threat Assessment* report drew support from a public that had looked askance at the subculture while damning Insane Clown Posse as among the world's most hated bands and Juggalos as the "most obnoxious fans in the world," in the words of the music scholars at Salon.com.

"No matter what you think of the music and Juggalos, everyone knows discrimination is wrong," J-Webb, the label flack, says.

Is there a fear that any form of popular embrace would damage the cred of ICP and the label?

"We'll always be the most hated band in the world," says J-Webb, a former legislative aide to the mayor in Dayton, Ohio. "You can't just turn that off. There will always be that elitist attitude toward us."

Violent J: "We love it. We're the most hated band in the world—that's our claim to fame."

Law enforcement in Legend Valley, an old-school shed with the main stage at the bottom of a jagged, steep hill, is provided by the

Licking County sheriff's office, which keeps a trailer on site for all of the shows at the aged outdoor venue. "It's an area that we mostly have country music shows," Colonel Chad Dennis says, watching the Juggalos set up their tents, campers, and trailers. "This one is a little unusual for this place."

As it was in 2006, the last time the Gathering was held in the county, down the road a piece at a place called Frontier Ranch Music Center. The cops had riot gear at the ready because of their intel on Juggalos.

The gear was never unpacked; cops encountered much more trouble at the country music shows than they did at the Gathering Frontier Ranch.

One night, as the main stage acts raged, Captain Slayman cruised the perimeter of the Gathering. A drunk guy who had fallen asleep in a stranger's car was as out of hand as it got. Slayman eased the young man—Matt, from Pennsylvania—out of the car and got him on his stumbling way.

Slayman sees Juggalos as any other group he has to police. The country music concerts, he said, tend to have the most violence. "They get drunk and fight. That's just what some of them do," he says. "I was raised very conservative and I am a Christian and that's who I am. I also believe in America and the Constitution and everyone has rights"

Including one of the most inalienable, the right to be stupid. And that includes the right to gobble hallucinogenics and wander around naked, clutching a cell phone, which is how officers found one festival attendee early Wednesday morning, walking down a main road bordering Legend Valley.

"He told us someone was chasing him," Slayman says. Sadly, he had a warrant and had to spend at least one night in the Licking County Jail.

Which makes the Gathering like any other festival, minus the drunk rednecks pounding on each other.

✦ ✦ ✦

It was pure good fortune that in 2014 landed the Gathering in Licking County, a farm-strewn block of land east of Columbus. The festival left its home since 2007, Cave-in-Rock, Illinois, after a dismal year, where a meager three thousand people showed and law enforcement and vendors sued Psychopathic for unpaid debts.

The year before, 2013, the Festival lost $700,000. The stunning loss caused layoffs and penny-pinching around the Psychopathic camp, and in 2014 some of the various events' hosts were being asked to pay for their own costumes.

Add a batch of misdemeanor disorderly conduct charges and a few felony drug raps to the kick in the coffers, and it was time to move to a new place—and hopefully pick up some new Juggalos on the way.

For a second they landed a spot at Cry Baby Campground in rural Miller County, Missouri. Concerned residents, however, contacted State Representative Rocky Miller, a Republican whose district includes the campground. They wanted him to wave his magic legislative wand and make the Juggalos disappear. But they were barking at the wrong guy: Miller is the owner of an engineering firm and is most certainly the only state lawmaker to have a Juggalo as an employee.

"He's a fantastic guy," Miller says. "I'm not a Juggalo, but I like some of the musical acts they've had at the Gathering, especially George Clinton. It's funny that people think I have enough power to stop the Insane Clown Posse."

Of course Miller has to get elected, so he gave the issue some lip service in his monthly newsletter to constituents. "I got a lot of contacts on the latest music festival coming to the area, 'The Gathering.' After some research, I discovered this festival is headlined by the Insane Clown Posse (ICP). The followers of the ICP are known as the Juggalos. This does not seem like the type of music I enjoy, but it does take all kinds.

So far we have notified the Departments of Natural Resources, Health, Transportation, Public Safety and Tourism. In addition we have contacted the secretary of state and attorney general offices.

We are also researching to see if the music promoters can be bonded to verify that all of our law enforcement and other tax-paid services will be paid for.

This festival has a bad reputation from what I can obtain from the Internet, but I am hopeful that if they can follow our local and state laws, everyone attending can have a good, safe time and all other visitors and locals will be protected.

That went nowhere to assuage the freaked-out locals, who were sure a new brand of lawlessness was headed their way.

Next the locals went to the local prosecutor's office. And when he found out about the pending invasion of the Juggalos, Miller County district attorney Matt Howard hit the books and found a law that restricted rock festivals. This law came about in the wake of a 1974 concert that featured a pre-fame Aerosmith, Blue Öyster Cult, Bachman Turner Overdrive, Bob Seger, Lynyrd Skynyrd, and various other now classic rock bands playing for stoned kids. The mayhem gave the establishment the incentive to do whatever it could to shut things down.

"We had seen all the news reports, and this group is particularly infamous for rowdy behavior," says Howard, who in a letter had advised Psychopathic that it could face legal problems if it moved forward with the Gathering. "Also, though, it's good marketing for Insane Clown Posse to get out word that they are banned or asked to leave. They want to be this scary thing, and it works. The phones were burning up; people were starting petitions to keep them from coming. When we told most of the people around here that they were going somewhere else, 90 percent of people were cheering from roof tops."

Cry Baby Campground manager Bee Enowski had already been popped for weed discovered growing in the outback of the property a couple of years before and was now facing some Juggalo-inspired hysteria from the locals. She was even getting threats for agreeing to base the Gathering at Cry Baby.

"I had to back out, with the threats and all," Enowski says. She's in her late seventies and has no appetite for this kind of bullshit. "I signed an agreement with [Psychopathic] not to talk about it, but they were very understanding."

Around this time Steve Trickle, operator of Legend Valley, which has hosted everyone from Willie Nelson to Bon Jovi since the seventies, reached out to Psychopathic.

It was an Altamont-like rescue. Like the Rolling Stones in 1969, who wanted to stage an outdoor free concert and had a hard time finding a place to put it, the Insane Clown Posse and its label were struggling with establishment backlash stemming from the FBI report in late 2011 that claimed Juggalos were a gang.

The report ranked Juggalos next to Bloods and Crips in terms of dangerous gangs, a ludicrous legal pockmark that resulted in a federal civil rights lawsuit from the ACLU against the US Department of Justice.

As a result of the FBI designation, ICP was persona non grata in numerous places, including many potential Gathering sites. Even before the gang thing, though, reputation trumped truth in many places.

"You know they worship Satan—I heard the services, the noise" in 2006, says Claudette Van Dyne, who lives just outside the Frontier Ranch Music Center in nearby Pataskala. She pauses for a second to consider the serious charge she just levied. "It certainly wasn't God, which is who I worship."

Van Dyne said she heard the services from the backyard of her home, which is right across the river from the venue. "They look so weird, with all their makeup and their tattoos from head to toe."

She claims the Juggalos also teased her about her Siberian Husky, who was barking at them—which only added to her anxiety, given her belief that Juggalos harbor a proclivity for ritual slaughter. "They also take animals for their sacrifices," she adds, calling the Gathering attendees "Jiggalos." "We had four head of cattle that we locked up when the Gathering happened."

When the Gathering came back to her area in 2014, she was distressed.

"Oh no, does the county know about this?"

Of course.

In May a number of people, including a woman purporting to represent local residents troubled by the idea of face-painted music lovers in their midst, met with Ohio state senator Tim Schaffer at his Columbus office.

"The gang thing was brought up," said Schaffer spokesman Justin Stanek. "The citizens had done a lot of research and came in with articles on vandalism and violence, not just at other concerts but in general."

Which brings us back to the evolving Juggalos, who as people will always sit gleefully on the margins, despite growing public attention. The media list is generally capped at seventy-five passes, and it's become a job to sort through the requests and discern between bloggers and other scammers who are trying to skate on the admission along with serious publications including the *Daily Beast*, *Village Voice Media*, and *Vice*.

As recently as 2009, there was little interest from outside the Juggalo world, much less an established media outlet.

National attention to the Gathering and Juggalos simmered for years before it finally bloomed with the FBI designation and wider reports of deaths at the Gathering, even though there are deaths at any concentration of people.

"The media really started to pay attention when someone died in 2011," says Kenny Fritch. He's from Mesquite, Texas, is in his early thirties, and has been a Juggalo since he was in sixth grade. He's also an Eagle Scout, works in a car stereo shop, and takes his week paid vacation to hit the Gathering every year.

"People die all the time at [electronica festivals]," Fritch says. "We've had what? Three deaths in fifteen years? They have three deaths, at least, every year. But the public and the media seemed to start watching us as soon as those started to get publicized."

He's right. One can watch any number of ill-conceived "documentaries" on Juggalos and assume that loading up on cheap beer and low-grade weed is a daily ritual for just about all of them.

Nothing could be further from the truth, of course.

But the mythologized Juggalos are more breathtaking, with painted faces and warped minds that adore tales of murder and serial killers delivered by ICP. It's the admission to a world of freedom, silliness, and, yes, sometimes intoxicated idiocy. Just like some of the mental patients-in-waiting from the 1986 documentary *Heavy Metal Parking Lot*, which chronicled the scene outside a Judas Priest concert, Juggalos have performed for cameras in full-blown, shit-faced drunkenness, much to the detriment of the group at large.

Pan a camera at a gaggle of football game tailgaters, though, and you'll see drunken idiocy in truly full blossom, intoxication that is somehow aimed at supporting "the team," whichever team that may be. And let's not forget the paint—in team colors, of course.

"No matter what they do to the Gathering, where they have it, what they close and open, it's always good to be home, which is what the Gathering is," says Hippie Joe, a fortysomething pipefitter and father of four from Detroit. He packed up eight people in his Ford Flex and headed out. "This is not a place where you're going to be judged," he says. With that, he takes a huff off a morning joint and moves into the throng of jovial patrons.

Later that day Hippie Joe does a phoner with Toledo radio station WSPD radio personality Scott Sands. "It sounds like you're much calmer than what I expected a Juggalo to sound like," Sands says to him, as if there is a wild blueprint for all Juggalos. "Hippie Joe, what makes you a Juggalo? What does that even mean?"

Hippie Joe is a movin' kinda slow, but he explains, somewhat incongruously, that it's all about family. "It's a time of year I only get to see certain people," Joe says. "I've met people here from Germany, Alaska, Australia . . . "

Sands is patient as he listens to Joe talk on.

"The media would have people believe that the Gathering is a twenty-four-hour pot-, alcohol-, and drug-filled orgy," Joe says. "We're not all drug crazed and kinky and looking to get laid."

There's some awkward silence, and soon the interview is over.

It took a few years of fandom before Bart Spanfellner began to hit the Gatherings. "I saw this Gathering on the Internet, and I said to my wife, 'I'm going to see this.' I'd been going to shows for years, but after that first one I knew that any time they have one of these things, I'm going. Everybody else has a family vacation, I have a Gathering vacation."

His wife has been to one Gathering and dug it, but not as much as Bart. So here he is, with a bunch of friends in their little compound of trailers and tents.

Spanfellner has had some bad luck in the form of a scrub-styled beatdown from the cops. Just a month earlier he was pulled over around 9:30 a.m. on Memorial Day Saturday in 2014 for the hatchet-man and Twiztid stickers on his car not far from his home in Flat Rock, Ohio, about an hour southeast of Toledo.

The cops smelled smoke.

"You don't smell it from me," Spanfellner said.

"Yes, I do. Please get out of the car," the officer said.

In the car were hash oil and a vaporizer pen. The bust made front-page news in little old Norwalk County. Spanfellner lost his job of fourteen years as a palletizer over it. Now here he was, with his other family. And with the blessing of his wife.

Having the FBI as an enemy in the age of anti-Fed sentiment is a good thing for the Juggalos, who may eventually be seen as those lovable, Faygo-swilling/spilling music fans. There is no questioning their fellowship and effort to dispel misplaced preconceptions.

"It seems like they go out of their way to make sure they contradict their image," says one sheriff's deputy, sitting in his car at a gas station across from the Gathering site. "They have the tattoos, the face paint, and the tattered clothes, then they hold the door for people and say 'thank you' and pick up after themselves."

Indeed, in a world that seems bent on social stratification, the Juggalos are still busting things up. They don't even need a drug bridge to do it.

> John Lemmon mans the gate outside the home of the man putting on the Gathering in Licking County. Steve Trickle lives in a wood-framed house one hundred yards from the main stage, and his long, narrow driveway is gated and, when events hit, manned by a guard, although not all as cheerful as Lemmon.

"Oh, I've seen them all here—ZZ Top, Rod Stewart, Allman Brothers," says Lemmon, who began going to shows at Legend Valley in the seventies. "The Grateful Dead were regulars here every year for a while."

Juggalos, though?

"We put anything in here that people want," Lemmon said. "They're awful nice kids. It's almost like they are aware that people expect them to do something nasty and they are trying to make sure to prove everyone wrong."

They will no doubt do something wrong. Everyone does, and Juggalos will forever be unfairly stereotyped. But for better or worse, this is what subculture is in the twenty-first century, where sameness is celebrated and ownership of creative outlets is compressed into the hands of a few multibillion-dollar corporations headed by individuals who make more money in a day than most of the patrons of their company make in a week, or month, or year.

The Juggalos are one last revolution, and the children of the revolution come armed with Ritalin prescriptions, FDA-sanctioned diagnoses of depression and anxiety, fatherless children, and incarcerated spouses and siblings. They come also with ebullient, irrepressible spirits sprung from their often-broken lives.

These outsiders, often with nothing in common other than their collective dysfunction, share one thing for certain: a spiritual connection to a couple of white-trash dudes who themselves come with the baggage of molestation, addiction, and crippling neurosis.

Insane Clown Posse are them, and vice versa.

ICP and their fans are a lonesome outpost in a blur of sameness, perhaps one last chance to outrage parents and any other authority. Little Richard, Elvis, Alice Cooper, Iggy Pop, Marilyn Manson—they drew outrage but were also tolerated because someone was making money off of them. ICP and the Juggalos are a pisser because the business is all done on the inside—no massive sponsorships, no branded stages.

It is the last American subculture, and it stands alone. And it is caustic and condemned, creative and coarse.

3

Cops Hate Weirdos

*Insane Clown Posse is a "horrorcore" rap-metal act
known for its scary clown make-up and elaborate,
theatrical concerts that have featured open fires, chain
saws and liters of soda dousing the audience.*
—SIOUX FALLS ARGUS-LEADER,
SIOUX FALLS, SD, SEPTEMBER 10, 2014

Never mind that ICP has never
used real chainsaws during a show. It's all part of the fountain of
misinformation has been spewing for a long time. In Juggalo land,
rumor and outright lies are part of the conversation, sometimes just
for the fun of it. Violent J is dead? Sure, let's go with that. Juggalos
have been deemed a hate group by the Southern Poverty Law Center? Sure. (Not true.)

The painfully misguided gang connection to Juggalos was
launched a thousand miles from Sioux Falls in Salt Lake City, Utah,
where ICP fans first became an FBI target.

The crime theme of the region is crazy white motherfucker, which cues the Juggalo stereotype. In Utah, like most other places, a second-degree felony becomes a first degree if the alleged actor is deemed a gang member.

FBI agents in the agency's safe streets/gang unit had observed, reviewed, and interviewed Juggalos in and around Salt Lake City for several months by late 2010. Given the city's legacy as a Mormon fortress, polygamy and closeted antisocial behavior of all types provided the perfect impetus for anyone with a decent sense of justice and a knack for fucking things up.

So a Juggalo could get himself into all kinds of trouble. Three wives is no big deal behind closed doors, but slapping on some cheap face paint and rockin' Twiztid—now that's some serious shit.

The cops had long been averse to anyone who dared to step outside the mainstream. Punk rockers were harassed, and law and order—not to mention a good dose of blind allegiance to authority—is a whole other article of faith.

The fact that most Juggalos in Salt Lake City are harmless blue-collar boys and girls, men and women, working in the service economy didn't dissuade cops from being positive they were purveyors of a high level criminal enterprise, led by a couple of misfits who liked to sing carny-inspired songs about fantasy serial killers.

In the fall of 2010 the Salt Lake City Police Department went full bore on the Juggalos as the federal gang report was being compiled. Nine gang officers were assigned to take care of the Juggalos. An affidavit for a search warrant was executed in November 2010 on a Juggalo living in an apartment complex who allegedly sold some pot to a confidential informant. The officer seeking a legal order to enter the suspect's apartment noted that officers "have observed the suspects and others seen with the suspects, all wearing clothing similar to a drug-related street gang known as the Juggalos ... members of this gang have a high propensity for violence and commonly carry and use knives, hatchets and other edged weapons."

In West Valley, a Salt Lake City suburb, the police department began tracking Juggalos in 2004, certain that the thirty or so in their midst were gang members. "Their lyrics are very violent, very vulgar," Detective John Lefavor, a gang specialist with the West Valley City Police Department, told a Salt Lake City TV crew in 2006. By the next year Lefavor was embroiled in a full-tilt propaganda war with Juggalos, and he had some company.

A youth pastor out of Virginia named Danny Holland was making the rounds, spreading the bad news about Juggalos. He convinced the parent groups and gang investigator units he spoke to that they were extremely violent and aggressive.

Holland hit Salt Lake City in 2007 as the keynote speaker at the seventeenth annual Utah Gang Conference. At that time his credential was as president and founder of the group Parent and Teen Universities, Inc., a for-profit corporation that has since called it quits. As he scared the attendees by assuring them that the average juvenile spends more time listening to music than going to class between seventh and twelfth grade, he also let them know that much of that music was violent. Worse, he said, "It's not just the music they're listening to—it's part of a creed. They're saying this is what I believe in life."

And there was Lefavor to pick up the propaganda.

Lefavor told the crowd that there were nearly four thousand Juggalos in Utah, but "I don't believe the majority of them are gang members," he said. "They're right on the edge."

Of course they are. Lefavor refused to do an interview for this book. There's just no way he'd allow his blathering to be contested.

Lefavor's ill-informed positing is similar to the one-percenter theory with regard to gangs, a term with a disputed legend in biker lore. After the Hollister Riot in California in 1947—in which drunken bikers from a gang called the Pissed Off Bastards went berserk for the sheer hell of it and tore up Hollister, then a town with a population of forty-five hundred, just an hour outside of San Francisco, later fictionalized in the Brando flick *The Wild One*—the head of the

American Motorcycle Association claimed that 99 percent of motor-cyclists were good folks who would help your grandma cross the street. The rest? Outlaws. The association today claims no one from its ranks ever made that statement. But because it was reported in a *Life* magazine article, it remains a part of the lore.

Federal law enforcement agents, like most cops, live on the main-stream side of the fence, in a world where different is bad. They've forever chased perceived wrong-doers, from whiskey bootleggers and rogue bikers to coke dealers and mafia dons.

To a lot of folks, Juggalo or not, they're not helping. No one in their right mind would burn a field of perfectly good marijuana, but then again, federal agents may not always be in that right mind.

Never before, however, have federal agents ever singled out a col-lective of music fans and made them subject to enhanced criminal penalties, as a so-called gang affiliation does.

In any state, when someone deemed a gang member is detained, their tattoos are photographed and entered into a database for fu-ture reference. In some states a gang member can receive a sentence of up to five years longer than any other violator for some crimes.

Since at least the mid-2000s the Feds believed that Juggalos were a gang, but they were having a hard time collecting anything other than anecdotal evidence.

A memo from 2008 out of the FBI's Springfield, Illinois, unit claimed that there had been twenty-two drug-related arrests at the 2007 Gathering of the Juggalos, the annual festival put on by Psycho-pathic Records. It also falsely stated that ICP merchandise includes actual hatchets for sale.

In November 2010, noting that Juggalos had already been deemed gangs in four states, an FBI agent in the Salt Lake City office began a deeper look at the situation. He delivered the information to an agent in the National Gang Intelligence Center in Washington, DC. From there, the federal crusade against Juggalos was launched.

On March 15, 2011, a classified FBI memo came out of Salt Lake City, titled "Juggalo." The unit was seeking approval from

Washington to proceed with a full-blown investigation into this threat to national security.

Law enforcement in Arizona, California, Pennsylvania, and Utah had already classified Juggalos as gang members years before an FBI analyst named Ryan Bausch launched the probe that would land Juggalos on the FBI's biannual gang assessment report, sitting next to the most infamous and violent gang-bangers in the land.

In one click of a mouse Bausch sent thousands of Juggalos into law enforcement purgatory, caused them to be targeted everywhere for their hatchetman tattoos, ICP T-shirts, and bumper stickers pimping Psychopathic Records.

Over a two-year period the FBI's Bausch, who was officed in Virginia, sent e-mails to law enforcement agencies across the United States, asking questions about their encounters with Juggalos:

> My name is Ryan Bausch. I am an FBI analyst assigned to the National Gang Intelligence Center.
>
> I am attempting to gain a national perspective on Juggalo activity within the United States in an effort to identify current threats and trends. I have narrowed down the areas in which Juggalo activity was initially reported when the National Gang Threat Assessment was submitted. In order to get a better sense of the emerging threats and trends associated with Juggalos, I am reaching out to areas where this gang is already established or has migrated to in the last couple of years. Below are the questions most pertinent to my research. Thank you for any assistance.
>
> I am looking for information regarding any criminal activity in your AOR that is Juggalo-related.
>
> Do the documented Juggalo gangs in your area have an established name to represent their group (Killer Klownz, Juggalo Rydas, etc.)?
>
> How organized are they as a gang?
>
> Is there an established hierarchy or leadership roles?
>
> What types of crimes are they committing?

Do they identify themselves as a gang?

What is the typical age/race of the members?

Do they have any rivals or alliances?

How long has this gang been a problem?

Are you seeing any unusual or new trends?

Are there any areas outside of your immediate jurisdiction that you know this gang has a presence? If yes, please identify the respective location.

Thank you again for taking the time to answer these questions. This information will be analyzed in order to monitor the growing Juggalo migrations, identify emerging trends in other parts of the United States, and help to better understand the dynamic evolution of this emerging STG.

The Feds refused to provide that list of questions to the public in response to open records requests, most proficiently carried out by MuckRock, the erstwhile repository and public records requesting machine.

Responses to Bausch's note came from the low levels of jail operations supervisors in California all the way up to an "intelligence analyst" in Nashua, New Hampshire, who e-mailed him back a local newspaper article about a 2009 home invasion in which the cops alleged that one of the perps was into Charles Manson, White Zombie, and Insane Clown Posse.

One respondent from a police department in Texas had spoken on Juggalos at the Texas Gang Investigators Association in 2006—a seminar titled "gangs and music"—and had met a number of officers working on "Juggalo gang crimes." Another from Oregon pasted in a link from an anonymous blog called "Juggalo holocaust," which calls itself an "anti Insane Clown Posse and Juggalo group."

More than anything concrete, though, the respondents provided media coverage. Uncritical and presumptive articles based in many cases only on the speculative assertions of cops.

The material that came pouring into the FBI's headquarters merged misinformation, police paranoia, sloppy journalism, and reckless accusations. The saga of Juggalo Daniel Crawford is a good example.

Crawford grew up in Carson City, Nevada, a typical gambling town set in the Sierra Nevada Mountains. His is a typical Juggalo tale: a dad who split when Crawford was eight, a mom who was not around all the time.

At Carson High School Daniel hung with the outsiders—they would be called scrubs in Michigan—as they were the people who had shit in common, usually a broken home and a lot of downtime. Toss in a general lack of intellectual curiosity, and you've got a wayward kid in the making.

Enter the Juggalo lifestyle. Daniel heard Insane Clown Posse's *Riddle Box* and never returned to his old life. He got a hatchet tattoo on his back, a signature cartoon that Juggalos sport as part of their fealty to the cause. He started smoking pot and ended up selling it as well. But when he got popped for distribution, he wasn't considered just a kid who sold a little weed on the side: he was a piece of the Juggalo crime puzzle that the authorities were selling to the public. Daniel got a six-month suspended sentence, and the cops got another Juggalo-related crime to feed to the FBI to bolster their hypothesis that the Juggalos were in fact an organized crime syndicate.

Some of the material Bausch collected was compelling in a gone-mental, sometimes violently voyeuristic fashion. New Hampshire police provided Bausch with a newspaper story from the trial of Steven Spader, who was seventeen when he murdered forty-two-year-old Kimberly Cates and assaulted her eleven-year-old daughter in a home invasion during the early morning hours in October 2009. The main weapon was an axe.

The lead prosecutor claimed that Spader was a fan of ICP and that his favorite song was "Pass the Axe." The *Telegraph* in Nashua published a post to Spader's MySpace page from Quinn Glover, one of Spader's codefendants.

Aug 11 2009 9:56 AM

NORMAL FRIENDS: Never ask for FAYGO.

JUGGALO FRIENDS: are the reason you have no FAYGO.

NORMAL FRIENDS: Call your parents Mr/Mrs.

JUGGALO FRIENDS: Call your parents DAD/MOM.

NORMAL FRIENDS: bail you out of jail and tell you what you did was wrong.

JUGGALO FRIENDS: Would be sitting next to you sayin "Damn . . . we [explicative] up . . . but that s— was fun!"

NORMAL FRIENDS: never seen you cry.

JUGGALO FRIENDS: cry with you.

NORMAL FRIENDS: Borrow your stuff for a few days then give it back.

JUGGALO FRIENDS: keep your shit so long they forget its yours.

NORMAL FRIENDS: know a few things about you.

JUGGALO FRIENDS: Could write a book about you with direct quotes from you.

NORMAL FRIENDS: ASK WHAT A FAYGO SHOWER IS

JUGGALO FRIENDS: SAY "WHAT TIME AND WHERE? IM [explicative] AMPED NOW!!!"

NORMAL FRIENDS: Will leave you behind if that is what the crowd is doing.

JUGGALO FRIENDS: Will kick the whole crowds ass that left you.

NORMAL FRIENDS: Would knock on your front door.

JUGGALO FRIENDS: Walk right in and say "I'M HERE B—!"

NORMAL FRIENDS: Are for awhile.

JUGGALO FRIENDS: Are for life.

NORMAL FRIENDS: Will take your drink away when they think you've had enough.

JUGGALO FRIENDS: Will look at you stumbling all over the place and say "B— drink the rest of that you know we don't waste s—.

NORMAL FRIENDS: will talk s— to the person who talks s— about
   you.

JUGGALO FRIENDS: Will knock them the [explicative] out.

NORMAL FRIENDS: Would ignore this.

Glover got twenty to forty years for burglary, robbery, and conspiracy to commit burglary. His first parole date is March 2017.

Later it was disclosed that the axe used in the slaying belonged to
the father of one of Spader's codefendants. Spader was convicted
and sentenced to life. The article provided to Bausch was the only
one that mentioned Juggalos. The kid was just a garden-variety
stoner with a homicidal bent and a love for horror rap.

But the cops could build a Juggalo case anyway.

One of the biggest coups for Bausch came from the California Bureau of Prisons. It spoke to everything you could possibly fear in un-
mitigated Juggalo hatred and violence.

In July 2008, Travis Phillips and Chad Hughes severely beat a known
homosexual inmate in a federal prison in Kentucky. The inmates assaulted the victim by repeatedly kicking him about the head, facial
area and upper torso. The victim was beaten because he sat at a
table in the dining hall which is frequented by white supremacist,
gang-related inmates. Staff transporting the victim believed the
beating is so severe that he would not live. Hughes is a known gang
member and Phillips is an admitted Juggalo with a "hatchet-man"
tattoo and "ICP" tattoos. Both had white-supremacist tattoos
as well.

According to court documents Phillips, the "admitted Juggalo,"
denied any gang affiliation throughout the investigation. The victim
lived, and a subsequent investigation found that the beating had no
basis in gang activity. In the pursuant case filed by the Bureau of
Prisons against Phillips, it was found that correctional officers had
questioned Phillips in violation of his rights.

Also included in the materials sent to the FBI was a report from the Sacramento Police Department Criminal Intelligence Unit from 2009 that didn't even name anyone as the perpetrator. The subject became "an admitted Juggalo gang member who is currently on active parole."

> The parolee detailed the criminal activity of his cell or "family" of Juggalo gang members. One of the important items of interest gleaned from this interview was the fact that there are two active but very different factions of the Juggalos: The music fans (Insane Clown Posse and other bands on the Psychopathic Records label such as Twisted [*sic*], Kottonmouth Kings, Dark Lotus and Axe Murder Boys) and the criminal street gang. The true difficulty for law enforcement officers is telling one from the other. The de-briefed parolee said he believes about one-third of all Juggalos operate in cells or "families" . . . most Juggalos are anarchist and hate all things establishment.

The flimsy, fact-omitting, and error-prone document was a shitshow of assumptions and allegations that would never stand up in court.

And there was more.

From Cañon City, Colorado, Bausch was sent a story from the local newspaper that quoted a local police officer, Maureen Sheridan, asserting that Juggalos "are all over our school system right now" and that they "do not like authority."

The cops in Cañon City were confiscating students' Juggalo trinkets, including bracelets or bags with the hatchetman on them. Sheridan said that if kids were wearing that kind of thing, "chances are they're smoking pot."

Almost as absurd as Sheridan's *Onion*-esque claims is the notion that a reporter could listen and write such crazy, *Reefer Madness*esque hysteria. The article was published in November 2010, and shortly after it came out "the cops came to our school and took anything that was related to Insane Clown Posse or Psychopathic Records," said a seventeen-year-old Juggalo who told the reporter his name was Milenko, copped from the ICP LP *The Great Milenko*.

Milenko attended Cañon High School West Wing, the "alternative" school for misfits and deadbeats.

"It was a shakedown based on nothing. And the kids who had any other band stuff—like the Deadhead kids with marijuana leafs on chains around their necks—they were left alone. It was all about getting the Juggalos."

Milenko said his friends, Juggalos and Juggalettes alike, went from social outcasts to alleged criminals in almost one day following the article. "No one ever stopped living a Juggalo life—digging the music and reading about ICP and the label or going to the shows. But they did stop talking with anyone else about it."

As for any parental pressure, "most of us only have a mom, and none of them cared. Some of them are Juggalos too."

The FBI report indicting the Juggalos as a criminal enterprise was a little late, actually. Police departments across the country were already figuring that the Juggalos were easy targets, marks for their well-funded gang units to justify their existence. These departments are always clawing for grant money for one thing or another. In this case, demonizing a lower-class fan base would work just fine.

✝ ✝ ✝

ops hate weirdos.
They've historically hated hippies, and all you have to do is take a YouTube gander at footage from the sixties and you can see the gleeful contempt in the nightstick-swinging cops' violence.

Check the 1968 Democratic National Convention, when the longhairs came to town in full protest mode. The year before, cops in Chicago admitted that they couldn't tell a radical subversive from a college kid on a rage-against-the-machine bender. To them, "a long-hair was a longhair." The FBI deployed a thousand of its own agents for security, while the ground troops came in at a seventeen thousand, including police officers and National Guardsmen.

"They were trouble—we read about them, and they spoke of causing trouble in our city for the convention," said Chicago police officer Ernie Bellows. "Poisoning things, having sex on the streets, and hurting delegates. It was all bad, and we could hear it coming down the pike, and smell it too."

Surveillance footage by Johnny Law of the MC5, the influential proto-punk band of *Kick Out the Jams* fame—playing outside the convention on a Sunday summer afternoon, the wind blowing, the patrons blissed out, tossing plastic bottles, talking to each other, smoking and drinking—is an early example of a Gathering.

The cops put a stop to that. The weirdos were in for an ass-kicking, and 650 of them were arrested. By February 1969 the FBI would have a file on the MC5 that ended up spanning 150 pages. They were not only weird, but they also advocated, loudly, for total revolution in the form of "rock and roll, dope and fucking in the streets." It was cultural carnage wrapped in music.

Flash forward to October 24, 1980, at a little place called Baces Hall on Vermont Avenue in Los Angeles north of Sunset Boulevard right before it jogs south toward Silver Lake and downtown.

The Los Angeles cops hated punks. The notion that a bunch of white boys posed a threat to a police force composed of well-armed jocks is curious until you remember their mentality: different is bad. Not only is it bad, but it pisses someone off who is predisposed to be a bully. So cops routinely shut down clubs that hosted punk bands like the Germs, Black Flag, the Dils, and Middle Class. As a result of the notoriety, the bands became even more popular.

Baces stood for Bulgarian-American Cultural Educational Society, and it sat right in the middle of a community of Eastern European immigrants.

The Bulgarians were cool with renting out the place for shows, and it was soon hosting everyone from the Go-Go's to Black Flag, The cops swarmed on occasion, but it was part of the game. There were various other entities that also hated on the punks, including the considerable and sometimes violent Mexican gang community.

On that fall evening in 1980, Black Flag was getting ready to play when the punks started goading the cops outside, taunting them. Showing zero restraint, the mace came out, the helicopters swarmed, the fire hoses blasted, and the billy clubs cracked skulls. It happened repeatedly over the years.

By 1985 the cops had decided that punk rock led directly to gang behavior. They managed to plant stories in the *Los Angeles Times* and the *New York Times* about the mythical Fight for Freedom, or FFF.

The *Los Angeles Times* wrote,

Their origins are in punk rock and heavy-metal rock. In part, these groups bear the stamp of the Satanism, Nazism and nihilism found in much of that music.

A Fight for Freedom member's sketch that was confiscated by police, for example, shows a swastika crossed out, a pistol shooting a bullet through a detached head and a punk rocker choking someone so hard the skull pops out of its skin.

That's pure punk-rock fare, the experts say.

The Feds came out with a report in 1995 that connected punk rockers to "a wide range of loosely organized criminal acts, characterized by perverse and negative behavior, including vandalism, drug use, homosexual assaults, and even homicides."

Even as recently as 2011 at the Key Club on Sunset, a three-band punk bill drew the law. When some people started throwing shit at cops, it's hard to blame the officers for wanting to bust some heads.

Juggalos are weirdos squared, and generally without the good fortune of having lawyers for parents. This gives law enforcement some extra confidence in such cases, where agents can feel free to disparage without likely blowback.

This dislike for the outcasts is how the Juggalos came to be a national gang, with full-on criminal implications for anyone professing to be down with the clown. In older times gangs were a problem for the local cop shop—they could club all the punks and hippies they wanted. But in 2010 the fear-everything lawmakers in Washington had gotten involved. In 2006 something called the National Gang Intelligence Center was created with a price tag of $10 million a year. The Public Code contained an obscure thousand words to create this center and was tacked on to a violence-against-women bill sponsored by Jim Sensenbrenner Jr., a Republican from Wisconsin.

It would require sharing of information between a bunch of agencies that may or not be qualified to size up anything outside a jaywalker. They would report and deliver assessments to Congress on just how bad it was out there on the mean streets.

And the deadline was closing in for the Bureau's 2011 National Gang Threat Assessment report, the primary objective of the FBI's fifteen-person gang team, composed of one agent and fourteen intelligence analysts.

Along with a number of other agents across the United States, Bausch was working on the report.

The Springfield FBI memo in 2008 was an opening shot at the Juggalos. It failed miserably to provide any details on just what the event was, though. Instead, it simply recounted some events of dubious veracity and origin.

The Gathering is a five-day orgy of clown love, where Juggalos from all over the world descend on an expanse of land, which invariably has to be changed every few years. Most memorably, between 2007 and 2013, the Gathering was held at 115-acre Hog Rock Campground in southern Illinois. Survival tales from bystanders are filled with drama, in which hipster-journalists from Brooklyn come back mortified with stories of unbridled intoxication and bad behavior.

To be sure, in a world of straight-laced, big-business-funded music celebrations like Bonnaroo or the Austin City Limits Music Festival, most people weren't prepared for the open-air drug market that is the drug bridge, or Lake Hepatitis, a green foam-covered puddle where bikini-clad women and their beer-bellied boyfriends frolic after ingesting cases of Keystone.

Cops weren't allowed inside the gathering by agreement with the Hardin County sheriff's office. But local FBI agents had been infiltrating the Gathering since 2001, when the event moved from an exhibition hall in Novi, Michigan, to a more spacious site in Toledo, Ohio. What those agents saw gave them enough intel to horrify and alarm their colleagues.

By 2012 there were already cops on boats in the river that runs past Cave-in-Rock, binoculars stuck to their eyes, getting an eyeful of topless Juggalettes and the carefree smoking of weed. One could imagine the blood vessels bursting as they watched, in a mix of titillation and outrage, open drug consumption and carefree public nudity.

Then the ATF made a move, and not for the first time.

"We had to lock the backstage down in 2012," says George Vlahakis, who booked the Gathering for years, working for Psychopathic. "They came into the park, but they didn't do anything. They drove in and then out and never even came backstage."

It was the first Gathering after the FBI gang thing, and "it looked like they were just keeping an eye out."

It had taken time to convince the Feds of the terrifying goings-on. But when the Gathering moved to Illinois in 2007 due to the need for even more room and a growing sense of resentment among the locals, the FBI took an interest in this phenomenon, a cast of characters better suited for a *Batman* episode—Cesar Romero would be proud—than a serious criminal investigation that would cost millions.

✝ ✝ ✝

A week before the FBI report came out, complete with a press release, J talked with the O Music Awards people, a group owned by media giant Viacom, about the importance and the force of Juggalos.

Although there was an awareness in the ICP camp of the four states that had given Juggalos gang status, it was a gnat bite, hardly anything that affected Juggalos as a whole. The interview was a bitch about what was about to go down.

> The things they say about Juggalos: "They're a bunch of fat losers or idiots." That's the things they write about us, as cold as that sounds. That's what we hear. You could take twelve Juggalos and stick them with twelve members of the Supreme Court Justice, and not one of those groups is any more important than the other one.

The annual FBI gang assessment came out on October 21, 2011, and delivered a full-on, erroneous assessment of Juggalos, who were mentioned thirty-one times in the document's one hundred pages.

The very next day Brandon Bradley of Sacramento, California, walked down a darkened street on his way home from work at an assisted-living facility. He'd been harassed for a couple of years already and was nineteen years old. He was wearing a Twiztid T-shirt and a hatchetman jacket.

Two patrol cops hit him with spotlights.

"Where you going?" one asked him.

Home, he said. His apartment wasn't far.

"How come you're walking in the street and not the sidewalk?" the cop asked.

The street was wider and in the dark less likely to have a rut in it, Brandon said. He was a scared kid.

The cops looked at his clothes. They wondered whether he was one of the sixty-nine kids in the district's Juggalo database. It didn't matter, though, as he wasn't doing anything wrong. They let him go.

Later Brandon would replay the episode, which would repeat it-self until he simply decided he'd had enough. Someone has to take a stand against these bullying police, even if it was a scared, skinny kid with a fading dream of becoming a cop when he grew up.

4

"Insane Clown Posse Clothing Is Banned"

*Yeah, I was in a gang. Everybody had a gang. We named
ours the Insane Clown Posse. We had members who were
Latinos, African Americans, whites. But we always got our
butts kicked. So we switched to being a music posse.*
—VIOLENT J, 1995

*Any music you can think of, there are gang members
that listen to that type of music.*
—SHAGGY 2 DOPE, 2015

*Every city in the world always has a gang, a street gang,
or the so-called outcasts.*
—JIMI HENDRIX

In the fall of 2011 no one was
gonna tell J or Shaggy about page twenty-two of the FBI Gang Assessment report.

Leah, Kodi, Andi, Dirty Dan—they were all working through their Friday at Psychopathic headquarters in what was supposed to be a celebratory mood. Insane Clown Posse's American Psycho tour was delivering the goods every night like the circus was in town.

They'd blazed through the heartland, Des Moines, on to the middle west, Denver and Boise, on to the West Coast, Portland, Anaheim, back to the East Coast, Philly, Worcester, and Massachusetts. They were now in Florida, then would work their way north to New York City at the Hammerstein, then some dates in Columbus, Indianapolis, and Milwaukee, and were finally headed home to play their annual Halloween show, Hallowicked, at St. Andrew's in Detroit.

J, Shaggy, and Billy Bill were up and at it early in the morning on October 22, sleeping on the bus outside Firestone Live in Orlando, where they had played the night before.

But the crew that morning at Psychopathic, usually spirited, especially amidst such a successful tour, was tame. They talked among themselves and once in a while broke into whispers. Then someone would look at a computer screen, reading, then look away, head shaking. There was conversation, and it came up, inevitably.

Then there was a morning phone call, just some basic label housekeeping, J, who was in Florida, was patched in. Everyone was talking, disjointed voices that you hear on a conference call.

"The FBI report . . . and Juggalos are a gang . . . " were the words J heard.

"What? What is this you're talking about?" he said. "There's something you guys aren't telling me."

They were holding back. They didn't want to break the bad news, but here it was: the FBI had released its biannual report on gangs in America, and Juggalos were not only in it but addressed explicitly on page twenty-two: "Most crimes committed by Juggalos are sporadic, disorganized, individualistic, and often involve simple assault, personal drug use and possession, petty theft, and vandalism. However, open source reporting suggests that a small number of Juggalos are forming more organized subsets and engaging in more gang-like criminal activity, such as felony assaults, thefts, robberies, and drug sales."

The FBI classified Juggalos alongside the Crips and the Bloods. It claimed Juggalos had infiltrated the Army and the Air Force, meaning the Juggalo ranks include "military trained members."

It went on to say that "law enforcement reporting suggests that Juggalo criminal activity has increased over the past several years and has expanded to several other states. Transient, criminal Juggalo groups pose a threat to communities due to the potential for violence, drug use/sales, and their general destructive and violent nature."

How do you break that news to your boss? Especially when he has ten days of tour left. But there it was. J dialed up the news on his laptop.

"At first I thought it was cool," J says. "I didn't realize what it meant for Juggalos. I was like 'fuck 'em. We are a gang—that's Juggalos.' We didn't understand the way it would play out and how much it affected our business. But most important, it takes everything we've done and shits on it and says, 'This is nothing but a street gang.'"

It had the same impact on Shaggy.

"I first thought, 'That's fuckin' awesome that Juggalos have this network that's a gang and people think Juggalos pose a threat.' I know they don't, but I thought it was great that the FBI thinks Juggalos are like MS-13. You know: 'Fuck yeah, Juggalos—we'll fuck you up.' But I was really thinking it was cool as in fictitious, the same as our music is. We don't roll around with dead bodies hanging out of our car, and we aren't gang members. But this was real life."

The cover of the second record, *Ringmaster*, which features a character with claws that represent rival gang signs of forks up and forks down, is a joke played by a couple of guys who failed miserably when they wanted to form a gang in the late eighties when they were teenagers with a bent for theft and *Clockwork Orange*–style violence.

No one would join them, and they figured they could be a bit more effective as musicians. Millions of sales later, it looks like a solid move. Then this, twenty-five years later, they finally front an alleged gang. It's bigger than they had ever dreamed of.

"To think that can happen to us—I was like, 'What's going to happen? Are we going to go to jail?'" J says. "If they can do that to a worldwide fan base, can they lock us up?"

Five miles and another world from Psychopathic HQ, Rob Bruce was walking through the parking lot at Community EMS on Eight Mile Road when he learned his brother was the head of a criminal gang.

"Hey, you hear about the Juggalos?" one of his coworkers asked him as he headed to the office to pick up the keys for the day's work.

His coworkers knew he had left Psychopathic Records to check into a new career as an emergency technician. There was a lot more to it than that, but Rob was happy to be doing something else for now.

Rob shook his head: no, he hadn't heard about it. He didn't listen to the news, which was broadcasting the FBI's declaration on the hour.

Media outlets that had previously ignored ICP and Juggalos were blasting photos of painted-up gang members as well as J and Shaggy. Local newspapers did their best to link Juggalos to anything in their small burg.

> A musical fan group with a local following that was thrown into the spotlight following a killing this summer has been identified by the FBI as a possible criminal gang.
>
> Juggalos, face paint–wearing devotees of the Detroit hip-hop duo Insane Clown Posse, appeared in the agency's 2011 National Gang Threat Assessment as a "loosely-organized hybrid gang."

Unlike traditional gangs, hybrid gangs have a "nebulous structure," according to the FBI report, and "are difficult to track, identify and target as they are transient and continuously evolving."
    —The *Keene Sentinel*, New Hampshire, November 6, 2011

The international press did its best to make the story germane.

But then, this is ICP we're talking about, and if their fans are half as dumb as their music, they might just be persuaded that a horrorcore gangsta is something to be.
    —The *Guardian*, November 3, 2011

But anyone who had grown up in Detroit knew Juggalos were just another part of the landscape.

Rob got inside and checked the Internet for the news.

"Cool," he thought. "Juggalos are going to think this is great. They're in a gang."

But as the day moved forward he considered how unfair this might get. He began to get angry. He'd already been considering a return to Psychopathic. He was married, had a daughter, and was sick of the stress of life as an EMT. It's one thing to dig into suffering on a fantasy level, but the day-to-day was wearing him out.

It was the first step toward his return to helping run the business his little brother and his friends had hatched. He'd been gone for four years, and maybe, he thought, they needed him. Even better—or worse—the Juggalos needed him.

"Some bones are harder to digest," Rob says now. "And that one got harder and harder. I really didn't see it going as far and having such an impact. But it got very heavy."

✚ ✚ ✚

That same **Tuesday** Paul Mohler left his house in Austin, Texas, to do his thing.

Mohler's job as training coordinator with the Texas attorney general's office was his best yet in his thirteen years with the state. He was paid $58,000 a year, in part to give presentations on Juggalos to law enforcement groups.

It took him to conferences large and small, in state and out of state. Eight months earlier, at the end of February, Mohler had presented to the South Carolina Gang Investigators Association in Myrtle Beach. Before that it was the Virginia Gang Investigators Association in Virginia Beach. At the Wyndham Virginia Beach Oceanfront hotel—now that was a good gig. Mohler's show was even hyped on the handout for that one: "Juggalo's [*sic*] in the U.S.," with the possessive apostrophe misplaced like someone who is not very bright might do.

So Mohler left his home that day to keep ensuring the world was safe from Juggalos. He took his PowerPoint presentation to a small meeting of the Texas Juvenile Detention Association, a group that focused on the correctional side of youth crime.

Mohler's pitch for his show was strong if you can get past the sad-ass writing: "This training workshop will explore the non-traditional side of gang life by looking at the Juggalo subculture. This workshop will explore the diverse subculture with concentration given to crimes prosecutable under gang or organized crime statutes. Participants will develop an understanding of the subculture, including characteristics that may be useful in the investigation and prosecution of criminal activity."

The PowerPoint that day told the juvie detention cops one thing up front: "Not all Juggalos are gang members, use caution when labeling any group."

Mohler proceeded through his slides. Under a slide that defined "basic identifiers," Mohler wrote, "Fago soda obsession." Who could be troubled to check the spelling on Faygo? Another slide featured what has become the main resource for intelligence on Juggalos: the Internet.

"Social networking websites are a potential gold mine of raw information, intelligence and on occasion proof of a crime. Court has ruled that social networking information is admissible [in court] in gang cases," read one slide titled "Gangs and the Internet."

The slide headed "Juggalo Crimes . . . just a few" noted four shootings in which the cops allege the perps were Juggalos. None were in Texas.

Then the biggie for prosecutors: "If they have common identifying signs and symbols (WC, hatchet man, whoop whoop), leadership structure (Juggalo family small cell structure) commit crimes (drugs to murder). They may fall under Texas statute for classification as a gang and for enhanced punishment."

In parting, Mohler advised to look for weapons and drugs when in contact with a Juggalo, and once more, "Not all Juggalos are gang members."

That's a tired line, like someone trying to fend off racism allegations by saying, "Wait, some of my best friends are black." The implication is clear despite any protests.

The Texas attorney general's office fought when it received a public information request for more information on its Juggalo workshops. It balked, insisting that releasing the information "would allow members of the public to anticipate and outwit current investigative and surveillance techniques" and undermine "law enforcement efforts to detect and prevent criminal gang activities."

That argument was a loser in the eyes of the state arbitrator. The information was ordered released.

Mohler's work was just another day, a million miles away from Psychopathic HQ.

No one's ears were burning back in Detroit, even as they were being discussed and dissected in an overly air conditioned conference room fifteen hundred miles away.

Mohler was one of a number of agents around the United States who fed the Juggalo information to street cops, gang sociologists, and investigators over the years. He was, however, a typical presenter, from the misspelling of Faygo to the hopeful connection to gang behavior, which made them eligible for broader and longer sentences.

No one thought back to Daniel Shellhammer when the FBI's bomb dropped, but someone could have seen the hate and just how far cops would go to attack Juggalos early on, when the paint was still relatively fresh on the weirdo label slapped on Juggalos.

Shellhammer was fourteen years old in 1999 and enjoying summer vacation like most kids in August. Also like most kids, Shellhammer was smitten with sounds—the loud and boisterous kind, the stuff with big guitars and rap vocal delivery. He liked bombast and ceremony and theatrics. He dug ICP, just like a few of his pals in Northwood, Ohio, population five thousand. The Toledo suburb is solidly middle class, white, and law and order with a coveted school district and low crime.

Except for Shellhammer. On August 3, 1999, he was walking with a friend down one of Northwood's main streets wearing a black ICP T-shirt that featured Santa Claus on the front with a gaping bullet hole in his head and, on the back, a picture of ICP and the holiday message, "Merry Fucking Xmas Bitch."

Northwood had ten patrol officers at the time, and Joseph Conley and Al Williams were among them. The two were on patrol when they spotted Shellhammer or, more importantly, spotted the shirt. Conley was the first out of the car, and he approached the two boys, who were holding—of course—sixteen-ouncers of just-purchased Faygo.

"You need to take that shirt off," Conley told Shellhammer. "Insane Clown Posse clothing is banned in Ohio."

The teen stood, stunned. He was a little impressed that any band could get its clothing banned, but he was also scared of the cops. "I can just turn it inside out," he offered.

"No, it comes off. The shirt is banned," Conley told him. "I'll tear that shirt off your back. Hand it over, or you're going to be arrested for disorderly conduct."

Shellhammer took the shirt off—it was a warm summer afternoon—and went home. His grandma went to the department the next day to get the shirt. And she was pissed off.

Then Raymond V. Vasvari Jr. heard about the incident. He's the wrong guy to alert on such things, as he was, at the time, the director of the American Civil Liberties Union chapter of Ohio.

"We would get 8,000 complaints a year, and about 150 were worth looking into," Vasvari says. "And that one was very much in that 150."

It was a few months after Columbine, and Vasvari had his hands full of goth kids being mistakenly ID'd as the anti-Christ. Shellhammer was a gift.

"He was not all that concerned about it, but then he was fourteen years old, and I'm not sure he understood it all," Vasvari said.

The ACLU filed a complaint in January, and speaking in strictly legal terms, Vasvari whipped the cops.

The city settled in May without even giving a reason for the blatant attack on Shellhammer. It gave $4,500 to Shellhammer, $500 to his mom, paid the $2,500 ACLU legal fees and issued an official apology.

Conley was later made head of community relations for the detective bureau for his solid work. Williams earned the rank of sergeant.

It was psychopathic manager and ICP svengali, Alex Abbiss, who had heard about the case and alerted the ACLU. He took no credit. He was already learning that lawyers were going to be good friends to the Juggalos.

They had to be—the religious people had stopped protesting them in the midnineties, when a batch of god lovers threw holy water on the door of the venue ICP were playing in Port Huron, Michigan. "Now it was becoming more of an indignant bunch of people who were against us," says Bill Dail, Psychopathic's CEO.

Those people had more than self-righteous moral outrage; they had the potential to stop the music.

✝ ✝ ✝

One thing the Texas investigator Mohler had right was the importance of the Internet to Juggalos.

In the early 2000s there were over 130 Juggalo sites, a number that dwindled as Facebook became the favored, cheaper alternative. Search Facebook today for Juggalo, and you'll have to take the day off to follow up.

Insane Clown Posse and Psychopathic saw early on that Juggalos were jacked up on the Internet, a reasonably cheap form of expression on both ends.

"ICP were way ahead in knowing their crowd," says Chris Fuller, who has managed Detroit act Electric Six since the nineties. "They recognized that they could give this strong core audience certain things that it wanted, and then it freed them up to do certain things."

So special giveaways, events that were spread only via social media and other favors, were made possible just by keeping everyone engaged. It was a smart advance of their own love of "promotion," a word they used as a verb when they were starting out as Kinko's regulars.

Those days of posters and prints and handbills were the only way to get the name around. They knew they were hardly major-label material, a hard lesson that would be learned down the line through their dealings with Disney, Island, and Jive and would result in their DIY management and handling of things.

On more than one occasion they'd be caught with the posters and glue used to slap them on a building. Cops would make them go back and remove all of them, which could take a whole day if they were caught at the wrong time.

Insaneclownposse.com was registered in 1997, the same time a lot of bands were hitting the web but a year ahead of their peers, Kid Rock and Eminem. All three were in a battle for the ears and wallets both locally and nationally through newsletters and in-store appearances as well as live shows.

While Kid Rock and Eminem were boosted soon enough by major-label backup—Atlantic and Interscope Records, respectively—ICP relied on themselves, their growing legion of Juggalos, and their own label. Psychopathicrecords.com was registered two years later, as was Juggalogathering.com, a year before the first Gathering was held.

Investigators could check up on Juggalos through Facebook, where an errant comment made from home, maybe from someone drunk or otherwise altered, could be interpreted and used as proof that some Juggalos were ready to do some crimes, that they were actually living out the stories ICP spun.

It's no wonder that Mohler in Texas cited the fact that "ninety percent of intelligence comes from open sources" for gang investigations in his presentation. The Juggalos, with an abundance of news sites thick with comments fired off in typically straight-up fashion, were easy prey for whatever interpretations cops and other onlookers needed to justify their agenda or view.

As a teenager, Farris Haddad cruised Gratiot Avenue and checked out the freaks. They wore face paint, blared *Ringmaster* from their half-assed car stereo cassette players, and were cool as shit.

Haddad was from West Bloomfield Hills, a relatively wealthy neighborhood, as opposed to the rest of Detroit—hell, the rest of Michigan—where the economy had been gutted long ago by antiquated taxing systems and a union-informed work ethic that actually believed in a forty-hour workweek.

Haddad didn't buy into that shit, but he sure did dig that Insane Clown Posse. A girl he knew was into Snoop Dogg, which was fine. But he needed something that struck him as more "real." That was ICP.

"I'd see the Juggalos in face paint every weekend, and through that I met the ICP street team, and to us, they were huge," says Haddad, a slight, thirtysomething of Arabic descent. "I bought all their CDs. I went to all their shows. I followed them on the Internet."

He bought the tapes at a local chain. ICP managed to finagle a way around placing parental advisory stickers on a couple of releases, so "I could get them without my mom approving them."

Haddad began identifying as a Juggalo in 1994.

In May 2012 Haddad was at the Partridge Creek Mall in suburban Macomb County. He was there with his girlfriend to get a puppy. It was a benign task in the region's most benign place, a collection of outlets that puts the "chain" in chain store.

Haddad got the dog. He and his girlfriend walked toward the parking lot, puppy in arms.

And there at the ATM, with son, JJ, and daughter, Ruby, and wife, Michelle, was Violent J. He was bigger than life, the tattoos on his beefy forearms jumped out like neon—"Detroit" on the underside of his lower right forearm, "Juggalo" on his lower left forearm, and, if that weren't enough, "RWBL" on his right knuckles, the initials of his brother Rob, or Rob William Bruce, and "love" as a symbolic appreciation. The "L" stands for Lee, as in Bruce Lee, one of their idols. Joe has "JFBL" on his other knuckles, for Joseph Franklin Bruce Lee.

Haddad froze.

"Man, that's Violent J," he said to his girlfriend. She knew of his fandom.

"Go say 'Hi,'" she urged. "Get a picture."

She understood her starstruck boyfriend. She had been hearing the music for years, listened to Haddad talk about growing from pedestrian street rap into the more intense rap-rock, of being a kid and led by his older friends into something that was universally hated enough for him to love it.

Haddad had met J before at a meet-and-greet, but this was different. He'd paid for the occasion before. This was free and was like seeing a bear in the wild.

Plus, J had a reputation for being prickly if you approached him in public.

Haddad took a bath and walked up to J, who was just getting done taking out some cash. No one else was approaching this local star, and Haddad couldn't believe his luck.

"It's great to see you—I love your music," Haddad said. He was gushing and couldn't keep himself from it. "You're a true storyteller and the best rapper going."

Haddad was an esteemed defense lawyer who had been in the local news for his solid work. If you were on the receiving end of a drunk-driving rap and wanted to get it knocked down, Haddad was one of the better men to sort it out. But for him that was nothing compared to being the platinum star that was J.

They talked briefly, fan to star, while JJ and Ruby petted the puppy that crawled around everyone's feet.

"I'm a lawyer, and if you ever need anything done, I'll do it for free," Haddad said, handing J his card. Although he had heard of the FBI report, he didn't know what was coming.

But the next day he had an e-mail from J when he woke up. "Farris—it was good meeting you yesterday. I would like to talk with you about a problem we are hoping to address. When you get time, please give me a call.—J." He left his cell number at the bottom.

The call Haddad made was the start of becoming a Juggalo celebrity, with lifetime all-access passes to the shows and a costarring role in what would become one of the first cases of a musical group suing the FBI.

He had a one-word answer when J asked him to be part of the legal team taking on the FBI: "Yes."

There was little more to say.

PART II

Crime, Carnage, and Renegades

5

The Mighty Bruce Brothers

Mom, I had a dream of a clown.
—JOE BRUCE, AKA VIOLENT J, TO HIS MOM, 1990

Dig this: Linda Bruce is stopped at a traffic light in Clawson, Michigan, a few years ago. Sitting in her minivan, which was bought for her as a gift by her son, Joe Bruce—whom she has never once in her life called Violent J—a Jeep Wrangler pulls up with all of its doors off, top back, four Juggalos bouncing to a song. She looks, listens—a sixtysomething lady—and starts nodding her head in time to the song, which she's heard before. "Hokus Pokus"? "The Bone"?

The kid in the passenger seat, early twenties, looks over at her with a furrowed brow—she's nodding in time . . . eh?

Linda looks back at him.

"ICP?"

"Yeah. How do you know?"

The light changed before she could answer. Not that Violent J's mom would tell the kid she was the mother of the music.

✝ ✝ ✝

Once in a while, when he's got a little time and, well, the streets just look familiar enough to be enticing, Rob Bruce steers his truck into the old neighborhood.

It's the shittiest part of Berkley, Michigan, and that's saying something. The Detroit suburb, eleven miles from the center of the city, packs fourteen thousand people into two-and-some-change square miles, most of them white and solidly middle class, as in "Don't think you're going anywhere."

There is no crime to speak of—some garden variety thefts and burglaries, but rarely a murder. Hell, there isn't a single mean street in Berkley, and that's what Rob remembers of growing up there with his younger brother, Joe, and older sister, Theresa.

Joe Bruce, who would become Violent J, was born in April 1972, a couple of years after Rob and four years after Theresa.

They were raised mostly by their mom, Linda, a lifelong Michigander from the Detroit area who'd had a run of bad luck with men. Rick fathered the kids and then left straight up after tossing a television set down a flight of basement stairs at Linda. When Linda and Rick were splitting up the money they had in their joint bank account, Rick took it all. It was 1974.

The next man in Linda's life was a fifty-year-old lineman at Chrysler named Lester. The kids were single digits old, Linda was thirty. It was 1978. Lester beat on the boys and sexually molested Joe on numerous occasions.

He was soon gone, and Linda worked low-skill jobs that almost paid the bills. Working as a night janitor at a church in upscale Birmingham was solid work. She also cleaned houses in the same ritzy area in her spare time.

They were also on welfare, food stamps, and any other do-gooder social program you could get on, and in Michigan circa midseventies, that's a lot of programs. They got the presliced orange processed cheese, the powdered milk, and the blocks of butter.

Other than that, the refrigerator was bare save for whatever the church would bring by as part of its outreach to the poor. Maybe some Faygo in there on a good day. It was cheap and it was local and it came in different flavors—red pop, orange, fruit punch, grape, root beer. Alongside the pop, inexplicably, was grapefruit. They ate it without sugar, which was too expensive.

Linda worked hard to make the family into a unit. "We had a really good childhood in the sense that we had each other," Rob says. "We were always away, always out and having adventures on our own, thinking up things to do. We were poor, but we didn't need anything. We had our imaginations. We were always going out with our friends and into the forest, and in the neighborhoods we had all the kids. Sometimes it was hard, sure, but we didn't let it get us down."

Joe was the baby, born in 1972, hazel-eyed with red hair dusting a high forehead. "Everybody's got a fucked-up childhood," Joe said. "Everybody has tons of heartbreaking stories about how bad they always had it while growing up. But my childhood was probably the freshest on the fuckin' planet. I wouldn't change one thing except for what my mom went through with her husbands. My childhood was without a doubt the greatest time of my life."

They got to school age, and Linda drove them to Angell Elementary in a shady Buick with rust spots the size of the fenders. When it was her turn in the carpool to take a bunch of kids, some of them asked to be dropped off around the block so as not to be seen in the sputtering heap.

The Bruce brothers didn't care. They'd moved three times in the last ten years in Berkley, which was only two square miles. They knew everyone, and everyone knew they were broke-ass poor.

The Bruce brothers were nerds. They wore thrift-shop clothes and in the summer sported the striped white tube socks and Payless sneakers with gym shorts. They rode Huffy bikes when everyone else was cruising on Schwinn Stingrays. They loved anything dealing with fantasy. They didn't swear until they were teenagers. They never drank or smoked.

"It was out of respect for my mom. She had it tough enough—she didn't need some foul-mouthed kids running around, or some drunk kids or high kids," Rob says. Theresa covered enough of that ground for the whole family. She was in and out of trouble, and the fights between Theresa and Linda were epic, loud, glass-breaking, throwing-shit affairs.

The Bruce brothers remained outside of it. They were geeks. "I wore the same pair of sweatpants all year long," Joe said. "In grade school in Berkley the school would serve a hot lunch. It cost $1.10. My mom never had the money, so they would let you borrow it at school from the office. You had three days to pay it back. After that they would announce your name and say that you owed the office money over the morning PA announcements. It was always the same names all year long, every year: Rob and Joe Bruce."

"Every year the church my mom worked at would have this big sale, and that's where we got our clothes," Rob says. The Bruce family got a discount, half off, because Linda worked there.

They got into their fantasies, a life where no one could reach in. For Rob, it was role-playing games like Dungeons and Dragons.

"I got into D&D at ten years old, and I was playing with kids who were thirteen or so," Rob says. "My imagination was so sick—it was this great escape from reality. And it worked. If your imagination was strong enough, you could do anything you wanted and be anyone you wanted. It was so intense that the first time I kissed a girl was in a game, and it was almost like it was real. I lay awake in bed that night like it really happened."

For Joe, his escape from the everyday at first was ninja movies and pro wrestling. When they tried to engage in what was normal, it didn't work. Rob grew up stout and handsome, dark haired and smart. He had a couple of years on Joe, so girls hit his radar earlier.

"I used to have this crush on this girl in middle school, Margo, and I used to try to work up the courage to talk to her," Rob says. "We were poor, of course, so we had this group that gave out food to families. Whenever they came by, my brother and I would get really excited because there would be some great things in there, like candy bars. One day we were outside playing and we saw the car with the food box pull up."

Rob and Joe tore ass down the street. Rob stopped running when he saw Margo walking up to his door, box in hand. She and her mom were delivering the food to the needy. "I was so destroyed," Rob says.

A short time later the Bruce family moved again, trading one working-class suburb for another. Linda married a Vietnam vet named Ron, and they went south to Oak Park, where the border stretched to a particularly shitty scrap of the fabled Eight Mile Road. It was racially mixed, as opposed to the straight-up white Berkley. That would help Joe figure out that he liked music. It was 1981.

"I got the single of 'Freeze Frame,' by the J. Geils Band," Joe says. "I had a babysitter; she took us up to Harmony House. It had 'Center Fold' on one side and 'Freeze Frame' on the other, and I bought that bad boy and I just played it and played it and learned all the words to the songs."

Joe and Rob took jobs caddying. Joe was thirteen years old, and the caddy master from the Birmingham Country Club came to the school to recruit some kids who may not be as privileged as those in the country club's orbit. They were right, and next thing he knew, Joe and Rob were hauling clubs for some of the wealthiest guys in the metro Detroit area.

"They bought their own clothes for school, bought an Atari—they did really well," Linda says. They did it for three summers, and she took them back and forth, sometimes when she was going to and from her own job in Detroit's richest zip code.

And when he got a large enough stash, "Joe decided he wanted to know what it was like to take a ride in a limousine," Linda says. "So he saved his money and took this girl he liked, but the girl's mother made him take her sister as well. He rented this limousine, and they went to the McDonald's and said hello to everybody. What kind of kid does that?"

Joe's spark grew. He was a personality, with a larger-than-life, born-to-entertain-people inclination. He liked to talk. He liked to perform. He loved the idea of becoming someone else and having people watch him.

Joe studied things. He watched and learned. His schoolwork was crap, but his dance moves were smooth.

"People were saying Michael Jackson was the greatest break dancer and all that stuff," Joe says. So he studied Michael Jackson videos as soon as he could find someone with MTV. Then he ran his mouth.

"Man, you know I can dance like Michael," he'd pipe up, over and over, sitting in the caddy shack the next summer. His colleagues were bored with his boasting. On other days Joe would amuse them with stories about the night crawls he and Rob would make, like putting on all-black clothing and walking to the corner store through backyards and ditches, avoiding detection or even the glare of a headlight.

It was another way to create another world. And it worked.

So one day, when Joe asked one of his fellow caddies for a buck to get a cold drink, he was challenged.

"Sure, I'll give you a buck," he was told. "But you gotta dance like Michael."

Everyone else laughed. Except Joe. He got down and did an impressive worm in the dirt. He even did the Michael Jackson spin. They laughed again. His clothes were filthy from the display and he didn't care. He got his buck.

Joe also had a mouth to match his eroding sense of propriety. He realized he had nothing to lose—he'd spent his life at the bottom.

"Are you rich?" Joe asked one of the well-heeled gentlemen he was working with one day. It was a weekday afternoon, and most people Joe had ever heard of worked every day, all day. If they worked the night shift, they spent the day sleeping, not golfing.

"No, I'm not rich. I'm just average," the man said, casting an air swing with his Maruman driver. It was one of the most expensive pieces of golf clubs known to man, made in Japan and used by the best.

Joe chewed on that one for a while.

How the fuck can he be average? he thought. *He should be claiming himself rich. That fucking bastard.*

Joey Utsler was born in 1974 with an abundance of energy. He hops when he walks, a long stride with long legs and gangly arms, like a spider on two legs. Upright and skinny, he grew to six-foot-two.

He was always that way—an intense but amiable wanderer. Joey was the middle of three kids, including his older brother, John, and his younger brother, Mike. They shared a home in nearby Ferndale with a batch of stepsiblings, a hairdresser mom, and a stepdad.

The houses on the block were standard-issue World War II vintage: boxy, maybe a small garage, mostly one story with a patch of front yard and, in some cases, a larger patch of backyard.

The Utslers real dad lived in Oak Park, which at the time had better schools, relatively speaking. The Utslers went to Berkley then Oak Park. They knew no one in either place very well and didn't care. Primary schooling was not a thought, just a law that said they had to be there. Joey was still in elementary. John went to middle school with the Bruce brothers.

One day John bumped into Joe Bruce in the hallway.

John never hated or made fun of the Bruce brothers. He kinda dug them and their "own world" vibe. Joe looked up to John and Joey.

Joe's musical tastes had moved on from J. Geils, bouncing to an infatuation with Michael Jackson and the rap music that he was hearing every day, day in, day out, blaring from cars cruising down Greenfield near his house. Rob too was digging into rap—not that they could afford to indulge in their tastes, though. Cassettes were running $7 a pop.

John came home one day and told Joey they were heading over to hang with the Bruce boys. *Cool*, Joey thought. He was easy like that.

"My brother brought [Joe] back to the house in the back of my mom's old sixties station wagon," Joey said. "He put me in a sleeper hold like a little woman. I was ten. The first time I met him, he made me cry."

Once they all started talking—Joe, Joey, John—as Rob was off playing games with his own crew—they all discovered that they loved two things: music and wrestling.

They were all fans of the kung fu movies that were on late nights and Saturday afternoons. Charlie Lum's *Kung Fu Theater*, *Martial Arts Theater*, *Kung Fu Classics*. There was more low-fi video of martial arts on Detroit TV in the eighties than there was in China.

They also dug wrestling, the big-time stuff with all the glitz and performance art. They loved it enough to build a wrestling ring in the backyards of both the Utslers' and the Bruces' and start Tag Team Wrestling, or the TTW, their own federation. They changed it to National All-Star Wrestling. The ring had a rubber hose strung around it. Alex was the ring announcer, speaking in a tone that would make Michael Buffer proud. He stood out in the center as the guys got their costumes on in the house. When they were ready, they'd communicate with Alex via walkie-talkie, and the entrance was made. They wore masks and took on fantasy names. Joey was the Rhino when he didn't wear a mask; the White Tiger when he did. Joe was Darrell Dropkick Daniels.

They offered free hot dogs fresh from Ma Bruce's hot dog steamer and Faygo to anyone who showed up.

Joe loved the gimmick out of the gate. It was all style and bombast and smoke screen. Wrestling personified it. Rap embraced it. Joey understood as well that to make great art, you have to start with something people want to get into.

And it always came back to the sound of music.

For Joey, music was being pushed at him since elementary school, where "it was just like a melting pot, so you got a little bit of everything from everybody," he says. "Like obscure urban music to rap to soul to rock—anything you could think of."

"My older stepbrothers were hard-core Ozzy fans, we always used to call them wolves, you know the long hair and jean jackets," he said. "And my parents were hippies, so they played stuff like Seger, Queen, Motown music. I never really got into that all that much."

He fancied himself a baseball player when he was going to elementary school. The Detroit Tigers won the World Series on his tenth birthday in 1984, and he thought they won it for him. He forgot about sports when he started to teach himself to draw and DJ.

Collectively, they all realized they were from another place mentally. "We just weren't part of the rock scene at all," Joe says. "We were suburban gangster wannabes."

Their friendship was sealed when the Bruce boys moved to Ferndale in 1988. Linda and Ron had scraped together enough cash to buy a $30,000 house. It was a real step up, a little frame off Nine Mile Road. They now lived a couple of blocks from John and Joey.

John was schooling Joe on the music he and Joey were digging.

They were getting on the city bus to catch shows, "those big package rap shows—Big Daddy Kane and Third Bass and mix with everybody," Joey says. "One of the best was at Royal Oak Music Theater with Boogie Down Productions. I had to see everything. I was just checking it all out."

One of the first rap groups Joe loved was pre–"Baby Got Back" Sir Mix-a-Lot, when Anthony Ray was an emerging rapper from Seattle putting out singles on his own label, Nastymix. They all went to see Mix-a-Lot in Detroit and came out of there stunned.

"We gotta do something," Joe said the next day when the three had absorbed what they had seen. It was a massive bill, with Awesome Dre, Prince Vince, and the Hip Hop Force opening. They were local and they killed. Joey agreed, as did John.

So the fake white gangsters, bored kids with a bent for music, formed the JJ Boys. "Our names all started with J, see?" Joe explains.

They knew a kid with a karaoke machine who called himself Scratchmaster T. Whatever. They experimented on and exploited the kid—fuck him. They went over, played with his toys, and walked out with a song, "The Party at the Top of the Hill."

It started like this:

> We're the JJ Boys on the microphone stand,
> Kickin' it live with a Faygo in our hand.
> Master T is on the table, not working in the stable,
> And on his Adidas jacket is the Faygo label.

Joe became Jagged Joe, John was Master J, and Joey was Kangol Joe, named after the UK-based hat maker he favored.

They used a couple of tape players and some ragged beats, and they did their own cassette tape, scraping up money from the $80 a week or so Joe earned caddying and then teaming that with some blank cassettes Joey boosted from the local Harmony House record store.

The Faygo name drop was simple: "Run DMC always talked about Adidas and the Beastie Boys would put White Castle Hamburgers in their songs," Joe says. "So I said Faygo because we always had some. It was our trademark."

They were sporting a poor man's hip-hop look, with patent leather basketball shoes, track suits, and anything with the Adidas name on it. Flea markets sold the fake gold chains, and they draped them on. Joey loved stealing hood ornaments, like the Beasties used to wear—VW, Mercedes, whatever. They'd droop them around their necks. It was a monkey-see thing, but it was a start.

At the same time, there was substance. Joey was in love with music. More than John and more than Joe, he was collecting singles, setting up turntables in his bedroom, and figuring out how to make the sounds he heard in his head.

He got the Herbie Hancock single "Rockit" and used it to learn DJ scratches. Afrika Bambaataa singles were popping, and Joey was on it. When the movie *Beat Street* came out, Joey followed the South Bronx dreamers in the cast seeking musical fame. He began collecting music via theft. Joey could steal anything like a pro, a combo of foolhardy guts and nothing to lose.

They'd head up to a nice part of town and go through the stores, turning an item they liked around on the rack. Joey would come through and snatch anything facing the wrong way. He was like David Copperfield. And soon enough everyone had some nice duds. He was just a kid—what were they gonna do? Send him to prison?

They met Bill Dail in the neighborhood. Bill and his brother Doug had a stable home, with a regular, stay-at-home mom and a truck driver dad, the latter of whom was in remission from cancer. The Dail family had a work ethic that made the ethics of the other locals look sick. To make up the money lost from Mr. Dail's lost trucker revenue, the family took on a Detroit newspaper route that covered eleven hundred subscribers.

Up every morning at two o'clock to get to the paper drop site at three and then to fold and pack the papers. Holidays, weather— nothing kept the paper from being delivered.

Bill stopped going to school in ninth grade. Before the cancer took his dad down, he wanted to ride with the old man on the truck, but then the paper route took up his time. He dug rap, like most of the other kids around him—N.W.A. and anything else associated with Dr. Dre in particular.

"I was just a music fan when I met Joe and Joey," Bill says. "I never wanted to play or anything, but I just liked them and what they were doing."

The JJ Boys sucked. They became the Inner City Posse, but there was little music involved. It was a street gang—whatever that entailed for confused, broke kids with no money and few pals.

While they were playing at becoming MTV heroes, Rob enlisted in the Army, 1st Sustainment Command, and trained at Fort Bragg in

South Carolina. While he was there J missed him terribly. "Joe was kind of left out," Ma Bruce says. So J took his thumb and hitchhiked to Bragg.

"Don't worry—he got here," Rob told his mom when J arrived. Ma Bruce was freaked out with worry. Hitchhiking?

J was a little lost, and his big brother was there for him.

So was Burt Reynolds.

The military had one of its shows of appreciation for the soldiers, and Reynolds was hosting. "Joe wanted to go, so I gave him one of my uniforms so he could get in with everybody else," Rob says.

Just like they did at wrestling events back in Detroit, they snuck backstage to meet the talent. In this case the talent was happy to see them, J and Rob, standing there in their Army fatigues. "I want to thank you guys for all that you've done and that you do," Reynolds said, looking at J, then Rob. And J was ready.

"Man, you know that movie, *Cannonball Run*? I loved that movie, and remember that line, 'Why do you do it?'"

Reynolds was ready. "For the hell of it," he quoted him back.

J was ecstatic. It was one of his favorite lines ever.

J was homesick, though. He missed Detroit, so he hit the highway once more. It was an adventure.

Once he got back, Joe kept on trying to figure out how to have a life.

The wrestling at Joe Louis Arena—"The Joe" to locals—became a monthly thing. Joe and Joey met Rudy Hill at one of the professional wrestling extravaganzas they went to in downtown Detroit. For $1 they could catch the downtown bus. They could sneak into the porous, mammoth arena, the city's primary sports and concert venue. The place held twenty-one thousand souls. And when anything wrestling went down in the late eighties, Joe and Joey were skulking around the back docks, where the equipment loaded in, looking for a leak, be it an unlocked door or a security guard on a smoke break.

For Rudy wrestling was a religion. He was Rude Boy inside his head, a pro wrestler with no match. He too rode the bus over to the arena from Mexicantown in Southwest Detroit, never missing an event.

On a fall day in 1986 he was waiting for the doors to open, stalking the back entrance in hopes of catching a wrestler coming in. He got autographs, pictures, and a few "fuck yous" for his vigilance.

On this day he had a fortuitous meeting with two strangers. Joe and Joey, on a patch of grass, were performing their own wrestling moves to kill some time.

"What are you idiots doing?" one of the bystanders asked them, looking on. There was a small ring around the two, but no one was impressed. Until Rudy joined the crowd. When they finished showing off the best of their moves, he came up to them as everyone else walked away.

"Hey, you guys are really good at this," Rudy said to them. He looked up. Joe and Joey were already growing into their thin frames, and both already had some height.

"Thanks, man. We have our own wrestling federation. You should come and check it out," Joe said. "We live in Ferndale."

Rudy checked it. *These guys are fuckin' rich*, he told himself. Rudy's dad humped the line at the Chevrolet Gear and Axle plant in Hamtramck, and it was a solid living, especially considering that the family had originally come to Detroit from Juarez, Mexico, where $3 a day was considered making it. But when Rudy got a load of Joe and Joey's world . . . well, compared to Mexicantown, everyone was rich.

"And it was all togetherness and love up there. I had never seen such a thing like that, even though my family was great," Rudy says.

Then Joe and Joey came to visit Rudy.

A match was made. Friends for life.

"My parents loved both of them. They were so damn respectful and well mannered. They'd say 'frick' when we were all saying 'fuck.' They'd come over, and we'd go get some quarts of beer, and they just didn't care. They didn't drink."

They drove around Mexicantown, where there were real gangs instead of the imaginary street hoods that Joe and Joey and their crew were conjuring in their heads. The Latin Counts, X Men, Young Guns—it was for real here.

"Wow, look at those dudes," Joey said, seeing a group standing off a street corner one night. He lifted his finger, pointing.

"Put your fucking hand down—you're gonna get us killed," Rudy told him.

One night they were out cruising in Joe's Plymouth Volare. His stepdad, Ron, had bought it for him in hopes it would inspire him to work for a living. For now it was just getting him around in this new world of street thugs. Joe hated violence—he was the first one to try to talk it out—but he loved the scene, the imagery.

They drove to a local street festival—Joe, Rudy, Joey, and Rudy's cousin Randy.

"Did you miss that turn?" Randy said to Joe. He was ragging on him pretty good from the backseat. "I thought someone from the richy area would know better."

The shit continued for a while until Rudy had heard enough. It was 3 a.m. "Joe, stop the fucking car," he said.

"What? This is Clark Park, man. We can't just stop here," Joe said. Clark Park is just off the Fisher Freeway, a bad place to be at the time.

"Stop the car!" Rudy repeated.

Rudy jumped out of the front seat, pulled some kid from their crew from the back, and beat him severely with a series of punches to the face and head. The kid stayed down.

Rudy jumped back in.

"We're just going to leave him?" Joe asked. He felt bad, even though he had been the target of the kid's insults all night.

That sealed the deal. Joe moved in with Rudy's parents. Life at home was getting harder, with pressure from his parents to *do* something with his life. Rob was serving his country. His mom was all over him to get a job. "You're screwing around and nothing is going to happen," she told him. Then, "If you're not going to work, you're not going to live here."

So Rudy's it was. A world away from Ferndale, but it felt like home: most families were on food stamps and struck with poverty, working bottom-rung service jobs—McDonald's, Wendy's, whatever.

Joe did some jail time for scaring a local girl he was pursuing. More likely, he scared her dad.

"He threatened on the phone some girl he liked," Ma Bruce says. "I never thought he would end up in jail over something like that. He called her, and they were fighting, and he would hang up, and she would call right back, and so he said something like his crew would take care of things or something."

The girl's parents must have thought Joe had an actual crew.

They pressed charges, and Joe landed in front of a judge who handed down a restraining order. And when Joe went to a school dance that the girl was also attending, she narced him out. Next thing he knew, he was in the county jail. The bail wasn't much, but it was more than the Bruces could come up with, so he spent the Christmas holidays in lockup, only seeing his relatives in the visiting room.

He got out, and he and Joey continued to hit the matches constantly. They also loved music and kept seeing as much as they could while keeping their dreams alive.

Oddly for all the crime and poverty, no one fell into drugs—that was for losers.

Joe and Joey were not going to be losers, despite the overwhelming evidence to the contrary.

So when they decided to do another music project, they just took the Inner City Posse name and used it.

Joe wrote a song, "Something to Say." It was a stunningly unoriginal gangster rap lift, but when he busted it for everyone, they loved it. So he made a tape at home, bouncing sounds from portable tape player to player, like so many other kids were doing in bedrooms all across the world, as no one could afford studio time. He would take his songs to his mom to see if she understood what he was trying to say. If she did, he was communicating. If not, he would try to explain, which would help him rewrite.

Enter the Ghetto Zone was a shabby stab at rap, but Joey and John dug it so much, they wanted to do something like it with all of them together. The Inner City Posse started recording tapes and handing them out. Rudy distributed them in Southwest Detroit. Rob was jamming it for his soldier pals in Saudi Arabia. People said they liked it. ICP felt encouraged. Rob had a friend he met while gaming, Alex Abbiss, who co-owned a record store, Hot Hits, in Roseville, on Detroit's east side. "Take the tapes over there and see if he'll sell 'em. Drop my name," Rob said.

"Yeah, you're Rob's little brother," Alex said when Joe brought the tapes in. He agreed to carry the tapes: $5 a crack—he keeps $3, and ICP gets $2. He sold nineteen tapes in four days. To them, it was like going platinum.

Joe and Joey were still hustling for work, and they lost jobs as fast as they got them. But one job they got together would shape their music, set it aside, and eventually make them special. And it started at a rock joint in downtown Detroit called St. Andrew's Hall.

"Mutt and Jeff" is how one DJ there recalls them: Joe worked the register and Joey watched the crowd, as he could spot a troublemaker from fifty feet. "They were really nice, really white-trash high school dropouts" is how a coworker, John Liccardello, aka Speck, described them. Speck was a brawler bouncer, a rough guy from Orange County, California.

To him they were just wide-eyed kids "and hard workers who really knew what they were doing. It was like this was a place they understood."

It was. Joe and Joey studied the hard-rock and punk bands of the era—Helmet, Rage Against the Machine, Bad Religion, Monster Magnet—and they started to see the merits of guitars.

"We were in the middle of all of this rock," Joe says. "There were these songs that we learned that everybody moved to."

They went into working at St. Andrew's as straight rap, Joey says. "Then it started morphing. We got this bigger picture, we broadened our horizons, and we got these rock influences."

They also watched a host of hapless local bands walk on stage and tune and meander and dick around. Joe and Joey learned that it paid to hit the stage with drama and rage right away. That's how the winners did it. And failing to do that is how locals stayed locals.

Soon they went to a proper studio to record something else. There was $5,000 from Alex's mom, a daring bet that Linda Bruce wouldn't have taken even if she were flush, but she wasn't. "I tell you if I would have had that $5,000, I wouldn't have given it to them," she says. "I had faith but not that much. She must have had it to lose, or at least if it didn't work out she wasn't going to suffer without it. She had courage."

Dog Beats came out in early 1991, a four-song cassette featuring a guy in clown face paint on the cover.

They released it on their own label. At first it was going to be called Mad Paperboy Records. "There was this kid in the neighborhood who was a funny paperboy. We loved him—he had this crazy hair," Joey says.

They decided instead on Psychopathic, with Joey as in-house artist. He modified the paperboy, replacing a stack of newspapers in his hand with a hatchet. Later, cops would think the hatchet was a primary part of the violence they claimed ICP embodied. Imagine if they had kept the newspapers: How would the police have spun that? Alex stayed on to manage them.

Dog Beats taught them a new skill that they discovered was just as important as delivering songs: promoting.

It was the name they used for marketing, and Joe and Joey spent days and nights in the local Kinko's creating flyers and artwork for their endeavor. ICP would print up thousands of flyers. "They would come in and have to load them out on a hand cart," a former Kinko's worker says. They had no social life. Nights and days were spent on the band. Inspired by the image of the clown-faced buddy they put on the cover of *Dog Beats*, they became Insane Clown Posse. They'd paint their faces and be wicked clowns. They would operate under the Dark Carnival, a traveling entourage of spirits. It was creativity and fantasy to the nth degree, a backstory and its own universe. Each of their albums represented a Joker's Card, which would reveal an element of life, from birth to death to salvation. It was heady stuff for a couple of dropouts.

In terms of pushing themselves as musicians, they had no mentors. The St. Andrew's experience opened a door.

"I'm glad we didn't learn from anyone." Joey says. "We smoked everybody. People are lazy. We knew we had to do everything twice as hard as everyone else."

Their first album was *Carnival of Carnage*. It came out in fall 1992. John, Joey's brother, played on a couple of songs, but he was committed to chasing girls, while Joe and Joey were monastically focused on music. John was out before the record was.

On *Carnival* was a song called "The Juggla."

Juggla juggla fuck with the juggla
You can't fuck with the juggla

By 1994 ICP was selling out shows all over Detroit and doing damn well in some other areas of the Midwest, playing most of the songs on *Carnival*. At one show, as they wrapped up "The Juggla," Joe looked at the kids, faces painted, devouring every lyric.

"I'm a juggla," he said, looking down at the front row and scanning to the back as best he could in the lights. "That makes you Juggalos."

With those four words he launched a million identities.

6

In the Milenko Zone

*Humanity has advanced, when it has advanced, not
because it has been sober, responsible, and cautious, but
because it has been playful, rebellious, and immature.*
—TOM ROBBINS

His Twitter account declares him
a "Skiny Tatted Up Sk8boardin Rappin Fuk Machine WyteBoy," but
his name is Jimi Kanklez, and he shattered a kid's elbow with one
savage blast of a baseball bat one March night in 2012. It was in the
parking lot of Mac's Bar, a locally legendary beer joint in Lansing,
Michigan, that has hosted everyone from Ryan Adams to Blue Cheer
over the years.

On the night Jimi hit a home run off the dude's funny bone, there
were a batch of Juggalo bands playing, local acts with a decent draw.
The victim was talking smack about a Juggalette, and he'd driven in
from out of town to do it.

Jimi couldn't take it, so there you go.

In July 2012 Jimi played the Underground Stage at the Gathering before he was picked up for the assault. He wasn't thinking about that dickbag with the busted elbow, although he still remembers the scream coming out of his quarry's mouth as being something other-worldly, like a rabbit being eaten alive.

Kanklez was arrested in November 2012 on his way to a show by Anybody Killa, another band on ICP's label. "I got in my damn van and left after I hit him," Jimi says. "I shoulda known there were consequences, but I didn't get caught for almost eight months."

The lazy effort to round him up is a testament to the seriousness with which the local fuzz takes Juggalo-on-Juggalo crime. But Jimi was charged with assault with a dangerous weapon. His bond was $5,000, and he didn't have it, so there went the Subway job he'd held for six years. You can't make a Cold-Cut Combo from the county slammer.

If the national narrative is to be believed, the episode was one more instance of Juggalo-related violence. Jimi sports a red hatchet-man tattoo on his upper left arm and the Great Milenko tat on his right forearm, proclaiming his loud and proud allegiance to the Juggalo world that has been part of his life since he was nine years old.

When he checked into the county jail the deputy noted the tattoos and duly wrote "gang" on his check-in sheet. But other than that, there was no grief.

"I don't get harped over the hatchet," says Jimi, who truly is skinny and tatted in additional to being tall and gentle. The tats creep up his neck as blue vines and scorpion talons and then spread every-where—hands, back, stomach, and arms. He puffs clove cigarettes and says "dear lord" when he's frustrated or hears something he can't process, like a shitty song by a shitty band.

But apparently a gang member is in the eye of the beholder. One man's hatchet is another person's ticket to jail.

A month after the bat incident in Lansing, Charlene McCallister held her wrist upward and outward in a courtroom in Carrizozo,

New Mexico. On it was the hatchetman, and Judge Karen Parsons took it in.

"That tattoo shows gang affiliation," Assistant District Attorney Elizabeth Williams told the judge.

"She would be considered a 'Juggalette,'" added Ryan Wright, Mc-Callister's probation officer.

McCallister had pointed a gun at a woman in a dispute over a parking space two years earlier. She'd fared poorly on probation, Wright said, landing her in front of the judge for sentence reconsideration.

The hatchet sealed it: the judge gave her eighteen months in jail. Her defense lawyer asked if perhaps his client could get a furlough to enroll her son in Head Start. "Someone else will have to do that," Parsons said. "She is going to be in prison."

Some parts of the country were clearly outraged over the Juggalos, clearly. And after the FBI's declaration of gang connections nationwide, reporters aped every word that cops, prosecutors, and probably their moms said about Juggalos, and it was all aimed at demonizing those wicked clowns.

But before the cops tormented the Juggalos and ICP, the media crucified them. For so many people, kids in clown paint and homemade tattoos shouting "whoop, whoop" and chugging cut-rate soda are easy targets, walking punch lines.

No one cared when Insane Clown Posse was selling out eighteen-hundred-capacity places in Detroit. Hell, the Motor City was so in love with crazy, edgy music that it would send a record of traffic sounds to number one as long as it included the crashes.

Violent J and Shaggy 2 Dope started making money in 1994, when their second album, *Ringmaster*, became a national sensation. *Rolling Stone* gave it one out of five stars, and there was no radio or video airplay.

Ringmaster went gold.

"I went out and bought some shoes," Shaggy recalls. "Nikes. I didn't even have to steal them anymore."

The next one, *Riddle Box*, also went gold. Their label, Jive, didn't promote it outside Detroit. So they did it themselves.

They did a Bay City Rollers to create a marketing plan. Just as the Scottish pop act of the seventies got its name by tossing a dart at a US map, striking Bay City, Michigan, ICP did the same to decide where they would move to for a month and hammer the place with promotion.

Dallas.

"We took all our money, $60,000, and bought three vans and wrapped them with the *Riddle Box* cover," J says. "We went to every high school we could, every day, handing out samplers for the new album. We were selling in Michigan, and after we were done, we had, like, twenty thousand sales in Dallas."

It was six white hip-hop dudes with a stack of cassettes, stickers, T-shirts, flyers, and just about any other thing you could hand to kids craving something new. They had some black-and-white Insane Clown Posse comic books that Shaggy had drawn. And full-page ads were purchased in the local alt-weekly, the *Dallas Observer*.

It was a road-show version of a time-honored tradition in indie music of street marketing. All it takes at its most basic level is some poster paste, a staple gun, and a copy machine. Bands from New York to Los Angeles engaged in the practice. But taking it to another city for some concentrated flyering was a new concept.

The guys from Detroit jammed into a hotel room on the sordid south side of town, splitting the mattress in the room to create two. A couple of people had to take the hard floor, and they switched off every night. That was what it took.

"The principals in the schools would let us in—it was nuts," Shaggy says.

It made no sense, of course, to let the guys onto the school grounds.

"We made sure not to put parental stickers on the samplers," J says. "We'd go to record stores: 'Hey, can we do a window display?' They were all cool with it."

"After the high schools in the day, we went to Deep Ellum every night, which is where all the music was," says Bill Dail, one of the Psychopathic crew.

They read the music show ads in the record stores and local rags. "We'd find a show where people who might like us would be and head over after the show," Dail says. A George Clinton show was a gold mine. People coming out saw the crew handing out free shit and jumped all over it. "People started recognizing us as those crazy guys from Michigan."

They'd hit titty bars, handing samplers to the DJs and dancers, and if there was a wrestling event, they'd hit that too. They went to the Sportatorium, a now-razed tin shack/pole barn that put on the biggest wrestling events in Dallas for six decades. It sat in the shadow of the city's mixmaster and was in bad shape, with third-rate grapplers on four-fight bills for the Confederate Wrestling Alliance that few cared about.

Except the Psychopathic crew.

"Anything where we thought there would be people who would want free shit," J says.

Tracy Fuller was all of fourteen years old when he was handed an ICP poster outside his school. He'd heard the ICP guys—really, the actual dudes in the band—were hanging around Deep Ellum and handing out more freebies.

Tracy was a troubled kid. He was a cutter, and his parents had a contracting business and were together, then not, then back together, bouncing Tracy around. As a result, the business suffered, and Tracy lived in a rough neighborhood. ICP, of all things, gave him some solace. Next thing he knew he was standing in a line outside Deep Ellum Live, a warehouse with bad acoustics but a stage that bumped right up against the crowd.

Fuller's girlfriend's dad drove them and accompanied them to the matinee. But first they stood in line for five hours, weathering a cold rain—it was December, and the venue wasn't exactly worried about the care of Juggalos, or whatever these kids were.

Fuller and his buddies had been passing around mix tapes for months, jamming to Marilyn Manson at first, and then graduating to ICP. They finally got into the place, and it was like going to the circus for the first time: colors everywhere—purple, pink, yellow, blue, red on and behind the stage and on the poles at each side of the stage.

He remembers the opening song twenty years later—it was "I'm Coming Home" off *Riddle Box*. The Faygo drenched him because he had moved to the front and stayed there the whole show. When he walked outside his clothes froze stiff.

"Goddamn, what a memory," Fuller says now. He's the father of two boys and two girls and works for a concert security group. "It was this great time in my life. After I found ICP I stopped cutting. My parents got back together and straightened out. And I shed this negative trance I had been in, trying to kill myself and all that. It was this positive outlet."

The Dallas show was part of a ten-city ICP tour. Some unsuspecting reps from Jive, the label that had put *Riddle Box* in a partnership deal with Psychopathic, came to check it out in St. Louis. They'd never seen the band live before and were all about it for the first few songs, standing at the front. When the Faygo came out they ran. If they could have run all the way back to New York City, they would have.

Juggalos were in love with the Dark Carnival, as Insane Clown Posse called its muse and overriding mythology. The albums were referred to as Joker's Cards, each one detailing an element of the human condition as a march toward some kind of answer or salvation.

Juggalos adored all of it. But then the rest of the world heard about ICP, and Juggalos became a punch line.

✠ ✠ ✠

Holy shit, Mike Clark thought, *we're like the Sex Pistols. We're going to be signed to a big label and it's going to go like that.*

Meaning, things will not end well. Insane Clown Posse, like the Pistols, had a devoted following and an equally rabid band of detractors.

Clark had been producing and cowriting with ICP from the beginning, a virtual third member of the band who created the beats. He launched his music production career with the $500 his mom bequeathed to him on her deathbed.

He grew up with no dad and a hard-drinking mom whom he had to watch over. He worked sessions at a little studio called the Disc Ltd. for the stars: "George Clinton never paid me for the current session I would work—he was always one behind. So I'd be scheduling for a session with George, and I wouldn't show up until he paid me for that last session."

Patti Smith showed up for a session to record during her *Dream of Life* LP, and Clark informed his colleagues that there was a bag lady in the lobby.

He produced some Kid Rock stuff and met ICP when they wandered into the studio like the Lost Boys. "Damn, he was so good. We all just clicked," Shaggy says. They'd met a guy named Julian Raymond, who was working A&R for Hollywood Records, Disney's foray into the music biz, which was booming.

Hollywood's biggest coup so far was landing North American rights to the Queen catalog. Otherwise, the place was a mess.

Raymond loved ICP, saw their sales, and thought good things. He was the guy who landed the rights to the Queen catalog, and a righteous masterstroke it was. But he was also on board for grunge-crazed courtships like Fluid, who were signed in 1993.

"The Hollywood Records guys didn't know about rock and roll," said Garrett Shavlik, drummer for the Fluid, a Denver band that did one album for the label. "They knew about soundtracks for fuckin'

cartoons, Disney. Hollywood Records was in the Disney complex studio area, and all the boulevards are named after characters. They
were on the corner of Dopey and Goofy boulevards."

Raymond started his music life as a bass player in hair-metal acts,
playing for bands with names like Bang Bang and Black and White.
He loved the extravaganza of rock. KISS ruled. He liked the
spectacle.

"This should be right up your alley," one of his colleagues told him
in late 1996, handing him a video of ICP playing for a frantic crowd of
Juggalos. *The Faygo was flying, the sounds were amazing*, he thought,
and that crowd was absolutely crazed. It was like the KISS Army.

Raymond was already courting a Detroit band, Suicide Machines,
and through them he was put in touch with ICP's mercurial manager,
Alex Abbiss. Raymond hopped a plane for Detroit and drove down to
Toledo, one of the band's hottest markets, and met with Alex before
the show.

Alex guided him to a spot—"a Faygo-free zone," Raymond
says—and he watched the band tear the place apart. After the show
he went backstage to meet everyone and gave J and Shaggy Mickey
Mouse watches, a joke gift. They talked. Their record label, Jive,
wasn't doing shit for them. So after the requisite contracts, lawyers,
and label honchos, ICP was signed with the Mouse. What could go
wrong with Insane Clown Posse being on a record label operated by
Disney?

Miramax was part of Disney, and it was cranking out some terrific
ultraviolent art, as in flicks like *Reservoir Dogs* and *Pulp Fiction*.
Something like ICP was the aural version of that art. The first album
for Hollywood Records would be *The Great Milenko*. They were already writing it.

"And we didn't really have to do anything for Insane Clown
Posse," Raymond says. "They had it all. All the songs, the ideas. We
just tried to build up their show production and give them a budget.
All they seemed to care about was how to give the Juggalos a better
show."

He came to Detroit numerous times as they started to work on the new album for Hollywood. He came to the Funhouse. Clark greeted him at the door of the bungalow, which he shared with his diabetic cat.

Raymond had worked in big studios with big budgets. He looked down the narrow stairs leading to the Funhouse. "This is where you are recording the record?" Raymond asked. It was cramped downstairs, and the studio shelves were boards on cinderblocks. But the sound was huge.

"This is the only way we record. This is what we have," Clark said.

So it was, Raymond thought. He listened to the heavy thud, as heavy as he could find in any other studio. And the attitude was, well, punk rock. "They didn't care what anyone said," Raymond says. "Sure, they wanted some money and some fame and anything they could get, but they were only doing it for themselves and the Juggalos. Always this thing about the Juggalos."

People in the industry thought he'd lost his mind. They would tell him how horrible ICP were, what a lame gimmick it was. He didn't care. He thrived on the hate. Wasn't pissing people off supposed to be part of the program?

To give the LP some name game, Raymond pulled Slash, Alice Cooper, and Steve Jones to come in and play. Cooper did the spoken voice to the intro. Slash and Jones jammed on a song each. Neither Slash nor Jones made it to the final mixes.

The parts were done by Rich Murrell, a Detroit guitarist who was brought in on the third album, *Riddle Box*, when Violent J wanted a real guitar sound. "I wrote the guitar parts on both songs," Murrell says. "Of course we gave them credits, and I'm sure we left them in the mix somewhere, way down. And here I was in awe because it was Steve Jones from the Sex Pistols, and those guys had no idea how big that was. In the end my parts were used because it was the way [J and Shaggy] were used to it."

Slash came into the studio in Hollywood with a truck full of guitar gear and a personal roadie to set it up in the studio, a Spinal Tap indulgence no one in the Psychopathic crew was used to. "You guys need to leave while we set this up," one of Slash's reps told the ICP entourage. It took hours, and Slash layered ten tracks of guitar.

In 1997 *The Great Milenko* was released on Hollywood.

And things were never the same.

"Disney, Facing a Boycott by Baptists, Recalls Album"

Walt Disney recalls 100,000 copies of Insane Clown Posse's record "The Great Malenko," a hip-hop album laden with obscenities, days after it was released under its Hollywood Records label.

—*Wall Street Journal*, June 27, 1997

The *Wall Street Journal* couldn't even spell the name of the album right. The editors never bothered to issue a correction.

The *New York Daily News* then hammered Hollywood Records for kowtowing to a wing of Southern Baptists, who somehow got a copy of the record:

Bowing to pressure from Southern Baptists, Walt Disney has pulled the plug on an obscenity-laced rap album and recalled it from stores nationwide.

Disney yanked 100,000 copies of the new CD from fledgling Detroit hip hop band Insane Clown Posse six hours after the album hit stores.

The album, titled "The Great Milenko," features songs about an evil and seductive force a "necromaster" who pushes people to the brink of death and destruction.

The Southern Baptist Convention, the nation's largest fundamentalist group, was meeting in Dallas in June when the collective call for a boycott of Disney products was announced, a couple of weeks before *Milenko* was released.

In their twisted, self-righteous minds, the family brand had gone off the rails and embarked on a trail that was anti-Christian and antifamily. The reality is that Disney wanted to make more money, and Hollywood Records was one of the new avenues for that cash.

Hollywood Records scrambled to explain itself.

When the lyrics of Insane Clown Posse's album were brought to the attention of senior management, the decision was made that they were inappropriate for a product released under any label of our company.
—Hollywood Records statement, June 27, 1997

It was a woman, still unidentified, who brought the whole thing down. After a crew of Disney honchos watched the "Halls of Illusions" video and heard the record, she lost her mind, believing that ICP was the Devil himself. She said the losses would be in the millions in terms of image depreciation if the record were allowed to continue. It was around 9 p.m. the day before the release, which was scheduled for midnight in Detroit.

Abbiss, the ICP manager, got the call the next morning. He was smart enough to immediately call the *Los Angeles Times*. He knew a hot story when he saw it.

Predictably, entertainment biz people fell all over themselves. When was the last time this had happened? The record was out for all of six hours before it got yanked.

Disney denied it was bowing to pressure, but it didn't matter: people beat the shit out of them and, in the process, took gratuitous pokes at ICP.

A *USA Today* piece reported that

Rap publicist Phyllis Pollack, who declined to represent the band last year because she considers Clown's humor "an insult to hip-hop," suspects Disney assumed a white Midwestern rap act would be less threatening than black gangsta rappers. "Maybe Disney figured that white guys would be immune from scrutiny."

At the *New York Times* hallowed entertainment writer Neil Strauss noted that some chain stores refused to return the album.

> An employee of Hollywood who spoke on condition of anonymity said the only major chain that had returned copies of the album was Tower Records. But as of yesterday, Tower Records in downtown Manhattan was still selling the album, as were HMV and Sam Goody.

The *Milenko* tour was already booked, and ICP was preparing for a huge signing event in Detroit at several record stores. They'd done one the night before, at midnight, about the same time Disney was shaking in its Tom Ford slide-ons over the platter's content.

Just before a signing event at a chain story in Taylor, Michigan, Alex Abbiss told J and Shaggy that the album had been recalled. They made it through what was the biggest day of their lives turning into the worst.

"Everyone in the camp was hurt by this," Billy says. "But the labels wanted us to come over, since now everyone knew who we were."

The lawyers came in, people talked to cameras, and J, Shaggy, and Billy got in J's SUV and headed to Virginia Beach. They needed to be alone and away from the shit. But within hours a call came from Alex as they had breakfast at a Denny's. "You need to come back. Everyone wants to talk to us. CNN called—c'mon," he told J.

At Psychopathic Records the calls were coming in, and Rob Bruce was taking a lot of them. He told callers that "Hollywood had to clean up its act" in light of the boycott, "and it started with ICP."

It was convenient that a group singing of axe murder with a following of a million fans called Juggalos could be excised, although Disney said it wasn't doing so because of pressure. Instead, Disney wanted the world to believe that it had no idea of what was coming with the ICP record. Regardless, the world now knew all about ICP and the Juggalo fan base, which Abbiss told the *Los Angeles Times* was "insanely fanatical . . . one in every four ICP fans has a tattoo of the band on his arm or leg. And tattoos are for life, so there you go."

"I don't think any of us saw the impact right away of what the uproar with Disney meant for the album and for us," Rob says. "We didn't realize that when you say something is banned, people just want it more."

After Disney caved in to the moral purists, ICP wanted to get away from them. There was business to deal with, and lawyers on each side hammered out a deal in which the band would move over to one of the other four labels vying for them, Island Records.

"It was a huge headache, as Disney wanted all its money up-front—the money for the album—before letting us go. They didn't let us go, just like, drop us. We had to have someone pay for us."

Island paid $1 million to Hollywood for the rights. It gave another $1 million to the band. And ICP became a band on Island's roster, joining Melissa Etheridge, the Cranberries, and U2.

The deal was made for ICP to set up their own label, Psychopathic Records. They would have some cash to release records by other bands as well as their own, with support from Island.

"Once we got that all back, those rights, it was the end of trying to deal with outside people," Rob says. "They're always going to let you down."

Milenko sold fifty-two thousand copies in three weeks, and it numbered sixty-three on the Billboard charts, quickly going platinum. The tour was back on, and ICP played to sold-out houses.

J's mother could quit the janitorial business. ICP money bought her a new car and ensured she and her husband, Ron, were finally on solid financial ground.

Critics called *Milenko* "meritless" and "profoundly uninventive." The entertainment writer for the *Gazette* in Montreal concluded his savagery with "Evil clowns? They must be joking. How irredeemably uncool. One artistic suggestion: next time, guys, try mime."

It was around this time when J first coined his own proud legacy for ICP: "We're the most hated band in the world," he said. He still says it today, and the pride is still evident.

Juggalos, many of them feeling hated themselves, both inward and outward, really hung onto that one.

7

The Choppy Waters of Lawlessness

We're legendary. Dammit, we're the Insane Clown Posse.
We're the only ones with balls enough to stand up and
admit that you're a bitch and your husband's a doofy
junkie and that's the bottom line, all right?
—VIOLENT J, SPEAKING TO SHARON OSBOURNE IN
AUGUST 1999 ON THE *HOWARD STERN SHOW*.

If you're not affiliated with one of those major labels, it
gives law enforcement and politicians a green light—
you're fair game if you're doing something they don't like.
—LUTHER CAMPBELL

"**O**n their entire tour I think they
played to something like thirty thousand people. Altogether, collectively," Sharon Osbourne, manager to a select cadre of young metal

bands and wife of Black Sabbath vocalist Ozzy Osbourne, told a How-ard Stern radio audience in August 1999.

The words rolled off her face in an upper-class British lilt. Her glasses danced on the end of her nose, which she wrinkled every time she referred to Insane Clown Posse. She wore a dowdy black dress with a silver cross around her neck, dangling just to the top of her chest, and weighed in at an admitted 225 pounds. She was pissed because one of the bands she managed, Coal Chamber, was booted from an ICP tour after two shows. They weren't drawing, and at $12,500 a show, well, fuck 'em. After they were yanked from the bill, promoters had to refund all of fifteen tickets. There was no demand for the alt-metal band from LA, and ICP couldn't afford the dead weight. They'd said as much the day before on Stern's show. Os-bourne heard about it, called Stern, and asked to come on the show to face off with them.

J and Shaggy were already sitting on the couch in Stern's New York studio when she arrived.

"Sharon, I'm gonna ask you to stand over there if you don't mind 'cause—"

"Ohhh, Howard," Osbourne griped immediately.

"I'd put you on the couch next to them, but I'm afraid you guys will get into a fist fight," Stern explained.

"They smell," Osbourne said.

So it started on a classy note. She launched into the guys immediately.

Osborne vowed that ICP were "burning some bridges" when they messed with one of her bands.

"What is she gonna do? Get us yanked off some radio stations?" J said. "What stations? She's gonna get MTV to turn against us? We don't have no MTV. We have no help anywhere, nowhere. What can she do? There are no strings she can cut to hurt Insane Clown Posse because we don't have any favors. Everybody hates us already."

J and Shaggy had spent the previous twenty minutes insulting Osbourne and her husband, Ozzy, arguably the best-known heavy-metal front man in history. J called him a "heroin-infected junkie" at one point and "a half-retarded junkie" at another. J lampooned the classic Ozzy mic stance, straight up, delivering the lines: "It looks like he got gang raped by a motorcycle gang."

Sharon shot back, "Ozzy's farts have more credibility than anything that comes out of your mouth," and she promised to sue ICP for the $50 Gs they owed for the Coal Chamber obligation.

As Sharon defended Ozzy and threatened litigation, J verbally jumped her: "Listen, you crumpet, London bitch. I'll slap you."

"You're dead," she said, speaking not to them but to Howard. "Your career is over. I will bet them $50,000 that the next record that they release doesn't even sell two hundred thousand units, and they will get dropped by their record label. Let's bet $50,000."

"How about four hundred thousand—we'll make it official," J said.

"Darling, you've never even seen $400,000 in your entire life," she said.

"No, no," J said. He was referring to sales, and she misunderstood. Once squared away on the bet, Osbourne taunted them.

"You're over. You're history. You're yesterday's news," Osbourne pronounced. "You're going to have to pay me $50,000 because your next record will stiff."

On the heels of the platinum *Amazing Jeckel Brothers*, the next album, a two-album release called *Bizaar/Bizzar*, sold four hundred thousand and peaked at twenty-one on the Billboard charts. Osbourne never paid up, even after ICP promised to give the money to charity.

Toward the end of the thirty-minute combat J, in his best wrestling announcer voice, declared, "I'm speaking for all the Juggalos and all the bands out there that's put up with this bitch's antics forever."

Sharon was confused. She looked at Howard. Never mind all the name calling, the wager, and the so-called fed-up bands. She had one question for Howard:

"What is a Juggalo?"

✛ ✛ ✛

The fight on Stern cemented ICP as the leaders of the outsiders, the fearless crusaders for the underdog who beat the shit out of Sharon Osbourne, a lady who professes to make and break careers, the ultimate music-establishment figure.

While giving the finger to this royalty reject, ICP earned the scorn of people who had walked around paying little attention to them before. Now, beating on Ozzy—well, ICP was suddenly an adversary.

What happened to the time when taking on figureheads like Sharon Osbourne was noble?

Black Sabbath were pinned as worshippers of Satan for years. Ozzy loved it, and audiences lapped it up. He once told a reporter at *Hit Parader*, "I don't know if I'm a medium for some outside source. Whatever it is, I hope it's not what I think . . . Satan."

Rockers were outlaws out of the gate. Bill Haley, that middle-aged dude who looked like Duane Eddy's dad, with a cigarette dangling from his fingers, became radical when his tune "Rock Around the Clock" served as the soundtrack for *Blackboard Jungle*, the 1955 flick on teenage delinquents wreaking havoc in schools. The movie was a hit, and it became clear to the grown-ups who moved entertainment that the generation gap sold units. The song hit number one in May, when the movie came out, and stayed at the top until late in the summer.

Elvis was also on the scene with a 1954 tune, "That's All Right." Three years later he hit the *Ed Sullivan Show* and was filmed from the waist up. Network censors determined his stage dance to be indecent.

Eddie Cochran, Johnny Burnette, and Gene Vincent carried the ball of "fuck you." They were all mining black music, shit that the slaves played to each other to stay sane. Robert Johnson, Charley Patton, and Son House were the progenitors of rap. Johnson died at twenty-seven, Patton at forty-three, both living and dying in Mississippi. Son House, also born in Mississippi, lived to a ripe old age of eighty-six, probably by making his way north to Detroit.

The cops came down hard on the blues guys, likely due to an inbred, cultural aversion to blacks. But being black wasn't their only crime—these guys were cranking out some heavy noise, something that had nothing to do with white people's music. They were different. They were bad. Different is bad.

By the midfifties radio stations were playing Elvis and the black sound he mined. Then they weren't. Stations in Chicago were deluged with letters from listeners who urged them to stop with the rhythm and blues.

In Houston a group called the Juvenile Delinquency and Crime Commission made a list of objectionable records. All were on indie labels. All were by black artists.

"Smash the records you possess which present a pagan culture and a pagan concept of life," the Catholic Youth Center in Minneapolis wrote in a newsletter distributed to area youth. The place had been open for twenty years before the crazy sounds hit the airwaves and turned all to bust.

A bunch of crazy Negros from the South endangered all that proselytizing. Different is bad, remember.

Gang activity and music were linked immediately. What could be scarier than the notion of music-crazed youths rampaging collectively? This was before anyone really knew what a gang was or could be. The Crips would have been seen as invaders from another planet.

Link Wray was wicked before the wicked shit. He took rockabilly and slowed it down to an echo-laden tromp. So when the single "Rumble" came out in April 1958 it became the first instrumental ever banned from some stations because it was thought the title hinted at teen gang violence.

"There was a guy named Link Wray when I was in the student union of this major university, and I heard this music, 'Da da DAAA,'" Iggy Pop said in a TV interview a few years back. "And it was called 'Rumble.' And it sounded bad. I left school emotionally at that moment."

There's been lot of noise in the intervening decades about rebellion and oppression and rock 'n' roll all mingling together, most of it well chronicled by music-scribe types and tenured professors who think they rock and need a research project.

There were parental groups, moral majorities, moral minorities, and other strident foes of the First Amendment who felt music had gone too far. And that music was showing little restraint.

The sounds of the street, not to mention the daily vibe and the sentiments that drive that vibe, are slow to reach the rulers of the world. So it's no surprise that it took a year for the song "Fuck Tha Police" to hit the sensitive ears of the FBI.

In a letter dated August 1, 1989, a year almost to the day of the release of N.W.A.'s *Straight Outta Compton*, Milt Ahlerich, a seventeen-year veteran of the FBI, fired off a letter in anger to the promotions director at Priority, the distributor of Eazy-E's Ruthless label that had put out the LP. The subject was the song "Fuck Tha Police."

It went like this:

> Punk police are afraid of me, huh
> A young nigga on the warpath
> And when I'm finished,
> it's gonna be a bloodbath
> Of cops, dying in LA—

Over the year after the LP hit, cops were hearing about the song, talking among themselves about what it meant for them. Some of the police understood; others began complaining to their bosses, associations, unions, or whatever representation they had. The FBI at the time was hardly as bogged down in ineptitude as it is today. Not only was it larger, but it also was seen as the top cop shop, an agency that law enforcement types aspired to. Ahlerich was the agency's spokesman, and he dealt with the press daily. So after hearing from cops everywhere both in his office and outside of it, he composed the letter:

> A song recorded by the rap group NWA on their album entitled *Straight Outta Compton* encourages violence against and disrespect for the law enforcement officer and has been brought to my attention. . . . Advocating violence and assault is wrong and we in the law enforcement community take exception to such action. Violent crime, a major problem in our country, reached an unprecedented high in 1988. Seventy-eight law enforcement officers were feloniously slain in the line of duty during 1988, four more than in 1987. Law enforcement officers dedicate their lives to the protection of our citizens, and recording such as the one from NWA are both discouraging and degrading to those brave, dedicated officers.
>
> Music plays a significant role in society, and I wanted you to be aware of the FBI's position relative to this song and its message.
>
> —Milt Ahlerich, assistant director, Office of Public Affairs

Actually the number killed in 1988 was 195. By 1991 it was 148. All too many, to be sure, but the FBI makes stuff up, numbers especially.

"It was a matter of people coming to me and saying 'Hey, listen. This has caught our attention,' and I felt pretty strongly about it," says Ahlerich, who later went on to be head of security for the National Football League.

Ahlerich's letter was the first time the FBI had actively meddled in a musical release. Objection from the Feds in the late eighties didn't have the same implication it does now, as the government has, over the years, shown an inclination to retaliate against those who think differently. But in 1989 this was truly something new.

"The FBI should stay out of the business of censorship," said US representative Don Edwards, a former FBI agent and then chairman of the House Judiciary Committee's Subcommittee on Civil and Constitutional Rights. It's now the Subcommittee on the Constitution and Civil Justice and has nothing to do with the Feds' infringement on the First Amendment.

But back then Edwards could make a difference.

Ahlerich contends the letter was meant to make the label and its distributors aware of the content. "It was never aimed at the performers," he says. "They were just young guys, trying to make a buck and make some music, as they were artists. I'm not sure I agree with that type of art."

"But I made their career for them," he added.

A couple of months after the letter hit the news, Representative Edwards fired off a letter to the FBI:

> The FBI has developed an official "position" on a rap song by the group NWA and has conveyed that position to the group's record publisher, Priority Records. I am afraid this smacks of intimidation. The FBI should not be music or art critics. I do not believe that it is appropriate for the FBI to single out a particular song or film or book and write to its distributor. The only credible purpose of such an exercise is to encourage the distributor to drop its promotion of the work or the performer and that would seem to be censorship.

NWA was hassled all tour long, including an arrest in Cincinnati for violating the city's obscenity statutes. In Detroit, cops threatened to arrest the group if they included "Fuck Tha Police" in the set list. But nothing came of it. Along the way N.W.A. influenced a legion of rebellion.

Since the N.W.A. fiasco, the murder of cops has dropped until very recently. So much for bomb throwing from the FBI.

Then came Luther Campbell, a rap impresario from Liberty City. He had a head full of salacious party-time anthems in 1985, when he met the California-based 2 Live Crew, who had a Florida hit called "Revelation."

It was tame, not hard enough to be gangster and not soft enough to tilt the ballad machine. Besides, Campbell eschewed the gangster stuff, as he grew up in it—ditto the drugs. His bag was sex.

"So I put my own money into the group and then joined them," Campbell says. He wanted dance-party music with adult-themed lyrics, like the routines he saw Redd Foxx and Aunt Esther do on television. "I saw them on *Sanford and Son* and realized they were also hard-core adult-themed comedians. So [2 Live Crew] was going to be funny and fun."

Once Campbell was part of 2 Live, the party was on. The first LP, *The 2 Live Crew Is What We Are*, came out in 1986 and featured the single "Throw the D."

By 1992 the Feds were worried about speech in the moral-majority era, as obscenity prosecutions conducted by the Department of Justice rose from 37 in 1988 to 120 in 1989. Parental freak-outs were coming fast, and there's nothing like a raging housewife on *Donohue* to put your music in the front row, which is what 2 Live Crew wrought.

The foundation of today's right to hear anything you want—and the right of an artist to play and record and release it—started with a crusading Florida sheriff in early 1990.

The law in Broward County, home of then spring break capital Fort Lauderdale, was overseen by Sheriff Nick Navarro, who claimed his office was getting complaints about music by 2 Live Crew that was popping up in stores.

By then the band's second LP, *As Nasty as They Wanna Be*, an indie slab of vinyl featuring across the cover the asses of four down-for-it ladies, was selling like crazy. After obtaining a court or-der that the material might run afoul of obscenity laws, Navarro sent his agents out to advise record store owners that selling *Nasty* could result in obscenity charges.

"It was a watershed moment," says Bruce Rogow, Campbell's law-yer. "That run for 2 Live Crew was extraordinary. It was an oddity in that no one else in the country came after them. Luckily for 2 Live Crew, the sheriff in Florida decided to take them on."

In response to the sheriff's warnings, Campbell filed a lawsuit against the county, asserting his First Amendment rights. It placed the case in front of a federal judge.

In June 1990 US district judge Jose Gonzalez ruled against 2 Live Crew, the first time in US history a federal judge declared a musical recording obscene. The ruling put Campbell on the map as one dirty artist, in league with Mae West, Lenny Bruce, and the Miami-shot Deep Throat.

"I read [the judge's decision] and thought it was great," Rogow says.

Campbell, though, was devastated. He tore it up into little pieces and called it "toilet paper."

But Rogow knew something was about to break, even before the decision came. "No matter what happens in this case, you win," Ro-gow told Campbell. "If the government says you can't have some-thing, everyone is going to want it."

If the judge had not found the material obscene, it would have ended there. But with the decision to quash art, "he prolonged it," Rogow says.

Campbell wasn't thinking about the future, though. "I was think-ing about Bruce's argument, that we had proved our case so well, and when I understood my case, I felt it was an idiotic ruling," Campbell says.

Three days after the judge's ruling Campbell and two other Crew members were arrested after a nightclub performance and charged with obscenity for their act. The cops were there, armed with

Gonzalez's ruling. And if something is deemed legally obscene, you can't play it in public.

"I told the guys to be prepared to go to jail for this," Campbell says. "I knew the police were there."

Several months later a six-person jury, five whites (four women, one man), and one black woman, acquitted 2 Live Crew.

Meanwhile a three-judge panel of the 11th US Circuit Court of Appeals overturned Gonzalez, and the US Supreme Court, in declining to hear the case, solidified the appellate ruling.

2 Live Crew had fought the law and won.

And in the meantime the *As Nasty as They Wanna Be* went double-platinum. Not only was it dirty, it was good dirty.

Campbell notes that he went to the wall to defend musical artists' right to be protected under the First Amendment, all the while fending off zealots from the other side who accused him and 2 Live of making music that degraded women. "We had the Al Sharptons and the Jesse Jacksons coming at us saying this is wrong, against women and so on, and I said, 'You guys are not looking at the big picture.' I wasn't fighting for music or my livelihood—it was about the right to create something."

Campbell's battle has given him a profile among the First Amendment crowd but has earned him little praise from the music industry. "No one has asked me to talk at the Rock and Roll Hall of Fame about it, and we've never been recognized for it," Campbell says. "We're the Rodney Dangerfields of the executive and music business. I felt the establishment was after us in the first place because we weren't part of the record industry. I was selling records out of the trunk of my car, and the record industry didn't feel that we should exist. They weren't giving us any deals, and they were telling us we weren't going to make it anyway. I now realize it was political. We got no support from the music industry because we weren't part of the music industry. I didn't give money to the politicians the way the labels did, the way the corporations that own the labels do and did. If you're not affiliated with one of those major labels, it gives law enforcement and politicians a green light—you're fair game if you're doing something they don't like."

The same is true more than two decades later.

"We're easy targets. We're clowns," J says. "We've done it our way the whole way through. We didn't use the corporate mainstream machines. They all look at us as outsiders, and they want to fuck with us because we didn't use their power structure to get where we are. We used our own. They feel like we snuck in. We did sneak in. We're not supposed to be here."

8

Klebold's Coattails and the Miscreant Tribe

A hole was punched in Mr. Amphibian's hat and Tastes Like Chicken's leg was broken.
—POLICE REPORT IN TOLEDO IN THE WAKE OF
THE GATHERING OF THE JUGGALOS

A Couple of Clowns? Insane Clown Posse are Crude, Defiant and a Parent's Worst Nightmare.
—*FRESNO BEE*, AUGUST 1, 1999

You couldn't blame any school administrator in Colorado for being a little jumpy in the early twenty-first century. Columbine had shaken people up. Honchos had tried to blame everyone from Satan on down for the April 1999 slaughter of twelve students and a teacher at Columbine High School by Eric Harris and Dylan Klebold, a couple of kids who considered themselves outsiders.

It was inevitable that crazy kids with guns would come up with the notion of wholesale slaughter by themselves. Everyone from Marilyn Manson to the German industrial band KMFDM were blamed. Somehow Juggalos could be wrapped into the blame game as well.

The *Rocky Mountain News* came into an alleged e-mail sent by one of the two killers to the cops before the murders.

By now it's over. If you are reading this my mission is complete. I have finished revolutionizing the neoeuphoric infliction of my internal terror. Your children who have ridaculed [sic] me, who have chosen not to accept me, who have treated me like I am not worth their time are dead. THEY ARE FUCKING DEAD. Surely you will try to blame it on the clothes I wear, the music I listen to, or the way I choose to present myself—but no. Do not hide behind my choices. You need to face the fact that this comes as a result of YOUR CHOICES. Parents and Teachers, YOU FUCKED UP. You have taught these kids to be gears and sheep. To think and act like those who came before them, to not accept what is different. YOU ARE IN THE WRONG. I may have taken their lives and my own—but it was your doing. Teachers, Parents, LET THIS MASSACRE BE ON YOUR SHOULDERS UNTIL THE DAY YOU DIE. Am I insane? Maybe. Is it my fault? No. I did not choose this life, but I have indeed chosen to exit it. You may think the horror ends with the bullet in my head—but you wouldn't be so lucky. All that I can leave you with to decipher what more extensive death is to come is "12Skitzo." You have until April 26th. Goodbye.

Some people thought 12Skitzo is a reference to the song "12" on *Riddle Box*, which is about a guy who was executed and comes back to kill the dozen jurors who sent him up.

It's a stretch. True, Klebold, along with some of his classmates, hit up the library when the Internet was just starting up to check out the fledgling insaneclownposse.com website. Klebold didn't dig ICP—he was actually into industrial bands like KMFDM and the German metal band Rammstein.

"Dylan would tell me about how great Rammstein and KMFDM were, and I'd fire back with a spirited defense of Insane Clown Posse," Brooks Brown, a classmate, said later.

Early in 2000 J noticed the media's speculation. During a Pittsburg stop he addressed it: "We've been getting a lot of bad press lately about Columbine, and how the shooters were supposedly Juggalos. They've been asking us for sound bites. Quotes of the minute, if you will. Well, I've got this to say: if those two faggots in trench coats had been Juggalos, they would have gotten the whole damn school."

Later he was a bit more measured.

"Even if the killers left notes in their bedrooms saying, 'Insane Clown Posse did this,' it wouldn't be our fault," J said, speaking to the notion of an ICP-Columbine connection. "We know what Insane Clown Posse does is controversial. It's offensive. It's terrible to many people. But you don't see us on MTV. You don't hear us on any radio stations. We don't want to ever subject what we do to an audience that doesn't want to see us."

As mass shootings were new to the American landscape then, there were murmurs of gangs—the Trenchcoat Mafia?—fomenting plans of mass destruction and other forms of antisocial upset.

At Psychopathic it was decided that a multiday music festival for the Juggalos would bring them together amidst a series of public clouds amassing. Since 1994 there had been Hallowicked, held Halloween night in the Detroit area and drawing a full house from across the country. But this would be bigger. Like Woodstock 1999, which ICP had played the previous summer, but just for Juggalos.

The following July Scott Donihoo sat with a friend at the bus stop in Arlington, Texas, waiting for a twenty-nine-hour ride to the first Gathering of the Juggalos in Novi, Michigan. The ad for the first Gathering, held over two days at the Novi Expo Center, which has since been demolished, was over-the-top horror fantasy:

Imagine thousands of screaming Juggalos from across the nation gathered in one spot to become submersed in the chaos of the Dark Carnival culture. Soon this will be reality, and the only imagined thing will be the screaming you hear in your own mind.

It was July 2000, and ICP had gone from charting rappers with a weird little following to outlaws, a "parent's worst nightmare." Newspapers were peddling fear as always. In the early eighties it was punk rock, where whole families would be torn asunder if one of the kids "went punk."

Hollywood helped, with shows like *CHiPs* and *Quincy* devoting episodes to the perils awaiting those who embrace the punk-rock lifestyle.

In a post-Columbine world nothing could have been better. ICP was music for kids seeking weirdness in a world of sameness, where the nation had turned into rubber freaks for fear of AIDS and pissing in a cup was now SOP for anyone wanting a job.

Donihoo first heard of Insane Clown Posse in 1996, when someone played him the "Chicken Huntin" cassette single he had gotten when the ICP crew visited Trinity High School during the *Riddle Box* marketing blitz of Dallas a year before.

When *Milenko* came out he went to Best Buy and bought everything in the back catalog. He began contributing as a writer to a site called Faygoluvers that was devoted to Psychopathic Records and run by a couple of kids from Detroit—Jeff and Rick. A couple of years later he found himself sweeping floors in an auto parts warehouse for $7 an hour and writing almost every day on the happenings of these underground bands that, to the world, no one knew or cared about. To the Juggalos, though, his news was crucial.

"At the time there were, seriously, nearly a hundred sites devoted to Psychopathic and Insane Clown Posse," Donihoo, who soon adopted a Juggalo moniker, Scottie D, says. Indeed, a sweep of the URLs in 2001 shows dozens devoted to all things connected to Juggalos. Not all were active, and some were simply taken by business-minded poachers and others by Juggalos who hoped someday to be able to have their own website devoted to Psychopathic bands.

In 2001 Donihoo took over Faygoluvers when the other guys lost interest. Pretty soon it became the place to be for info on ICP, and demand kept crashing the server. The move to a larger server cost him $200 a month. Donihoo is still making it happen and has become the CNN of Juggalo news, a guy who knows just about anything connected to the label and the bands.

Today he's also a well-paid network administrator for a company outside Dallas and lives in an upscale home in suburban Dallas with his wife and young son. Every year he packs up a dozen bottles of 5-Hour Energy and heads to the Gathering in a large mobile home, where he documents every little utterance and posts it to Faygoluvers.

Back in 2000, as a kid in love with something new, he was ready for anything, and he and his pal Toxic D headed for Detroit. It was a shit show, logistically speaking, for him and Toxic D. The bus company lost their luggage. They were first denied a hotel because neither of them was twenty-one years old. The line waiting to get in was rambunctious—people throwing Faygo, hurling anything that might break, and making loads of noise.

Part of the Gathering was a scavenger hunt. When that hunt took them to Canada, the border agents refused them admittance. Toxic D was in clown paint.

"You're a disgrace to your country," an unhappy border agent told him.

When ICP came on to close the show, the Juggalos went crazy when J asked everyone, "Are we gonna burn this motherfucker down?"

The set ended after forty minutes when the crowd overran the stage. Outside the venue Juggalos wanted to torch the place, and fires were lit around the parking lot. It was a suitable ending. People could read about it on MTV's website, and many did so with shaking heads.

But even more compelling, more than the random destruction and mayhem, were the accounts of the devoted fans like Donihoo.

One kid told of traveling fifty-three hours by bus. Another of spending $700 on merchandise after receiving a trip to Detroit from Albany, New York, as a high school graduation gift from his dad. And then there were the Juggalos just trying to get back to where they came from. Four guys stood at the foot of the Novi Expo Center parking lot leading to the Interstate with a sign: "Denver ninjas need a ride home."

All for a bunch of white guys in clown paint trying to rap. In corners of the United States, music followers, critics, parents, moral overseers, and cops seethed.

✜ ✜ ✜

The Gathering moved to Toledo the next year and expanded from two days to three.

It was again a festival of mayhem. A Juggalo punched a police horse. Others ransacked the stage during ICP's set once more, and cops in riot gear mobilized outside the Seagate Center. The city claimed that Juggalos also damaged some fiberglass frog sculptures from a nearby art installment. "A hole was punched in Mr. Amphibian's hat and Tastes Like Chicken's leg was broken," according to a report from the city. The Associated Press reported the whole episode.

The venue was connected to a hotel. It looked like things were going to be called off, such was the disorder the Juggalos created. "They wanted us to get out of there. They needed one solid excuse to tell us to get the fuck out," J says.

So Shaggy found the master mic of the hotel—the one that the voice of doom comes through when the place is engulfed in flames to tell you to exit the building NOW. "Hey, listen up! It's Shaggy 2 Dope!" he screamed into the hand-held mic. The call went to every room of hotel. There was no "Juggalo rooms only" button to push. "Listen, everybody has to chill out or they're gonna kick us the fuck outta here," he said.

It worked, at least for the Juggalos. For the rest of the guests, well, it was going to be a long night.

ICP was banned from playing Toledo for the next decade.

The next year, Gathering number three, was held in Peoria, Illinois. Cops moved in when a girl was showing her tits. That was just too much, apparently, and when Juggalos resisted, the pepper-spray bullets came out. Juggalos fired back with water and the traditional—and ineffective—"fuck tha police" chants.

"Really, what was that?" J says. "Titties come out at rock concerts."

Over a decade later that situation still smarts. It was the first time the law had really come down on Juggalos for a suspect reason, but not the last. "There were no little kids there, and no one gave a fuck about this girl flashing her tits. They weren't smoking dope. They're not doing anything illegal. She has her top off. She's partying at some rock concert. You know, so you beat everybody's ass on your way to arrest her. Those are the only problems we have—people interacting with Juggalos. There are no problems between Juggalos. You know it's always people having a problem with what's happening."

Peoria police called in reinforcement from area agencies and emptied the Civic Center. Abbiss and Rob Bruce did some Paris Peace Talk–style convincing—*the place will erupt if you call this whole thing off*, was the thrust, a threat dressed as a statement—and the Juggalos were allowed back in and the event continued.

The news called the cop intervention a riot, which resulted in more national coverage.

This year's Gathering of the Juggalos was by far the biggest and best one yet. When you have over eight thousand Juggalos crammed into one place, the Peoria Civic Center, there are many opportunities for disaster and chaos. One such event did occur during the Gathering when a riot occurred shortly after police tried to stop Juggalettes from showing what their mothers gave them. Soon tear gas bellowed down the halls of the center and mass confusion set in. But this did not spell doom for the Gathering. Immediately assessing the situation, Jumpsteady and Alex Abbiss arrived on the scene and began negotiations with the police and the Juggalos present. It did not take long for the two dons to quickly bring things back to order. This however was one of the only bones that the Gathering witnessed; the entire three day event went crazy-smooth and almost everyone present had the best time of their lives.

—Statement by Insane Clown Posse at insaneclownposse.com the day after the Peoria Gathering

The Gatherings, coupled with ICP's relentless record-tour cycle, began to gain traction for Juggalos. And that wasn't gonna be good. Who the hell was going to heap praise on something so maligned?

Blender magazine in 2003 called them the worst artists in music history ("trailer trash"). You could file that in the same place as the four-page cartoon spread in the print edition of *Spin* in 1998 that disparaged Juggalos and depicted ICP as a couple of artistically bereft knuckleheads and dubbed them "Mooks of the Year."

The strip was drawn by a couple of Detroit wiseasses, Mike Rubin and Mark Dancey, with ties to the dead-as-hell rock scene. ICP took the high road and threatened them with bodily harm. Nothing came of it, although Dancey and Rubin used the pages of *Spin* to note that the threats were "considerably ironic coming from supposed First Amendment martyrs."

Pedestrian observations like that and more flowed every summer around the time of the Gathering. "All that stuff was getting run of the mill, those insults," says Mike Clark, who was gaining recognition from reviewers as the man behind the beats. "Everywhere you would turn, there would be slams in the paper. All the time. We just all got real thick skin. And our fans were just so fanatical and devoted. You hang out with them someplace, like at a show or a Gathering, then go into the real world, and you're barely hanging on."

Juggalo crowd at ICP show, Des Moines, Iowa. (PHOTO BY HAZIN)

"The Insane Clown Pussies"—Phil Anselmo refers to ICP during a Down meet and greet. Left to right: Phil Anselmo, Pepper Keenan, Danielle Keene, Jimmy Bower, and Kirk Windstein. The thumbs down is Anselmo's salute to Keene's hatchet man T-shirt. (COURTESY OF DANIELLE KEENE)

ScottieD, aka, Scott Donihoo, and his wife, Amanda. (PHOTO BY FAYGOLUVERS.NET)

The lake at Cave-in-Rock, Illinois, which hosted the Gathering of the Juggalos for seven years, was a fetid pool of filth dubbed Lake Hepatitis. (FROM THE PERSONAL COLLECTION OF JOEL FRAGOMENI)

Juggalos in their summer gear. (PHOTO BY CURTIS BOLT)

Juggalos on the USS *George H. W. Bush*. (COURTESY JASON FAANES)

Outside the Phoenix Theater, in Petaluma, California, a Juggalo takes a breather next to his ride. (PHOTO BY JASON SHALTZ)

Violent J, in the paint. (PHOTO BY CURTIS BOLT)

Juggalos: A fan club or a gang?

By Michelle Vasey

In the late 1980s and early '90s, two men from Detroit, Michigan, walked away from a gang they began, known as Inner City Posse, and tried their hand in the underground rap scene.

Changing their name from Inner City Posse to Insane Clown Posse (ICP), Joseph Bruce and Joey Utsler, or as they like to be called, Violent J and Shaggy 2 Dope, claimed to have been visited by the carnival spirit. They were told to send a message of society's need for cleansing or perish when the world ends.

They began their own record label called Psychopathic Records, and decided to send the message through six joker cards which became albums. Each album has a specific message and although the lyrics brought controversy, their fan base erupted.

The fans refer to themselves as Juggalos. The name Juggalo comes from Violent J's so-called alter ego, "The Juggla." Fans say that Violent J called out to the fans during a concert calling them "My Juggalos" and the name stuck. The lyrics speak of clown love and paying homage to the hatchet. The lyrics also speak of extreme violence and hatred toward society that has disrespected all those that society has labeled loners or outcasts.

Juggalos are fans of Insane Clown Posse but several groups of Juggalos have evolved into gangs.

In 2004, the Arizona Department of Public Safety Gang Immigration Intelligence Team Enforcement Mission (GIITEM) began investigating several incidents at Palo Verde High School in Tucson, Arizona. The juveniles, who were self-proclaimed Juggalos, were threatening a student for reasons unknown. Detectives began conducting research on the Juggalos and the Insane Clown Posse. Based on the information developed along with the Palo Verde case, the Juggalos were officially documented as a gang within the State of Arizona in 2007. The lead detective in the case, Hal Van Woert, noted, "Juggalos have adopted the message and philosophy of ICP and others on the Psychopathic Records label as a mission and a total lifestyle. They immerse themselves in the imagery and listen to the music whenever and wherever they can. They meet at annual and semiannual 'gatherings,' and they share their views and thoughts (such

These "Juggalettes" flash their gang signs.

as they are) on numerous Internet sites. In short, the message of ICP is, for the true die-hard Juggalos, not what they hear, but what they ARE."

Shortly after Det. Van Woert wrote his definition of the Juggalos, he found a similar definition written by a Juggalo on the Internet: "Many people often believe that Juggalos & Juggalettes are just another name for fans of Insane Clown Posse. Being a Juggalo is much more than liking the music; it is a way of life. A fan is someone who only likes the music either because it's the fad right now, or because they want to conform. Fans don't see the true message of the music, just the outer layer. Fans are quick to forget you as soon as the next big sensation comes along. They also will hound ICP for autographs and see them only as big famous stars. A Juggalo is one who lives their life by the hatchet. In other words, they believe in the true meaning behind ICP's songs [and] try to live by J and Shaggy's preachings. Juggalos are down with the clown for life, and will never turn their back on ICP because they are said to be 'uncool' ... They are dedicated to Psychopathic forever."[1]

Juggalos can be identified by the following indicia:
1) Any and all Psychopathic record label clothing and paraphernalia
2) Tattoos relating to Insane Clown Posse and Psychopathic associated artists to include

A fan club or a gang? Asking the burning question in a 2010 report from law enforcement. (FROM ROCKY MOUNTAIN INFORMATION NETWORK)

Juggalo photo handed out by the Agency of Firearms and Tobacco. (FROM ATF)

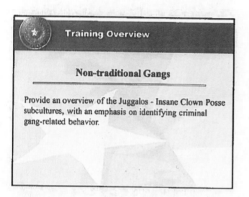

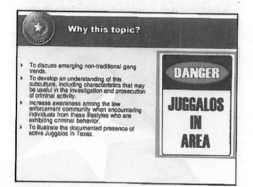

At the Texas attorney general's office presentation to law enforcement and community groups. This was delivered to the public twenty-two times between 2010 and 2014. (FROM TEXAS ATTORNEY GENERAL)

I pledge allegiance to the hatchet of the underground juggalo society.And to the ninja which it stands.One family under clowns,Full of freeks and mcgic neden for all

A page from a 2010 report assembled by a gang officer from the Denver Police Department titled, Everything You Never Wanted to Know About the Juggalos. (FROM DENVER POLICE DEPARTMENT)

In response to an open records request to the Salt Lake County District Attorney's Office for communication relating to Juggalos during the federal compilation of the gang threat assessment, this is what was produced.
(FROM SALT LAKE COUNTY DISTRICT ATTORNEY'S OFFICE)

Juggalo lawyer Farris Hadaad giving Juggalos an update on the lawsuit against the FBI, summer 2015. (PHOTO BY CURTIS BOLT)

"I'm a Juggalo, not a gang member" T-shirts came out soon after the FBI's 2011 gang threat report named Juggalos as a gang. (PHOTO BY HAZIN)

At any Juggalo event, arriving early is part of the deal. Three Juggalos at the pizza joint, The White Rabbit, in San Antonio, before a Twiztid show, 2010. (PHOTO BY JASON SHALTZ)

Twiztid at the Russell Industrial Center, in Detroit, for a press shoot. (PHOTO BY JASON SHALTZ)

From left: Shaggy 2 Dope, Violent J, and John Kickjazz. John was Shaggy's brother and left the band shortly before the first album. He died in 2015. (COURTESY OF PSYCHOPATHIC RECORDS)

Shaggy in Faygo. (PHOTO BY JACK GORMAN, HOUSTON PRESS)

Sarah at a gas station outside Cave-in-Rock, Illinois. (PHOTO BY JASON SHALTZ)

Long haired, broad shouldered, and bearded, Clark looks like a stereotypical roadie. He pounds on anything nearby when he has a novel idea or wants you to see something he just discovered on You-Tube or heard somewhere on the Internet.

Clark split with ICP in 2000. There were disputes over all kinds of things, money included. He wasn't the first to claim the cash was coming back to him a bit slowly, and Clark returned in 2007. But he never dropped his fealty to the Juggalos. Few did, in fact. Once you were in, it was your life. Then people started to get a little more haterlicious on them. There were more critical press reports, and more focused on the alleged actions of Juggalos than anything the band did.

Colorado Springs' largest school district banned garb associated with Insane Clown Posse on Monday after fans of the horror rap/metal duo were linked to violence at two high schools and a charter school.

—*The Gazette*, Colorado Springs, 2004

Getting banned was no surprise—it was getting to be a standard reaction from the establishment, from record labels to municipalities. It was old as Arsenio's fade, in fact. So a city in the home state of Columbine banned ICP stuff, the gear you could get at Hot Topic in just any mall in the United States or online at Hatchetgear.com. So what?

This ban, though, was the first of many to come. And Juggalos were being castigated for being Juggalos. Cops showed up at schools where Juggalos were part of the student body. Then came reports in Tacoma, Washington, of machete-wielding Juggalos who went on a rampage while painted up.

"The attacks over two nights would begin with the assailants calling to each other: 'Woo! Woo! Juggalo!'"—Pierce County Deputy Prosecutor Phil Sorenson told the Associated Press.

Next there were murders in Arizona being attributed to a "gang called the Juggalos." It was a shit show for anyone who dug ICP. And it was really on. "Fan or Gang?" blared a headline in the *East Valley Tribune*, a suburban Phoenix news site.

To some police investigators, the group—which calls itself Juggalos—is a gang.

Last month, a group of statewide gang investigators met to discuss the Juggalos in an effort to classify the subculture. They decided that while most Juggalos aren't considered gang members, a few emerging sects meet the statewide criteria for a criminal street gang.

"We're extremely divided," said Arizona Department of Public Safety gang expert Detective Michelle Vasey. "I've kind of made these guys my passion over the past year-and-a-half. You've got 90 percent of them that are true fans . . . but what we've found . . . is small groups of gangs breaking off and calling themselves some kind of gang sect."

Scottsdale police gang officers also met earlier this month with the city's school resource officers to educate them about Juggalos and how to identify them.

"I think the Juggalos have a pretty overt style with the face paint and the hatchetman," said Scottsdale police Sgt. Aaron Minor. The hatchetman is a cartoon drawing of a little man running with a hatchet that serves as a logo of sorts for the Juggalos.

Watching all of this from a cramped office in New York City, Thomas Morton recalled the Juggalos he'd gone to high school with in Atlanta. He had moved to New York, and there were no Juggalos there, so they more or less fell off his radar.

But in the summer of 2007 Morton was one of three writers working at the main office of Vice, a media empire born in Montreal that had spread to continents and countries with an insouciant flair. The scribes were poorly paid but had a waiting audience for stories that ranged from a guide to Slayer fans to goat slaughtering in

Jamaica. If you had some humor and a Gonzo instinct, all the better. So a story pitch to attend the annual MardiGrass festival in Australia, where ten thousand freaks gathered each year to smoke some good weed and talk about reform, well, that's a damn good idea in Vice land.

Morton saw Juggalos hitting law enforcement's radar and, at the same time, was reading the blog postings from the Gathering of the Juggalos, written by Juggalos. "It was the only thing out there at the time that really told what happened at the Gathering," Morton says. "It was this litany of horrible accidents and crowd incidents."

He also read the Wiki Gathering page and was treated to tales like this:

> The fifth GotJ was also held in the Crystal Forest. Tech N9ne, Ol' Dirty Bastard, and Vanilla Ice all performed. Kurupt also performed, but didn't quite understand what to expect at a Juggalo event, and ended up throwing a broom stick, striking a Juggalo in the eye. The Juggalos wanted to kill him.

"Juggalos had fallen out of my mind, but I had a friend who was into ICP and would keep me up on what was happening online," Morton says. "The Gathering had become, to me, this mythic sort of thing. I hadn't had any interaction with Juggalos since I was seventeen, and I recall when I was twelve or thirteen years old seeing metal heads and thinking that they really worshipped Satan. So I was getting this mindset of Juggalos, that they were capable of anything. And I figured going to a Gathering could be crazy."

It was apocryphal thinking. When he pitched the story—attending the Gathering and writing about Juggalos—the response was "Yeah, let us know how that goes."

His coworkers believed he might not return in one piece. For weeks he e-mailed the Psychopathic crew, trying to get a press pass. Finally someone e-mailed him and said they were too busy to deal with anything like that. Until Morton, there had been no outside media asking for such things. No one at Psychopathic was thinking that any outlet aside from their faithful blogger following would want to show up,

So Morton paid the $100 for a Gathering ticket, plus airfare to Nashville and a rental car and headed for Cave-in-Rock, Illinois. He drove four hours toward the site and spent the first night sleeping in his car.

The next day he entered the gate and was almost immediately struck by two things: *Wow, look at the fuckin' drug sales* and *Holy shit, everyone here is so damn nice.*

"I expected to get shit every day, and no one ever made fun of me. It was the shock of all shocks. I thought I would have to defend myself physically. And I didn't even see that many fights compared to a normal concert."

The closest thing to an insult came when he showed up wearing a military-green-colored shirt. With his small spectacles, someone noted he looked like Radar O'Reilly, the geeky, efficient corporal on the TV series *M*A*S*H.*

He'd been to Coachella, All Tomorrow's Parties, and various festivals around Europe, but never had he seen so many open-air drug sales. It was impressive, "like a cop's fantasy of how drug sales work."

Just the sheer availability was amazing. You could call out anything—acid, smoke—and someone would come to sell you whatever it was. Or they had a friend who could hook you up. "I think about it as a cartoon that I took part in sometimes," Morton says. "It was, though, one of the best weekends of my life."

The resulting story was a seven-thousand-word account that mixed observational humor with an inherent timidity and awe. Morton portrayed himself as a stranger in a strange land, only he was treated as one of them.

Whereas at the traditional big-buck music festivals the clientele is composed of mostly moneyed stoners, trust-fund kids, and cultural heeders, the Gathering was filled with real people from real America—the kind of folks most people don't ever want to hear about or from. But Morton, who graduated from NYU with a degree in English literature, was cool with the whole sordid situation. "I'd be standing in line for something, and they'd tell you these stories, just out of the blue," Morton says, "stories about being molested, and I'd end up in these hair-raising therapy sessions just standing there."

"And they had these seminars in a tent, where an artist would stand there and talk about things, and this whole notion of the Juggalos sitting around thoughtfully watching these seminars while pandemonium ensued behind them was just amazing."

When he headed to the front of the pit for the ICP finale he found himself getting jet streamed with Faygo. He wrote,

> In addition to a steady stream of people, anything too large to fling toward the stage was crowd-surfed in that direction. I ended up getting hit square in the face with boots, fists, chairs, bare tits, other people's faces, and an empty cooler. I also think I gouged some poor girl's nipple with my thumb while trying to push her overhead. I feel bad about that one.
>
> Following the longest 20 minutes of my life, I gave up and extricated myself from the maelstrom. I finally broke loose at the far edge of the stage by the space between the barricade and the stage where the crowd surfers were deposited after making it to the front. The folks who came out of this exit-chute did so in full, trance-like rap-dance. It was sort of like a filthy version of the *Soul Train Line*.

There were mistakes in Morton's article, the most glaring being the call "whoop whoop" translated as "whoot whoot."

"I never saw it written out before, so yeah, there was some of that," he says later. "But the piece was like the first article written on disco. There was nothing before like it."

Morton paved the way. His piece was widely read, commented on, liked, and shared. "And when it ran, I did get reimbursed for my expenses."

9

Magnets and Delinquents

Think of the press as a great keyboard on which the government can play.
—JOSEPH GOEBBELS

If you happen to see a Juggalo, don't freak out.
—NAMELESS GANG DETECTIVE, FRANCONIA, VIRGINIA

To ICP, science is dishonest witchcraft, and the practitioners of such deceit should be burned at the stake. As such, wonders like genetics, metamorphosis and even 'pet cats and dogs' will forever remain miracles to Violent J and Shaggy 2 Dope.
—NOAH HUBBELL, CITING THE LYRICS TO "MIRACLES"
AS THE WORST RAP LYRICS EVER FOR *WESTWORD*,
AN ALTERNATIVE WEEKLY IN DENVER

The studio in which some of the best Juggalo-pleasing work has been done is today tucked away in a bland neighborhood in Macomb County, north of Detroit.

Rows of sameness are jammed into blocks rimmed by four- and five-lane suburban Autobahns, where the eight-to-five shift is a religion.

For over a decade Mike E. Clark has created music in his basement studio, the Funhouse, named after the second album by the Stooges. The studio takes up most of the basement, which also offers a bedroom for performers who come and record.

In 2008 Clark wrote the foundation for Kid Rock's breakout "All Summer Long" there one morning as he was checking random songs in iTunes, crossing the piano from Warren Zevon's "Werewolves of London" with a beat.

Later that year Shaggy, J, and Clark hit the Funhouse and started to work on *Bang! Pow! Boom!*, the eleventh ICP LP. This was the one aimed squarely at Juggalos, more than any of the others. It was part of a flurry of work that also included DVDs, videos, the filming and production of their second full-length movie, *Big Money Rustlas*, and a massive tour to support everything.

ICP was also getting more attention from the media through some Juggalos' criminal activities. That scrutiny came mostly from journalists in smaller towns who were writing anything the cops told them as well as uptight music scribes who were mortally offended by the growing numbers of fans the band was earning. You'd see Juggalos almost everywhere these days, including jumping off the Metrorail in Miami in the noon sunlight of summer, fully painted or checking out Main Street in downtown Houston, Psychopathic T-shirts and ICP hats on cockeyed, walking along like they owned the place.

The crimes committed didn't grow, but the reporting did—a teenager in Santa Fe got pissed at the music being played at a party and stabbed the twenty-two-year-old host, who was jamming, of course, Insane Clown Posse. Somehow, the band's name made it into the second sentence of the news account, even before the name of the alleged assailant. In Salt Lake City some undercover cops claimed a dozen Juggalos attacked a woman who asked them to leave the parking lot of an LDS church.

And J and Shaggy were thinking about miracles.

The beats were already written by Clark, as usual, and J and Shaggy sang about the wonder of everyday things in a sincere fashion. It was a step away from the usual subjects, but they'd been leaning into newer avenues of emotions for a little while. They were secure with the love of Juggalos, and reflecting on the small things in life—pyramids, giraffes, childbirth, rainbows—felt good.

"Fuckin' magnets, how do they work?" Shaggy worked into the second verse about two minutes into the four-minute song.

Clark cringed. He'd done it before when J or Shaggy would spout a line that was sure to draw some shit. "Fuck the Beastie Boys and the Dalai Lama" from "Fuck the World" was another lyric. That one spelled the end of a potential relationship with one of New York's top publicists, Steve Martin, whose clients included the Beastie Boys.

But the line about magnets, well, that might even be worse, as it was playing right into the hands of the wheelhouse of critics, with their worn-out "ICP are stupid" line. "I knew then there would be some kind of noise over this magnets line," Clark says.

With all the hand wringing about the band, the haters screeching about how dim Juggalos were, the classist dislike of the lower-income class, the dislike of white rappers, the mounting efforts of police to criminalize being a Juggalo—that line—"fuckin' magnets, how do they work?"—is going to catch fire in a bad way.

When the video came out, it did.

The video was shot a couple of blocks from Psychopathic HQ in a production house with better gear. The creative was handed over to Universal Images and the hands of Tom Horvath II, who now handles animation for *American Dad* at the Fox Broadcasting Company. And he's smart enough to still pimp out that he worked on the video for "Miracles" on his LinkedIn profile.

The video took a while. It makes the guys look like they're standing on planets, pontificating and pointing and preening while spouting the simpleton words that flustered everyone from academics to janitors. Juggalos got it. Everyone else didn't, and that pissed them off.

For the video, "We told them to make it very literal, about everything J and Shaggy talked about in the song," says Brian Kuma, an in-house producer at Psychopathic. The video's ambition was beyond anyone there. It was beyond J or Shaggy, for that matter.

J brought in his kids, JJ and Ruby, to be part of the shoot. "And he just loved the video, he was ecstatic at the result," Kuma says.

People jumped on it as it went viral.

"This finally proves what I've been saying for years: Insane Clown Posse and their fans are like every stereotype about white American stupidity and poor taste made manifest," posted one brave soul at Gawker.

BuzzFeed named the lyrics to "Miracles" among the "Most mind-bogglingly stupid song lyrics."

The video came out the morning of April 6, 2010, and later in the day J came over, alone, to the Funhouse. He was inconsolable. "Man, they really hate us," he told Clark. He had written the song through the eyes of his young son, JJ, seeing simple things that were mystifying to a developing person. It was also about not losing sight of these things that truly are magnificent.

"I saw the hurt in his face that day," Clark says. "He really did not expect that reaction. He was just crushed."

Later that month "Miracles" was lampooned by *Saturday Night Live*, which called it "Magical Mysteries" and was delivered by a couple of cast members in face paint. J dug the *SNL* attention but was still saddened to think that some people didn't see miracles in the things that fascinate their kids.

For Juggalos it didn't matter. *Bang! Pow! Boom!* hit number four on the top-200 Billboard charts and sold fifty thousand copies the first week. It was seen by even the most strident ICP haters as a breakthrough, better even than *Milenko*. Juggalos were going nuts buying it.

"That was no joke to us," J says. "But apparently it was to everyone else."

✛ ✛ ✛

Juggalos were also no joke to the twenty law enforcement agencies in that bastion of bad actors, northeast Wisconsin.

Cops from seven counties in that region were convinced that Juggalos, also referred to in the report as "Big Money Hustlas," were perpetrating all sorts of mayhem along with the Bloods, Crips, Gangster Disciples, Mexican Mafia, and La Raza. Never mind that the region is 93 percent white; for these cops to be correct in their estimation, nearly every Hispanic resident in that tundra would have to be part of a gang.

So on top of being prone to ridiculous hyperbole, the police also somehow managed to connect the name of a movie made by Psychopathic, the parody of a street flick *Big Money Hustlas*, to the alter ego of a Juggalo gang. It was all wrapped into a seventy-eight-page document called the "Northeast Wisconsin Gang Assessment."

The Juggalos are a nationwide white gang, reported throughout the Northeast Wisconsin, and associated with increasing levels of criminal activity. In Sheboygan, they are considered a structured gang (with a member handbook describing ranks and duties), consisting of at least eight members and six associates, ages ranging from fourteen to twenty-one. They have been linked to crimes such as graffiti, possession of narcotics, and theft. They are often seen wearing red, black, and white colors. They also paint their faces with black and white face paint, resembling a clown. This group follows the music and "teachings" of the Insane Clown Posse, and have been equated with the "dead heads" of the Grateful Dead. They can be identified by Hatchet Man (cartoon character running with a hatchet) and/or "BMH$" for Big Money Hustlas Sheboygan. They also make the letters "WC" with their hands, which stands for wicked clowns.

Sheboygan Police Department reports that Juggalo members from Chicago recruited members in Sheboygan and established the Big Money Hustlas there.

Any criminal knows that slapping on some face paint before a heist is a smart move.

The report went on to claim that there were fifty-six gangs in Oshkosh, Wisconsin, alone, an amazing number given how few people live in Oshkosh (about sixty-six thousand). At the end of the report is what the entire seventy-eight-page document was really all about: money. At the heart of the claims of the state's Department of Justice was an assurance that there were programs in place to ensure that the good people of Northeast Wisconsin were protected from the terrible clowns. There was GREAT (Gang Resistance Education and Training), DARE (Drug Awareness Resistance Education), and a staggering assortment of other acronyms that were helping, with results that were "particularly impressive."

These programs were publicly funded, which is how cops make their dough. Why not throw the scare of Juggalos into the people?

GREAT is a federally administered grant program, throwing around $10 million in grants around the time the Wisconsin report hit. In 2009 the Feds received 270 requests for $19 million in funding through the program.

DARE is a cash cow, funded by taxpayers and fat-cat donors—it made $2.9 million on merch sales alone in 2000 and paid its director $276,000. DARE has been around since 1983 and has spent millions of dollars, despite studies showing that kids are more likely to get high *after* going through DARE classes. It hands out grants to cop shops that compete fiercely for that dough.

Project Safe Neighborhoods came about in 2001, which purported to combat gun crime. Gang squads found out about the $2 billion allocated for the program, and in 2006 the program was extended to include antigang efforts, lumping together gun crime and gang violence. The money is allocated through the Bureau of Justice Assistance.

Between 2009 and 2014 the amount of gang fighting grants allocated through the Bureau of Justice Assistance totaled $30 million. Recipients included the Ijis Institute, a nonprofit tech group based in Virginia, which spends nearly half of its revenue, most of it obtained through government grants, on salaries and benefits, including up to nine executives pulling in six-figure salaries. Out of the $38 million in public money Ijis received from the Bureau of Justice Assistance between 2003 and 2013, $1 million was devoted to chasing gangs.

The gang money flowed between these groups that helped chase gangs. In 2012 Ijis paid a group called the Institute for Intergovernmental Research $300,000 as a subcontractor. Meantime, the Institute for Intergovernmental Research was itself getting grants from the Feds for gang fighting—$19 million between 2004 and 2010.

The tales of gang war money flying around are legion. Google "funding for fighting gangs," and you get 19 million hits. Fighting gangs with money is a drug war gone mad, money swirling down a hole that pays for fresh new cars and flights and hotels and conferences and time away from the jackass thug who just knocked off a liquor store or shot the guy pumping gas.

Despite all the money spent, however, the number of gang members has remained the same since 1996, even by the government's own figures, which in 2012 placed the figure at 850,000.

In 2011 Congress passed the Fighting Gangs and Empowering Youth Act, which allowed the attorney general to dole out grants to law enforcement as well as public and private groups. This was in May. The gang assessment naming the Juggalos came out in the fall. The timing was perfect for application time.

Herbert Gans is a hard-ass sociologist from Germany who writes about how poverty feeds the upper classes. He's cranky but sometimes astute, and he examined the poor-as-victims situation with a lot of academic analysis that can be mostly chucked out the window.

But he also arrived at the conclusion that a whole group of folks, including cops and social workers, make a living on the backs of the poor and those just getting by. Gans said that someone benefits, and in this case these are local law enforcement agencies that are benefiting from these gangs and things like the Juggalos," says Alex Alonso, who carries that rare combination of street smart and academic. He's from New York City and lives in LA, and journalists call him a gang expert. He nailed the Gans reference. "Many small police departments want more money for their gang squads or to start building gang squads. They do the same with drug squads."

What so many forget about gangs—at least since the Jets fought the Sharks in *West Side Story*—is that there are a couple of things that used to define gangs. First is an outsized tendency to commit violence on a collective basis. Then there's the territorial thing. And leadership or some form of structure. This last qualification is never hinted at regarding the Juggalos. There would be immense ramifications if one were to cast Shaggy or J as leaders of a gang—a First Amendment affront of a higher order.

Then there's the issue of expert testimony. Cops are already on the record as being of the opinion that Juggalos constitute a gang. So when Detective Sergeant Tom Walker, supervisor of the Knox County, Tennessee, sheriff's office's gang investigation unit took the stand in the 2011 trial of a Robert Edward Fritts, a twenty-seven-year-old accused of hacking his mother-in-law to death with a hatchet, he told jurors exactly that. "I believe he is a member of the [Insane Clown Posse] gang," Walker told jurors, who added that Juggalos are an "almost cult-like religion."

He went on about Juggalos for quite some time while he sat on the stand. He explained the six Joker's Cards and the fact that Fritts was wearing an ICP sweatshirt on the day of the murder. Walker told jurors that he read some of Fritts's journals, which included writings that, he contended, referenced ICP songs regarding "decapitation, mutilation, and dismemberment," according to court documents.

Fritts had a hatchetman tattoo to boot. Fritts was a scumbag with a pregnant school-bus-driving wife and a job at Arby's. The two lived with the deceased, and Fritts killed her.

He was convicted and sentenced to life. That all could have been done without a reference to Juggalos.

In the inevitable appeal Fritts's lawyer said that Walker's testimony regarding the Juggalos "provided no assistance to the jury that if in fact [he] was a member of an ICP gang assisted the jury in determining as to whether or not his gang affiliation connected him to this homicide."

The appeal was dismissed. But the point was a good one.

The ease with which a cop's testimony regarding Juggalos is taken as truth is a brutal kick in the ass to justice. Anyone can claim they are an expert.

Law enforcement perceive Juggalos as lacking the money or the awareness of their rights to fight back. As such, they have become the perfect victims for cops. The media, which live on scare tactics, found that inserting the word *Juggalo* in a crime story ginned up some fierce fear. Who wouldn't be frightened by someone who may or may not wear face paint, has little use for the conventions of life, and listens to music that could be the soundtrack to a Stephen King movie?

About the same time the Wisconsin report hit, Michelle Vasey was getting worked up down in Phoenix, Arizona, over the confounding proliferation of Juggalos. Vasey was with the Arizona Department of Public Safety's gang task force, and she was a true believer in the evils of Juggalodom. She was convinced that the term Juggalo came from what she claimed was Violent J's alter-ego, "The Juggla."

Vasey prepared an essay on Juggalos for the Rocky Mountain Information Network, a conglomerate of law enforcement groups from Colorado, Nevada, Arizona, and New Mexico:

Juggalos can be identified by the following indicia,

(1) Any and all Psychopathic record label clothing and paraphernalia

(2) Tattoos relating to Insane Clown Posse and Psychopathic associated artists to include the six joker card album covers and the hatchet man which is the Psychopathic record label insignia.

She cited a hard investigation done most likely via a deep dive on Google by Tucson detective Hal Van Woert, who said,

Juggalos have adopted the message and philosophy of ICP and others on the Psychopathic Records label as a mission and a total lifestyle. They immerse themselves in the imagery and listen to the music whenever and wherever they can. They meet at annual and semiannual "gatherings," and they share their views and thoughts (such as they are) on numerous Internet sites. In short the message of ICP is, for the true die-hard Juggalos, not what they hear but what they ARE.

Vasey's essay on Juggalos was titled "Juggalos: A Fan Club or a Gang?," aping a headline in an Arizona newspaper.

In Salt Lake City, Utah, they were really a gang in the eyes of the local gang unit, with membership numbers second only to Sureños 13, an honest-to-god gang that actually got together and killed people for any reason.

Looking at the records, though, there was little Juggalo action in Salt Lake City in the last months of 2010, when the FBI was trying to round up gang information. Minutes of a fall meeting of the gang team at the department reflect that there was quite a bit of gang activity the department was working. When it came to Juggalos, however, they had nothing. "SLC straight-edgers are everywhere in junior highs," asserted one officer. "Bend Over Slut Crew is everywhere," reported another. There was no mention of Juggalos.

December 2010 e-mails show that an officer was assigned to oversee the Juggalos. And it was surely about the money. Sergeant

Bob Eldard, who was part of the gang unit and SWAT team at the Salt Lake City PD, wrote,

> Keep in mind that unfortunately the FBI financial resources are not set up to respond to fast developing cases. And right now due to Congress not having approved the federal budget yet, it's even slower. We can get the money but the wait will probably be about 2 weeks. What we are trying to do now is request buy money [*sic*] in chunks on several cases in anticipation of using it in the following month.

In Denver, Sheriff's Deputy Christopher Pratt compiled a twenty-seven-page report entitled "Everything you never wanted to know about the Juggalos." He introduced his presentation by stating, "During my short time on the Sheriff Department's Gang/Intelligence Unit one group seems to keep randomly popping up and catching my attention as I conduct various searches, member contacts, and so on. This group is comprised of fanatical followers of the rap group known as the Insane Clown Posse (ICP). On the streets they call themselves the Juggalos."

He noted that Juggalos wear baggy clothing to conceal weapons, and "for obvious reasons, contact officers should consider Juggalos to be armed."

> The Juggalo "code" (as one might loosely refer to it) encourages all sorts of miscreant behaviors. They are not beyond committing violent, sexual, or even grotesque crimes, and in fact, such acts give a Juggalo a sense of pride and street credit amongst peers. The Juggalos claim to be strongly opposed to racism, bigotry, and snitches, but everything else is apparently okay.

After fifteen pages of this, he ran out of things to say and printed off photos from the Internet, including ICP album covers, tattoos, art work, and Juggalo graffiti.

So when officer Michelle Vasey poses the question, "A Fan Club or a Gang?" the cops already know the answer.

✝ ✝ ✝

Certainly the LAPD knew.

Early in 2009 J, Shaggy, and most of the Psychopathic crew were in Los Angeles shooting *Big Money Rustlas*, the band's second full-feature film. Their first, *Big Money Hustlas*, was a parody of seventies street crime exploitation flicks. The experience sucked for most everyone, but the idea was cool.

Rustlas was a take on *The Good the Bad and the Ugly* with a *Blazing Saddles* tilt. The budget was $1.5 million, but all the cops saw when they pulled over the van containing J and some of the others was a street gang. The face paint was a giveaway, right? They were coming from the set.

"Insane Clown Posse is a gang in this area," one of the officers told J as the crew stood at the side of the road.

"No, there's a misunderstanding," J said. "Maybe there's a five-member gang that's also called Juggalos and happen to be wearing our T-shirts."

The guys thought it was funny. It was their first incursion with the gang thing in years, since they had failed miserably at bangin' in the early nineties. And here they were, roadside, in LA being accused?

"What's in the van?" one of the officers asked.

Nothing illegal. But the cops searched it based on their gang assertion. Rights tend to go away once the cops can rely on that gang thing.

J and the guys were cleared. But that little episode didn't bode well for others who might not be as clean.

✝ ✝ ✝

How J and Shaggy met Martin Bashir, a news entertainer with ABC:

J: "Do you know Michael Jackson?'

Bashir: "I did some filming with him, yes."

J: "Yeah! I'm a huge Michael Jackson fan."

Bashir: "Thank you."

J: "It's an honor, brother."

He reached over and shook Bashir's hand as a crew wired the ICP boys up for a *Nightline* segment.

It was March 2010, a couple of weeks before the "Miracles" video would drop, and J and Shaggy walked into a hotel conference room in Detroit to talk with Bashir. They didn't do the set-up nice or anything—chairs were stacked up at the side of the room, and the makeshift set included the bad wallpaper. It was a low-rent set, for sure.

The only reason they were doing the sit-down was because Bashir had done a series of interviews in 2003 with Michael Jackson, J's longtime idol. Although the interviews with Jackson were hatchet jobs—Jackson used the term "yellow journalism" to describe them—J was enthralled with the resulting documentary, *Living with Michael Jackson.*

So sure, Martin Bashir, cool. They knew Bashir was going to be about as uptight as it gets among the TV entertainers that masquerade as newsmen. They'd done an interview with Bill O'Reilly in 2001, who all but screamed to parents to lock up their kids when ICP came around. It paid off—Juggalos watched the video online, passed it around, and watched their heroes stand up to the man.

Over the next hour or so Bashir heard J and Shaggy speak of chicks, titty bars, choking people out in the thralls of wrestling, and how, although they have no trouble singing about violence, "ICP is a little more classy than that. Our shit is doper. Our shit is more of a worthy product."

Bashir nodded along.

"How should pedophiles be dealt with," Bashir asked. He pronounced it pee-do-files. J looked at him for a second.

"Pedophiles?" he asked, making sure he heard right. "In the most gruesome, ruthless manner possible."

"Even prisoners don't like those motherfuckers," Shaggy chimed in.

At some points Bashir would cite ICP lyrics. Once he chuckled himself when reciting them. "Got you laughing, didn't it?" Shaggy said.

The whole thing took about half an hour. When it was edited into a ten-minute piece, it was a parade of Juggalo crimes and sound bites of J and Shaggy sounding defensive. Some of Bashir's questions appeared to come verbatim from gang reports. The first minute of the show was a litany of courtroom shots and cops talking. He called ICP "one of the most successful music acts you've never heard of." They play, according to Bashir, music that celebrates "murder, suicide and decapitation." He even told viewers that ICP makes $10 million a year. But they have never come close to earning that much annually.

Then more cops, more crimes. Utah, Arizona, and Monroe County in Pennsylvania, he noted, all classify Juggalos as a gang. Kids wearing ICP T-shirts while committing crimes. "And the crimes are mounting," Bashir told viewers.

To the notion of ICP creating murderers via their music, "I say bullshit," J told him. "Just the way you're reading these off is like a brutal attack to make it sound like our fans are these dangerous people when it's the most misconstrued thing."

"Violent J, I didn't say that," Bashir said, holding his hand palms up in a sign of innocence. "I'm just reporting the facts of these cases."

Camille Dodero saw the online infomercial for the Gathering of the Juggalos in 2009 and was impressed. It noted that Juggalos were "The most misunderstood people of all time," and promised "if you've never been to the Gathering, this is the motherfucking year to go."

Violent J compared it to Muslims visiting Mecca. The video collage portrayed Faygo showers, face paint, trampoline jumping, people smacking people with all kinds of things, bloody wrestling; and the

MCs of the video, DJ Clay and Sugar Slam, reading an intentionally inane script.

Oh, and there would be helicopter rides.

"This video had gone viral, but to me it was something no one else was really writing about," says Dodero, who found herself in spring 2010 in her late twenties working as a web editor at the *Village Voice*. Growing up in a working-class family around Boston with eight half-siblings, she had known about Juggalos. They weren't in her social sphere, however; she was ready to move on to college, only the second in her family to do so.

So she had one foot in the working-class reality of the day-to-day life and another in the more lofty airs of the college-bound. She was grounded. She knew this was a group who was being maligned, and perhaps unfairly.

"I was editing more than writing, and I wanted to do this for a little while, so in 2010 I realized that maybe this was something no one else would do," Dodero says. "I wanted to humanize them, what they did, what they were like as people. All I could see on the Internet were things that made fun of the Juggalos. You could put up a picture of Juggalos and put some statement on it, and it was supposed to be a joke. These people were more than just a meme."

She had read Morton's Vice piece in 2007 and dug the humor. Then she read the *New York Times* story in April 2010 headlined, "Fools' Gold: An Oral History of the Insane Clown Posse Parodies."

The story explored the numerous Juggalo lampoons that were popping up, starting with a take on the Gathering commercial of 2009 and extending to the *SNL* "Miracles" satire. Naturally the story went over the heads of *New York Times* readers. One reader was sure it was all a capitalist scam: "We think we're having a laugh at ICP's expense, but they're laughing all the way to the bank," he commented.

Still, there was more to it, Dodero was sure. "It was this thing I was mystified by, and I wanted to know what was going on. I knew this was not a thing where you go and make fun of everybody."

The *Village Voice* refused to pay her way to the Gathering, so she paid her own way, $1,500 upfront, and took a photographer, paying his way too. She rented an RV in Nashville, and they flew in, picked it up, and drove to the Gathering.

Dodero got in via press credentials by sheer will. Psychopathic had no press liaison on the website. Dodero found Psychopathic rep Andrea Pellegrini, listed as such on LinkedIn, but she could find no e-mail or phone number. She tried variations on e-mails until she finally connected.

Friends, with a straight face, some of them who considered themselves enlightened and tolerant, told her she was crazy. She would be raped almost certainly. "My perfect story is one where someone is repelled, and by the end they become empathetic about a subject they dismissed," she says. "A class of people that America has forgotten about in every conceivable way. When I came away I wanted to remind people that they weren't freaks. That they were actually humans. In American culture there was no one who has reached out to this culture, the Juggalos, other than in this pejorative way. ICP offered them something to befriend them. Every other part of American culture has been reached out to for that kind of connection, and these people finally had something."

Dodero returned to New York, and for a month she worked on a five-thousand-word story that blessed the Juggalos. It was supposed to be one page in the music section. By the time she had finished it was a cover.

"You want to read the story that really made the impact, that for once really got the whole deal right, you read hers," says Scottie D of Faygoluvers. "It was the first time someone took the time to understand."

✛ ✛ ✛

A few months later detectives in Franconia, Virginia, asked the public to call them if they spotted a car with a hatchetman sticker and to give them the license number. These were some bad folks, they warned.

In February 2011 two detectives, who asked that their names not be revealed, told a group gathered for a "gang awareness" event that Juggalos had been responsible for a murder case in Fairfax County. But just as they didn't want their own names attached to the information they were dishing out, they couldn't tell them the name of the victim or the perpetrators. It was secret. Juggalos were also involved in assaults, robberies, and child pornography, they said, even as they could not name a single case.

"A lot of people consider them a cult," the nameless detective told the small gathering. But if you happen to see a Juggalo, "don't freak out."

10

Apocalypse for the Masses

*I think there's always a call for people who are bucking
the norm. But I don't expect it to happen now because I
think that more than ever the entertainment industry is
trying to serve as a distraction, to keep people from
thinking too hard.*

—GUY PICCIOTTO, FUGAZI

*You'll never go broke underestimating the taste of the
American public.*

—P. T. BARNUM

It's indie label heaven at Psycho-
pathic headquarters on Folsom Road in Farmington Hills, Michigan.
ICP bought the place in 2000. At one time it was teeming with thirty
employees and money was flowing. That number is now seven. Financial realities hit hard, and staff was pruned, as at just about every
corporation in the United States.

Folsom is home to the bevy of business entities J and Shaggy have formed—Insane Clown Posse, Wicked Touring, Bizzar Tours. Riddlebox, Carnival Trade, and Ninjas in Action are all businesses registered by and around Psychopathic. Some no longer exist.

The building sits just off Nine Mile Road in a bland industrial string of buildings. One block to the east is a Montessori school, but 32575 is a forty-five-hundred-square foot, Swiss chalet–looking atrocity, a design misfortune with deep brown paneling and fake brick outer walls with a flagpole in front. The front door is locked by code, and to the east is a barbed-wire fence and gate blocking off a seventeen-hundred-square-foot lot where trucks can move in and out.

Psychopathic Records is run as a design freakshow, where every nuance and color is approved and reconsidered. And it shows, from the elaborate stages to the artwork for any hatchetgear product and LP.

That doesn't translate to the headquarters. The place is aesthetically benign. Even so, stand around outside long enough on a summer day, and you'll see a kid or group of kids go by, cell cameras popping.

The blue shag inside is filthy, and the wall paneling does not make it look like a chalet but rather a teenager's basement bedroom.

The gold and platinum records and the full-color blow-up posters of J and Shaggy make the place look like, well, you know why you're here and who runs the place. On the ground floor, when you walk in the front door, there's a makeup room directly in front of you, with full-on mirrors. Look in the cabinets—full of Stein's face paint, the hard-to-get shit that KISS used during its ascent to fame.

Turn left and you'll sit in the Lotus Pod control room, the recording studio epicenter with waxed wood floors and thick office chairs around a large console. The control room leads to several small recording rooms that look like every studio you've seen—the sound is dead like the desert. Wall-sized posters of Psychopathic bands grace the walls, and then you'll see the wall of Michael Jackson presenting his divine inspiration.

Turn right and there's the office that doubles as a video editing room, with four desks. It's a communal place where video production and web management are carried out with much intensity, full of people staring at screens. Rounding out the space is a couch that may or may not have been among the first J or Shaggy ever owned—you don't want to sit there. All over the walls are photos of Juggalos and any other person who's encountered the tribe of ICP. They call it the wall of karma, but it's actually just a grab bag of underprovided snaps.

In one corner is Dean, a Jackson Pollock look-alike who fell into working at Psychopathic as a web designer. Dean went to high school in Dearborn Heights and had an Atari 800, an 8-bit early home computer, in 1979 when he was a teenager. Dean was the guy who came into your high school classroom with the projector, a classic tech nerd who you figured would later do something really important that entailed something you'd never understand.

He did the lighting in the high school auditorium and was cruising online bulletin boards as early as 1980. He and his pals were writing and playing their own games as well. He was fifteen. Dean grew up in the bar business; he was part of the Arena, a popular Detroit sports bar that featured Ring Girl competitions and, as of 1992, was the largest sports bar in the United States. At the same time, Dean was into dirt bikes and skiing and living the high life. He cooled out and formed his own computer business, specializing in design, programming—whatever was needed.

When he first answered a blind ad for a web dude, he learned it was a company called Psychopathic and thought it was, for some reason, a medical records company. But soon he was handling just about everything, so much that one day J's brother, Rob, asked him, "What do you do? As in, what can't you do?"

The next question was, "Will you come work for us?"

Out a door to the left is the warehouse—a Juggalo's dream jammed with the merch. Stacks of music—discs, albums, DVDs, and box sets—give way to rows and rows of T-shirts, jeans, thongs, lighters, hats, and socks.

Some of the merchandise ideas over the years have come from Juggalos—they used to have a deal where if your T-shirt design is approved, you get $50 and the honor of seeing your fellow Juggalos wearing your design. That idea faded after Juggalos realized they could make a lot more than $50 selling a trunk load of bootleg tees at $20 a shot. "Then we have to track them down, which isn't always easy," says Will Sigler, who oversees the warehouse. "What we found is that Juggalos have Juggalo names, and that can make it hard."

Sigler drives 187 miles, one way, every day from suburban Cleveland to work at Psychopathic. The license plate on his Chevy Malibu reads "2 Whoops." It takes three hours to make the drive on a good day. He lives with his mom and has a side business renting properties nearby. On his way up he keeps a laptop next to him—like a cop—and listens to movies he plays.

"I was an assistant to the assistants when I started," Sigler says. He started working for them as a teen, and he's now a gentle, stocky thirtysomething with a soft southern accent and a batch of homemade tats. He's also a former Marine, entering right out of high school, following in the military footsteps of his father. Juggalos will fuck with you like that—the kindly manner will cloak a career of discipline. On Sigler's LinkedIn page he identifies himself as a "Super Ninja," and that's exactly what he is. Sigler creates costumes, from stage duds to video outfits. He does clown masks. He's done sets for videos and stages. His mom manages a Jo-Ann Fabric store and gets him and, by proxy, Psychopathic good deals.

"I learned about ICP when I got the first LP at a place called CD Jungle," Sigler says. He always loved clowns "like the Joker," and ICP were the perfect meld of hard-ass music and carnival-esque makeup.

Every day Sigler comes in and fills orders. During the holidays they sell $5,000 a day worth of hatchetgear. Orders require a phone number, so on occasion he calls Juggalos to make sure their stuff got there in good shape and on time. "Sometimes they don't believe it's me," he says. "They actually know who I am, reading about me on the blogs and so on." He reaches out on Facebook and hands out his cell phone number to Juggalos in case they don't get what they ordered. He doesn't drink or smoke and, if the occasion merits it, cites Bible verses. He has no trouble telling you that in the Book of Revelation 11 there is talk of two prophets: "And they will prophesy for 1,260 days, clothed in sackcloth." They are, he continues, "the two olive trees" and the two candlesticks, and "they stand before the Lord of the earth. If anyone tries to harm them, fire comes from their mouths and devours their enemies."

Sigler can get devout if you talk with him long enough. And he can kill you with three quick moves, thanks to the US military.

Upstairs are more offices. A costume room is filled with four racks of stage clothes—you'll see the duds Shaggy and J have worn in videos and on stage. Along the walls are racks of masks, hats, charms, wigs, four-drawer metal file cabinets, and rolled-up rugs of all sizes and colors. The lighting is strictly Walmart fluorescent slodged in overhead fixtures.

Shaggy's record collection—crates and crates of twelve-inches, disco mixes, LPs, EPs—the whole lot of them—resides in the costume room for some reason. There's always a big sack of dirty laundry ready to go out for cleaning. The beat-to-shit meeting table near the door is weirdly imposing, flanked by fourteen office chairs upholstered in scarlet fabric. Brian Kuma is sitting at that table, mapping out a video with a local video producer, a cheery-looking blonde named Angela. He needs four packs of cigarettes ("any brand—we can hide the name"), an ashtray made of old-school plastic, a poster-sized map of Detroit, and, oh yeah, some C4 plastic explosive. Angela goes a little pale.

"Or something that looks like C4," says Kuma, who's in his midthirties. Wearing a Red Wings hat and a black hoodie over a Reebok jersey, he's as polite as Beaver Cleaver, paging through the sketches that will become the video for "Explosions."

"I'm going to give you $250. See if you can make it happen," he tells Angela. "And let me know if you need more."

He's not cheap—he's experienced. It's the algebra of need in the entertainment world. Give a dollar and it's gone.

Kuma didn't go to college to be a techno DJ, and he's played to tens of thousands of people at festivals all over the world. He played Berghain, in Berlin, one of the hottest EDM clubs in the world, but he won't tell you about that unless you pry.

He beat up a Juggalo named Sloth when he was in tenth grade in Fraser, outside Detroit. Kuma was the quiet kid—that's how empowered Juggalos are in Detroit, a rare status in the world. The Juggalo actually fucked with Kuma, ironically. Kuma irritated Sloth because he listened to boring, alterna-rock like Smashing Pumpkins and Radiohead.

"I have the greatest day job in the world, and I never forget that a million kids would like this job," Kuma says. He's an in-house producer for Psychopathic. He works on the albums and is the go-to guy for Shaggy and J when they want to get something musically cooking. He's so morally clean-cut it's almost distracting. When he says "shit" in a conversation, he qualifies it with "pardon my French."

Kuma landed his job via a Craig's List ad for a producer. Alex Abbiss was still on board, and when Kuma came in Alex did his eyes-closed affectation to put Kuma on the defensive. "So what kind of music do you like?" Alex finally asked him. He looked like he was reading Braille, his hands on his desk.

Kuma aced the test. He's been there since 2005.

Rob Bruce has a strategy about signing artists to Psychopathic. Being good is one thing. But you have to be able to hang. People have come over with all the jam in the world and lost the deal. The unnamed female rapper is exhibit number one. She swung for sure—chops, looks. Got into the Lotus Pod, fired it up. And up some more. And then started bossing people around like she owned the place.

"We had her cut a track," Rob says. "And she left and no one wanted her around, even though it was good."

She had talent but no skills.

"And no one ever heard of her again."

Rob was just out of the Army when he first came on board, working as a dishwasher and checking out the possibilities of civilian life.

"I was hesitant to leave my job," he says. "I liked it, but I said, well, let's just do this," he said. "I started in shipping."

Now Rob sits behind a desk strewn with paper and deals. He books the Gathering, then switches to any tours, then to Hallowicked, then to . . . whatever needs attention. The liner notes, the more spacetastic writing in the Gathering program—that's Rob.

In a closet in Rob's sizable, sparsely decorated office, he keeps games. Wall to wall, up and down, and sideways stacks of fantasy games. The same world he adopted when he was barely ten years old he still lives in at forty-five years old and counting.

"Oh, yeah, I am still in that world," he says, despite being a husband and the father of a daughter. He pulls a game out that he created called *Morton's List*. It's something you'd find at one of those comic book stores full of dudes with no girlfriends and bad hygiene. Rob created the game over the course of seven years, wrote a good portion of a three-hundred-page book, figured out the dice configuration—the whole deal. Like some of the other fantasy games like his beloved *Dungeons and Dragons*, *Morton's List* has roles to play and tasks to accomplish. "The beauty of the game is that it puts you in situations you'd never find yourself in normally," Rob says. "It opens you up to new experiences, and it opens you up to life.'"

He created a company, Dark Carnival Games, printed ten thousand of *Morton's List*, and sold nine thousand of them. Hot Topic carried it for a while, and when the Juggalos found out Rob made it, it sold like crazy. Then the Hot Topic wholesaler read the book that detailed the tasks one might perform playing the game. One element involved stalking. Another dealt with explosives. And the Hot Topic orders stopped.

To be clear on what the problem was, they ran the book by a lawyer. "We got back the book, and about a quarter of it was highlighted. He said we'd have to take all that out in case people got hurt doing things in the book, so we'd have to water it down. We had to make a choice—do we want to do that?"

The answer was no. But if you look hard enough, you can find yourself a copy of the game.

On the other end of the main upstairs hallway is the office of CEO Bill Dail. Sitting there, tapping away at a MacBook, he looks like any other office drone save for the Psychopathic hoodie. A burly guy with broad, slumped shoulders and a consistent scruff of black beard, Dail once beat down a guy who was waving an Eminem T-shirt from the front row during an Omaha ICP show in 2001. The cops said Dail choked the kid until he passed out. Dail said the kid never lost consciousness, but so what?

"You don't come into our home and disrespect us like that," Dail told a reporter. "My intentions were to get him out of the room. . . . When he tried to fight me, it was my intention to hurt him. I grabbed him by the neck . . . and threw him against the wall." He pleaded guilty to disorderly conduct and paid $100.

Dail was working as a cabinetmaker when J asked him to be part of Psychopathic. He came to the team as a production guy and a heavy. He loved the staging, the flashy part, and he loved the logistics—how to bring the band across for the Juggalos. He grew up with J and Shaggy, and this was helping his friends.

When they were just starting out Dail could create eight-foot flames. To create such a thing, he had to procure devices "that I should never have been able to get," he says. He'd go to a fireworks store and talk a little bit. During sound check someone would distract the local fire marshal so the fire could be tested.

The first time he ever ran lights he walked over to the light board. "Okay," the in-house tech told him, "this is your spot. This is yellow . . ."

Dail nodded. He was clueless what the guy was talking about. "Staging was all trial and error," he says. "A lot of error."

Pretty soon they had a crew of seven traveling with the band in an RV and a box truck full of gear and merch. They had smoke machines, strobe lights, and costumes too.

And the Faygo. Promoters hated it at first. The stuff got into the microphones, and ICP was paying for those after every show, in addition to sound board and speaker repair. On early tours they were coming home in the red just because of Faygo damage. Once they toured with their own gear, however, things got better. And the Faygo could flow freely.

"Yeah, that's me handling that as well—$20,000 for a tour usually. It's the only real hassle of touring. It's so heavy. You can only carry so much on the truck."

They can only carry three or four shows' worth at a time—a Faygo cannon can use gallons in minutes—and it all gets shipped from Michigan. So if there's a show in California, they have to get it shipped direct to the venue, then Dail needs to find a crew to unload it—usually local Juggalos. Slap a pass to the night's show on them, and they'll work. Four shows later he has to deal with the same thing again. "And in the winter we've had to rent heated trucks because the Faygo will freeze and blow up," Dail says. Yes, it's happened.

They canceled a Phoenix show because the wrong Faygo was delivered. They ran out in Texas and found some six hours away. But it wasn't diet—the stuff they usually use. "Otherwise, the stuff will peel paint," he says. The Phoenix promoter checked the stash sitting on pallets when everyone arrived. "You aren't using that," he said. The show was off.

"So sorry for the bone! But there is still a show in Tucson," ICP announced. It would have been cool if they'd given the reason.

Dail took over as CEO in 2006 when Alex Abbiss split with little notice; he claimed he was being followed and dogged by some sort of inside music-biz hocus pocus and got spooked. At least that's the myth.

Abbiss isn't talking. But as a result, Dail got the big corner office with the obnoxiously big desk that Abbiss used.

"I don't need it," he says. "I use it."

✛ ✛ ✛

It's really just a group of people who don't want to be messed with.
—BOBCAT GOLDTHWAIT, SPEAKING OF JUGGALOS

An underground isn't built for durability. It erupts, kicks loose some legends, and eventually loses its meaning and/or direction. The industry vultures inevitably sweep in and pick the bones, the worst of the remnants, and next thing you know, Lindsay Lohan is wearing a Ramones T-shirt.

In the seventies you had punk rock and TV shows like *Eight Is Enough* and *Quincy* weaving punk rock into scripts. TV documentary crews ran around like numbskulls trying to cash in on eyeballs and interest with outrageous features speaking of wild violence and a "fuck the world" attitude. Major newspapers dispatched entertainment writers and terminally square reporters to come up with the meaning of it all—better yet, to disparage it.

"Punk rock has all the makings of a musical wasteland nurturing on all that it is tasteless to even the most open-minded," one scribe in Lawrence, Kansas, wrote in 1977.

The same year a group of college radio people got together and determined that punk rock was all about the money and who can make it. "A key role in fostering U.S. acceptance of punk rock music was assigned to college radio broadcasters," *Billboard* magazine reported in the fall of 1977 from a college radio conference in Chicago. Fashion designers eventually arrived at punk lines of clothes you could buy on Fifth Avenue. It was all about the Gs.

Rap music had a variety of flavors—gangster, dance, new jack swing, go-go. And it too was wrangled into something for Madison

Avenue. Sugar Hill Records was swooped up in a savagely poor deal with MCA Records, and the sound of the South Bronx turned into a Pepsi commercial. Movies like *Breakin'* and *Beat Street* were marketed to white people, and clothes designed to ride low and branded hip-hop sneakers were all shoved into the mix, with cross-marketing of everything from perfume to cars. When grunge hit, same thing—more clothes, more sales, more big corporate investments.

With Juggalos, well, there was nowhere for the fat cats to go. No fashion. No "fostering" of any acceptance. No kids with legacy cash. Nothing to base an academic curriculum on.

"We're not in bed with any major corporations," J says. "We don't do advertising. We don't have something that people want to copy. We're just Juggalos, and you can't really market that."

Sure, Walmart carries some T-shirts, ditto Hot Topic, but that's it. No branded lunch boxes by Mattel. No duds at Macy's. Doc Marten had nothing to adopt, and there was no Juggalo counterpart to the flannel shirt.

Plus, clowns are scary, even if the official clown line is anti-Juggalo.

"ICP have nothing to do with clowns any more than KISS does," says Glenn A. Kohlberger, who is Clyde D. Scope, the clown and president of Clowns of America International. "Clowns are not this sensationalized-on-TV thing. It comes from the heart. You have to be a special kind of person to be a clown. But they are using makeup to help benefit their music."

Juggalos were becoming a punch line in places other than online boards, where their verbal assailants could hide behind Internet anonymity.

Writers for the Comedy Channel's *Workaholics* series created an episode where the three protagonists, using the term very loosely, attended a Gathering.

An episode of *It's Always Sunny in Philadelphia* offers an adolescent Juggalo who's about to get his ass beat by three jocks in the high school bathroom before Charlie, a janitor at the school, walks in on them.

"Okay, who did this? Who painted your face, kid?" Charlie asks.

"He did. He's a dumbass Juggalo," one of his tormentors says.

"Juggalos for life, bitch," the kid, Richie, says, sticking out his fat stomach.

"All right, you three guys outta the bathroom. I'm talking to the clown," Charlie says, then turns to Richie.

"Okay, what's going on with the clown makeup, though? You're sticking out like a sore thumb."

"That's 'cause I'm a Juggalo—ICP, Insane Clown Posse, yo," Richie says.

Once again mainstream media portray Juggalos as dumb and fat.

At a pizza joint in Austin, Texas, Juggalos are part of an opening joke for an amateur comic on an open-mic night. "I think it's good for a person to get up and here tell something embarrassing about himself," a fleecy, oversized thirtysomething told a small crowd. The boys and girls, also in their thirties, clutched their beers and tittered. "So I am here to tell you that when I was twelve, I liked Insane Clown Posse."

Laughter all around.

"I went to see them at Stubbs," he continued. "They were throwing soda around, like they do, and they took this plastic two-liter out and hacked it in half, then threw it into the audience. I caught half. I took it home. It was garbage, but I put that in my room like it was a trophy."

By then no one got the joke: *Why would anyone do that? What is this soda pop they were throwing?*

The surprise was that after the evening's roster of amateurs was over, the jukebox cranked on and offered the best of outsider music, bands that at one point in their career couldn't get arrested, like the Misfits, the Stooges, and the New York Dolls. All were heralded as groundbreakers later, but all played to many indifferent audiences in their day.

Juggalos have nothing to offer average people, the ones who take to pop music and culture. Punk rock at least had some fashion sense and inspired some ill-advised college courses on punk rock. UCLA actually has someone it calls a "professor of punk" named Jennifer Schwartz, who teaches "Music History 13: Punk: Music, History, Sub/culture." It's doubtful there will ever be a Juggalo studies class, although just the thought does make one wonder what the syllabus would include.

Their music's all about how much they hate everybody
and what they're gonna do about it.
—COP ON EPISODE OF *LAW & ORDER*,
2010, SPEAKING OF JUGGALOS

Before there was the official, nationwide gang designation, there was a classified intelligence report given to law enforcement agencies in February 2011 by the National Gang Intelligence Center. Much of the material would be used for the FBI's report in the fall. States with a scary Juggalo gang presence would be increased. In the prelim, Delaware, Iowa, Massachusetts, Michigan, New Mexico, and New Hampshire were left out. The word "hybrid" would be attached to the Juggalos, as they were "on the rise," according to the final report, "in order to make it more difficult for law enforcement to identify and monitor them."

There was plenty in the February report that was omitted from the larger assessment.

Juggalos exist nationwide and exhibit many of the same characteristics as a traditional gang such as throwing hand signs, wearing matching tattoos, and dressing in similar clothing. Over the years, two sides to the Juggalo sub-culture have emerged. According to an admitted Juggalo gang member, there are two active but very different factions of the Juggalos: the music fans and the criminal street gang.

The nationwide Juggalo membership, believed to be over one million fans/followers, vehemently reject the gang label they have received in recent years. The majority of the Juggalo sub-culture following, which constitutes the non-criminal element, likens themselves to a "family".

- The Lackawanna County Prison of Pennsylvania reported that the Bloods and Crips dominated the local criminal Juggalo groups and used them for recruitment
- The Unified Police Department of Greater Salt Lake City, Utah, reported Juggalo alignment with Kearns Town Bloods because they wear the same color (red)
- The Garfield County Sheriffs Office of Colorado reports that criminally active Juggalo members in their area are also members of the West Side Crips gang.
- Reporting from the Arizona DIPS indicates that most Juggalos on the Indian Reservations align with the Bloods gang and have been involved in a number of drive-by shootings as a result.
- The Texas Attorney General's Office cites reports from Orange County Texas that claim Juggalo groups in that county have become associated with 3-11 Mafia, claiming Ku Klux Klan affiliation. Additionally, Juggalos in Northeast and West Texas have been reported to affiliate in the county jails with dominant White Prison Gangs such as the Aryan Circle and the Aryan Brotherhood.

—Juggalos: *Emerging Gang Trends and Criminal Activity,*
report from the US Justice Department, February 2011

So the Juggalos were down with the Klan, the Crips, and the Bloods. Not just lumped in, as they would be in the fall report, but actually interacting, recruiting, and bangin' with those legendary gangs.

When you track outlaws like the Juggalos, you wear a lot of hats. Chuck Schoville wears a ton. A former street cop in Tempe, Arizona, at any given time he heads the Arizona Department of Public Safety State Gang Task Force, is president of the Arizona Gang Investigators Association, chief of the International Outlaw Motorcycle Gang Investigators Association, and Western US vice president of the National Alliance of Gang Investigator Associations.

It's that last title that gives him some heft regarding the Juggalo reports released under the aegis and authority of the FBI. "The gangs on the annual reports are always the same," Schoville, says, then corrects himself. "Or the types of gangs are always the same."

He says the biggest change that came in 2011, when Juggalos hit the list, was indeed the hybrid gang. "We used to have gangs hating each other, and now we see them working together for some joint profit. Gangs in neighborhoods are even doing that now."

It's a little different, according to Schoville, than the 1988 movie *Colors*, in which Sean Penn and Robert Duval play a couple of LAPD cops trying to make peace between the Bloods, the Crips, and some unspecified Mexican gangs. "The colors thing used to be important. Now the only important color is green," Schoville says.

The National Alliance of Gang Investigator Associations, he said, is an adviser group to the FBI, even though the FBI does the heavy lifting on the biannual gang threat assessment. Heavy, as in firing off e-mails and compiling news reports. "We help them by getting it distributed," Schoville says. "I try to get it to everyone—police chiefs, offices, schools, parents. The FBI puts it online so the public can access it, but if we could afford it, I'd send it to every house in America."

The National Gang Intelligence Center, he says, "is the best thing we've had happen at the federal level for the last ten to fifteen years because now we have a group of people in DC with the resources and the ability to gather this information, which they share with us at the local level. There's always been this disconnect between the national and local agencies."

And then there's the money. Lots of it, "and it's very competitive to get grants these days."

PART III

Unruly Ascent of the Clown

11

Misfits and Fringe-Dwellers Explode

A sheriff says reality TV actress Tila Tequila complained that audience members pelted her with stones and feces during an outdoor music festival in southern Illinois. Hardin County Sheriff Tom Seiner told a Carterville TV station it happened early Aug. 14, 2010 at the Gathering of the Juggalos. That's a weekend festival based around the band Insane Clown Posse and other groups from Psychopathic Records.

—CBS NEWS

TO: THE HARDIN COUNTY SHERIFF'S OFFICE

Under the Illinois Freedom of Information Act, 5 ILCS 140, I am requesting a copy of the following public record:

All police and incident reports, including full narrative and any additional notes, regarding activities at the Gathering of the Juggalos in Cave-in-Rock, Illinois pertaining to an individual named Tila

Tequila or Tila Nguyen (DOB 10/24/81) that occurred on August 13, 2010 or August 14, 2010.

Any sworn statements taken by any employees of the Hardin County Sheriff's Office, including volunteer deputies or anyone working on behalf of the agency, regarding the Tequila/Nguyen incident.

We never received any complaint from Tila Tequila or this other person.

—spokeswoman, Hardin County Sheriff's Office

Just before 2 a.m. on August 14, 2010, a white van pulled up to the back of the second stage of the campground at Cave-in-Rock, Illinois. It was day two of the Gathering of the Juggalos, and things had gone pretty damn well at the outpost on the banks of the Ohio River, considering rains had turned the place into a swampy, fetid mess. Tila Tequila hopped out of the side of the van and into her trailer. She was clad in pink tights under cutoff blue-jean shorts and a tattered black–and-white top that made sure her premier DD breasts were on full display. It's hard to expect anything less from the woman who was booked on the merits of her apt hip-hop single, "I Fucked the DJ."

"The thinking was, 'Oh my god, she's rapping now—let's go with her,'" says George Vlahakis, who booked the Gathering between 2009 and 2012. "We could have thought that one through a little better," he says now.

She was part of an evening devoted to female performers, Ladies Night. It was put together by Sugar Slam, the wife of Violent J and better known as Michelle Rapp when she went to Alief Hastings High School in Houston with Tequila, who was using several first names before graduating in 2000. Her favorite was Thi, which somehow later turned into Tila.

A couple of weeks before the Gathering, Tequila posted a note to the Juggalos on her website, Miss Tequila:

Hey Hey Everyone!!!

I JUST returned from my awesome UK Tour, and now I gotta get ready and gear up for more shows! That means meeting up with more TILA ARMY BABY! YAY!

Anyway, I just wanted to announce that I will be making my first big debut at the awesome "JUGGALOS MUSIC FESTIVAL!" This is their 11th year anniversary so I am honored to have them book me to be there and perform live w/the most amazing crowd and I can't wait! This year there will be so many amazing artists performing there such as: Method Man, Lil' Kim, Insane Klown Posse, And many, many more, including . . . MEEE! YAY! Ohhhh it's going to be so much fun!

It was the same vapidity that anyone who followed Tequila was used to. Born in Singapore, Tequila, who grew up Tila Nguyen, was primarily a laddy magazine model, gracing the pages of *Maxim*, *Stuff*, and *Penthouse*.

Her brash mouth, fake tits, and plastic–jawline looks got the attention of several MTV producers, and in October 2007 *A Shot at Love with Tila Tequila* debuted on the music television network. The show was a bisexual dating contest in which sixteen men and sixteen women vied for what passed for Tequila's heart. It was a cultural disaster, a ratings semihit, and was canceled after two seasons.

Dating websites, a fashion line, and, finally, a stab at making music followed. "I Fucked the DJ" was a single to follow up her self-released three-song EP, *Welcome to the Dark Side*.

The post to the Juggalos on her website drew over a hundred comments.

"this has to be one of tila's worst moves in her carreer. she will cry. i will laugh. tila you dont know what your getting into, your making a huge mistake. and we have every right to hate on a mainstream bitch trying to apeal to juggalos when shes obviously a fake bitch, were not asking for hardcore were asking for real."

"Lol, you have no idea what you're in for."

"Hope you enjoy the smell of piss."

"Wow you're gonna stick out like a sore thumb. These bands are all legit and badass . . . not a bunch of teeny bopper fans. You totally ruin the lineup."

"you better watch your head.YOU WILL BE BOOED OFF STAGE JUST DO EVERYONE A FAVOR AND STAY HOME!"

"im throwing rotten hot dogs at you that are gonna be sitting in a warm cooler filled with hot water out in the sun untill that Friday. . . . they have also been in my fridge for over a year. . . . i fucking hate you and i will teach you not to come back to the gathering."

The days' soaking rains of Midwest summer, one tumbling in after the other, created pools that made a loud squish! sound when the van tires drove through.

Everyone in the house knew that Juggalos had hatched plans to make things tough for her. They didn't care for her MTV bona fides or her fake dance music. It was one thing for people like Charlie Sheen to have a hit TV show—he could get up on a Gathering stage, take the abuse, and dish it out with credibility. It was a whole other thing to be the subject of a dating show, especially on MTV.

In the trailer she was paid her full amount upfront, $5,000. And Violent J walked in. "The crowd is going to be violent, and they're going to throw things. If you don't want to go on, or go on and decide you can't finish, you can keep the money. It's all up to you," he told her.

"I'm not a bitch like that," Tequila said.

These were some aroused Juggalos who were ready to greet her. She was quarry. They were predators. It had the makings of an event.

The move into the fire that was the stage went quickly: up the back stairs, past several serious-looking clowns—no sign of the ICP boys yet—and into the lights.

The first thing she saw was a large white sign with black letters reading "CUNT," and Tequila was immediately pelted with an egg, which struck her in the lower jaw.

As she tried to sing her first song, plastic Faygo bottles, water, soda, beer cups, a rubber dildo, citrus slices, a bag of chicken, and urine flung from water bottles flew at her all at once. She threw a couple of half-full bottles of soda back into the crowd, which only further enraged the thousand or so in the crowd.

"Show your tits, show your tits," the crowd chanted.

Tequila bravely kept going right into the next song, with two of the Gathering security team flanking her on the stage while her own stood at the back by the steps.

"I ain't going nowhere," Tequila said repeatedly, still trying to dance as projectiles bombed the stage. "I love ya and I don't give a fuck."

Comedian Tom Green, who was performing later at the Gathering, saw the disaster and ran onto the stage, dancing like a crazy man in hopes of deflecting some of the anger. Dumb can sometimes trump pissed, but not in this case.

"What the fuck is this?" Ron Jeremy, the porn icon who was handling various MC duties, yelled at several security guys. "Get up and help her."

As she went into "DJ," Tequila removed her top. Another security guard walked onto the stage and wrestled back into the crowd a Juggalo who was trying to get at Tequila.

Then rocks began flying, catching her on the right cheekbone and opening a gash. She refused to quit, even as blood streamed down her cheek. When a beer bottle glanced off her left eyebrow, the two onstage security dudes grabbed her and led her down the back stairs of the stage.

She hopped onto a golf cart to take her to a trailer to the rear right of the stage, and enraged Juggalos began to follow the slow-moving cart. They crept, watching the cart as it pulled up to the trailer.

Tequila ran from the cart into the trailer, trailing blood, and several members of the stage crew followed her. Juggalos began to pound on the trailer—it wasn't enough to smash her face with projectiles.

Another cart pulled up with Shaggy 2 Dope, and Jamie Madrox from Twiztid jumped off and into the trailer. The van was pulled up to the door and Tequila came out, flanked by the two men.

With that she was gone but not forgotten, set up to fail, warned fairly before she even hit stage, and abused by Juggalos, who fulfilled every stereotype of themselves imaginable.

Within ten minutes of Tequila leaving the stage Scottie D, who runs fan site Faygoluvers.net, received an e-mail from gossip site TMZ offering him $500 for any footage of the incident. He didn't have it.

To its credit, TMZ ran a story headlined "TILA TEQUILA: Attacked at Rowdy Concert"—refusing to go for the audience grab by including "Juggalo" in the header.

In response to an interview request the next day from TMZ, Tequila in tortured syntax, wrote, "Since their security SUCKS, the 2 thousand people ran after us, trying to kill me. They almost got me so they finally reach the trailor, blood all over myself, cant stop bleeding, then all of a sudden, all 2 thousand people surround the trailor and busts the windows!!! Even the guys INSIDE with me were shaking! Their hands were shaking cuz they were so scared! So 3 guys inside the trailor had to grab a table and push it over the broken windows and grabbed all the chairs they could find so hold the people from outside back. It was scary as hell!"

And she kept talking. Via Twitter she threatened legal action that would never come.

"Go to www.tmz.com violence against women like myself or anyone for that matter is not ok! Lawsuit is pending."
August 14, 2010, 12:25 p.m.

"Thank you everyone for your support. The people at Juggalos behavior was disgusting and I am filing a suit against Them now. Thanks 4 ur luv"

August 14, 2010, 3:15 p.m.

"Pretty soon the owners who run the Juggalos will be bankrupt. My attorney Alan is already on it. This is disgusting behavior from men."

August 14, 2010, 3:31 p.m.

"But to all of my fans, I appreciate your outpour of love and support! Xoxo"

August 14, 2010, 3:32 p.m.

"RT @ninaholtz @TilaOMG im 1000000% w/u. R U ok now? i hope so. praying that those losers will have even more pain in return! KARMA, BITCHES."

August 14, 2010, 3:33 p.m.

Camille Dodero is today an editor at *Billboard*, but she is recognized as the first journalist to understand that Juggalos are worthy of solid, objective news coverage when she wrote about them for the *Village Voice*. And she was sitting stageside for Tila's show.

"This wasn't something the Juggalos did for the media. It wasn't for outsiders. It was a very closed, tribal response to what Juggalos perceived as an insult to them," Dodero says. "For them the idea of Tila Tequila, the embodiment of what they had been abused and insulted by, MTV culture, was something they had built their entire identity around rebelling against. They had been excluded and abused in the first place and then found others who felt the same way, and this thing that represented all things mainstream was right in front of them."

After the whole thing calmed down—it took only about twenty minutes—Lil' Kim was supposed to play. She refused. "It sounds like everybody is a bunch of animals," Lil' Kim said when her rep told her what had happened. She was on her way to the grounds when one of her crew on the ground at the Gathering called and told her what happened. She turned around and headed back to the airport. No one blamed her.

> Fascinated by miracles such as, er, magnets, Insane Clown Posse should be a laughing stock. But their fans—the Juggalos—symbolise a growing reactionary culture in America, in which ignorance is seen as a virtue.
> —*The Guardian*, August 18, 2010

The loose-leaf binders for the Gathering are enormous and over-flowing, jammed to overflowing with stacks of paper, some clipped together and some ripped almost in half. Some stained with Faygo, and one, inexplicably, is partly burned.

Inside there are documents of every sort—contracts for cleaning crews, golf carts, lights, sound and stage hands, and, of course, artists. There are also ticketing and ambulance invoices, generator guaran-tees, tent-rental agreements, and more communications with the management of artists that may or may not be worth a shit. Negoti-ating for performers is an ugly business that would dishearten any true fan. It's best left to the heartless bastards who see music as a business rather than a craft.

The trouble is, George Vlahakis is anything but heartless and the farthest thing there is from the coarse and sometimes downright swinish conduct that befits heavy-duty rock promoters. Cigar-chompers like Bill Graham are the central casting favorites.

Vlahakis is a polished speaker with a studied coolness and cu-riosity about all things. He began booking shows when he was a teenager, not long after seeing ICP and Psychopathic label mates Twiztid at Hallowicked in 1999. His dad dropped him off and picked him up outside the Majestic Theater in downtown Detroit.

"That's being a pretty good dad," Vlahakis says. He came out soaked in Faygo. He was thirteen years old, and he knew what he wanted to do—not perform but to make the spectacle of a show like that happen.

"My buddy AJ rapped, and so I started booking him and doing shows," he says. The first was an American Legion Hall in the Detroit suburb of Livonia. It was AJ and some locals. He broke even. The first time he made money—at a place called the Bullfrog in another suburb, Redford—he left before collecting. The next day the club owner called him as Vlahakis was on his way to his homecoming dance. "Hey, you need to come over here and get your money," the owner told him.

George told his date he had an emergency at home and ran over to the Bullfrog. Success. Who knew you could make money doing this?

He began booking more locals. His pal AJ knew Anybody Killa, known best as ABK, a local who was signed to Psychopathic Records, then bounced over to another, lesser-known label to see if the grass was greener. George sent him on a jagged route that only a beginner could create, from Pennsylvania to Virginia back to Ohio and up to New York. George rented a minivan and followed him to make sure things went smooth at the show.

The grass was not greener, and when ABK went back to Psychopathic, George was asked to keep helping on the booking end for the label's lesser-known acts on the roster. Every call he made, the first question was the same: "Do they spray Faygo?" For ICP the hassle was worth it. For anyone less, not so.

One day Bill Dail, the chief of Psychopathic, asked George to book the Gathering.

"I was thrilled. It was a dream come true," George says.

✝ ✝ ✝

George Clinton and Parliament-Funkadelic showed up at the Gathering in 2011 with a busload of people and another car jammed with more. His entourage sat coolly on their bus, waiting, and when the band hit stage, the entourage surrounded the stage in the wings and at the rear. And when the drummer keeled over from the heat, someone from the side walked out, jumped behind the drums, and played without missing a beat.

MC Hammer was booked the same year but was a little nervous. A few weeks before the Gathering he was in Detroit for a show, co-billed with Clinton and his crew. Hammer's manager called Psychopathic and invited J and Shaggy and some of the office crew down to the show at an outdoor venue north of the city.

As the set ended Hammer looked to the side and saw J and Shaggy standing there. "Let me bring out a couple of friends," Hammer said as he started the last song. "Insane Clown Posse!"

There was a little ripple, and it wasn't positive. Then the two came out and did their best to keep up.

"I can't dance," J says. After the set was over they all sat backstage. To get onto the stage, Hammer had waded through the crowd.

"You probably don't want to do that at the Gathering," J told him.

A few weeks later Hammer time came. He didn't start the set on the stage. The music started, and there he came, dancing through the dirt with the Juggalos in the crowd. Hammer hit the Gathering stage and announced, "Let the world know: there ain't no party like a Juggalo party!" He danced, took a Faygo shower from the crowd, and mesmerized the fans.

He didn't need to listen to the advice. Unlike most, Hammer had already done his homework. "It sounds goofy that I have to tell a pro like Scarface to go out and say 'whoop whoop,' but this kind of thing matters," George says. "But they get it, and when they go out there and do it, they understand why. And if I didn't say it to them, you can bet ICP will. They're fans too. They want them to do well."

"No human can tell GWAR what to do," says Brad Roberts, drummer for GWAR, which played the 2009 Gathering. "We do what we want to do on this planet."

GWAR had toured with ICP the previous year, and it was a pretty good match. GWAR fans dug the insouciance, the outright balls of ICP. Juggalos, well, they like the idea that GWAR turns the stage into a bloody mess.

"The Gathering was great. I just wouldn't want to do it again," Jizmak says, then adds, "They should have coached Coolio. He walked out on stage, and someone bounced a nine-volt battery off his head first thing."

Ice Cube showed up and sat in his tour bus, waiting for stage time. J and Shaggy pulled Cube's road manager aside. "Listen man, we want to talk to Cube because he should know a few things about Juggalos," J said. The road manager advised J and Shaggy that there would be no audience with Mr. Cube. One of them could go talk to him—that was as good as it was going to get.

J took the honors and sat down on the bus. As soon as he started explaining things, it was clear Cube had no idea what a Juggalo was. To him, this was just another job.

"You just have to let them know you appreciate them as Juggalos," J said, adding that the "whoop whoop" is part of the deal, and it is *not* booing. Cube took every bit of J's advice to heart. He addressed the Juggalos graciously as Juggalos, and even thanked ICP from the stage.

But for Pauly Shore the Gathering was pure torment.

He was playing the comedy tent, which was something added down the line thanks to the hard work of Joel Fragomeni, a Detroit comedian who became Upchuck the Clown for the Gathering, a guy with a wig of various blinding colors—orange, purple, yellow—and a wiseass painted-on smirk.

Upchuck handled the talent at the tent, procuring drugs, talking them down (or up), and making sure the acts got on and off on time.

And Shore, ensconced in a hotel in Evansville, Indiana, wasn't sure he wanted to play anymore after coming from California to the Midwest. "So once I talked him into coming out—it was seventy-five miles or so, and we got him a limo—he wanted to go on early," Upchuck says.

Jamie Kennedy was scheduled—and paid—to open for Cheech and Chong. Kennedy showed up late, as the tent emptied after Cheech and Chong killed it. No one cared about Kennedy.

Charlie Sheen showed up with no jokes, and completely unprepared. So Upchuck, who has toured his act over the years, was asked to write some jokes. "I was at the drug bridge, and now I think I'm going to be putting one in my house," was one of them.

He didn't perform it. Still, the Juggalos dug his bullshit, especially when Sheen, being rained on with refuse of all kinds, caught a water bottle in midair and looked cool doing it.

And Upchuck was proud to have Bobcat Goldthwait appear one year—proud enough to give him a personal tour of the grounds.

Upchuck already had attracted a crew of haters for no good reason. Actually it was one guy who Upchuck had made fun of on a radio show. "So he started calling me on the phone—he was a Juggalo—and saying I'm a child molester, all this stuff. And Juggalos started believing it."

The campground tour went quickly awry. "So Upchuck the Clown had opened up for me and was trying to explain to me that it's not that bad," Goldthwait later told Dan Harmon for the popular Harmontown podcast. "Upchuck is like, 'This is a decent group of people,' you know, 'I'm here every year.' And then this clown, this huge guy, just burst out through the crowd—by the way, there's fires and fights goin' on—but this guy's all sweaty and crazy looking and he goes, 'Fuck you, Upchuck, fuck you.' And he just pounds the shit out of him. So he hits gas, and we just scoot out, and he's chasing us. It's a drive-by ass-kicking.

"So then he goes, 'You know, they know me. It's like family.' He's trying to laugh that off. And then a can of Faygo hits the golf cart, and it's all over us. Faygo, apparently, if it's diet, it doesn't stick or stain, and so Upchuck is like, 'It's diet—don't worry about it,' like he's a connoisseur. So he hits the gas, again, after the Faygo cola, and we're driving, and as he's trying to tell me, he says, 'It's not any more rowdy than a Dave Matthews concert,' at that point a can of unopened Faygo cola comes whizzing in and cracks him in the head like a baseball pitch. And he just slumps over and says, 'I'm hurt. I'm hurt really bad.'"

Goldthwait had to take the wheel from the passenger side and veer through the campground.

"And do you want to know what he put on his head for the swelling? Ice-cold Faygo."

It was good comedy at the expense of the Juggalos.

J and Shaggy love Vanilla Ice, always have. Once the Gathering was happening, he was at the top of the list as a requested guest.

They'd all met a couple of times: West Palm Beach when ICP played a half-full house early on, then a Dallas show that was off the hook. Ice came out for a cameo.

Then the Gathering, Toledo, 2001.

J and Shaggy told Ice one thing: "They're gonna love you."

Ice had no idea what to expect. "I had just seen three acts before absolutely play great, and the Juggalos booed them, threw shit at them," he says.

"Why would they like me?" he asked J.

J again assured him, "They are gonna love it, really. Just do your thing."

He was right. Ice was a Juggalo forever after that. So far he's played six times, and he's seen some acts fare poorly. Like a trashed Ol' Dirty Bastard in 2004. "He's this legend, everyone wanted to see him, and I was watching from the stage," Ice says. "And he was so messed up. I mean, I knew he was into some stuff, but this was really bad. And his beat guy was also fucked up, so it was this 'thunk, thunk, thunk.' And he wasn't even covering up that he was fucked up."

As he watched from the wings, a couple of shoes plunked the Bastard in the chest.

"Finally, a piece of watermelon hit him in the side of the head," Ice recalls. "That had to hurt."

In 2014, after years of hopeful reaching out by Gathering organizers to each of the three different management groups that handle them, Cypress Hill agreed to play. Rob Bruce, Joe's older brother, had come back in mid-2012 after leaving Psychopathic Records for seven years, and he took over the Gathering booking starting in 2013.

One of the first things he did was get rid of Ron Jeremy, unceremoniously. "The guy knows everybody, and he doesn't care about you unless you're a name," Bruce says. Jeremy didn't know who Bruce was when he came onto the scene in 2013. So he ignored him. Bad idea.

So when reports started coming back to Rob that Jeremy was taunting some of the girls at the Miss Juggalette contest, which he MC'd, that was not going to be good for Jeremy's future at the Gathering. "In the middle of the Gathering I told him he had to go, and I put him on a plane," Bruce says.

Getting Bruce back was a coup, to be sure. But the rest of the booking was becoming a nightmare as the federal gang pockmark festered.

Three tent companies pulled out of their contract after hearing that the Gathering was for Juggalos. "They do a review, and they see it's us, then they back out," Bruce says. Now, he said, some of the entertainment agencies are even cowed by them. "Or the agencies will say yes, and the artist will say, 'Hell no.'"

"The cash outlay is huge," Bruce says. "We don't have corporate sponsors. No one wants to be a sponsor. But that would help, and that's how the other festivals do it."

Indeed, the major festivals are an integral part of the entertainment industrial complex, ironically the very machine that many of these same attendees rail against in rallies across the nation. The greedy are running the asylum, in fact, where Miller Lite, owned in part by what was once Coors, holds hands with AT&T, which is in tight with IBM. They all team up with multibillion-dollar media conglomerates to sell like hell to attendees of Bonnaroo and South by Southwest.

These massive music festivals pull in 32 million people a year, many of them operating on a collective love for spending cash. Festival goers don't even flinch at paying upward of $7 a beer or $2 for water. Want a slice of pizza? $7. This is after the $375 to get into a clusterfuck-like Coachella.

Some of them stick you, symbolically enough, in a pen if you're drinking, safely away from the stages. Putting Juggalos in a pen would be an interesting proposition.

The big ones are put on by big corporations—Live Nation, for example, handles Austin City Limits. Michael Rapino, Live Nation CEO, in an August 2015 investor call, told analysts,

> Along with attendance growth, we have also grown per-fan on-site revenue this year by 18 percent to over $20 per fan in our amphitheaters and festivals as our new sales initiatives, particularly those focused on the high-end fans is paying off. With the growth of our Festival businesses we are also continuing to build our base of major advertisers, increasing the number of companies that pay us over $1 million a year by 15 percent, now delivering a collective $200 million to Live Nation in 2015.

Rapino was paid a package worth an estimated $11 million in 2014. And folks like him are taking the soul out of music, one dollar at a time.

Then there's Anschutz Entertainment Group, which does Coachella. Anschutz owns the Staples Center in Los Angeles, operates the Target Center in Minneapolis and the Sprint Center in Kansas City, and has a stake in the Los Angeles Lakers. This is a group that puts the C in corporate, and it's pimping what was once known as "the devil's music." Only now the devil—the one with the open palm extended at you—is running the joint.

Even Lollapalooza, which was once truly a magnet for freethinking rollers looking for a day in the sun with some of the day's best artists, has turned into a greedy cash grab.

When it began, it was $25 to get in for a day of bands, with small and large stages and no special tents for those who wanted some kind of special treatment or private bathrooms. Today five options are available, from the three-day GA up to the platinum pass for $3,600. Among the perks are catered meals, golf cart transport, concierge service, and an "exclusive festival merchandise gift bag."

For a nation that wants to appear concerned about the growing gap between the rich and the poor, music festivals do a good job of ensuring the haves and have-nots are kept separated. The Gathering seems Spartan in comparison. That's because it doesn't seek to be anything other than something for the fans, who are perceived as not having enough money to interest the Rapinos of the world.

The insider, buddy-buddy operation of these so-called music festivals have been part of a mainstreaming of America that keeps Juggalos on the outside.

Psychopathic has never approached any brand, and no brand has ever approached them, Bruce says. Monster Energy, he says, would probably do it, "but then we'd have to have their shit everywhere, and we'd be like every other music festival."

Faygo has for years been bantered about as the perfect brand sponsor. "I always thought we should do a microphone endorsement with the Faygo dripping off the mic," says Violent J. "'This is a mic tough enough for any band,' Faygo dripping off it and it still works."

That's never going to happen.

In fact, Faygo honchos have had meetings over the idea. "We discussed it several times over lunch, and it was pretty much 'This is a group that is not in the general population,'" says Hugh Mathew Rosenthal, a now-retired Faygo marketer whose Russian grandfather founded Faygo in 1907 using frosting recipes. "The feeling was that these guys are somewhat misogynistic, and they're the opposite of what a family brand would want," he said.

It's the Cristal line gone Faygo. Remember when Cristal got hinky about the rappers digging it? When Frédéric Rouzaud, managing director of Cristal producer Louis Roederer, was asked by the *Economist* in 2006 if he thought the rap connection would hurt the brand, he said, "That's a good question, but what can we do? We can't forbid people from buying it."

Jay Z, who had no business in the fray, called the comment racist and demanded a boycott of the brand.

ICP is too tough for that. Instead, they plunk down $20,000 a tour for a good supply of Faygo to spray. And even though Faygo is everywhere at the Gathering—on T-shirts, stacked by the two-liter in tents and in the stores surrounding the festival grounds—the event will never see a sanctioned Faygo tent or event.

Even the Faygo suits admit that ICP has increased demand around the United States, especially during a tour. "Every place Faygo was not found, sales managers complain because they spend so much time answering requests because the requests volume is so huge," said Al Chittaro, an executive vice president with Faygo.

Faygo brand manager Josh Bartlett has heard anecdotal accounts where ICP fans helped Faygo gain popularity in new places. "I've heard stories that in a handful of markets there have been requests for selling at certain retail locations because there was a significant cadre of ICP fans living in that market."

Fans from Texas and California, pretty dry states when it comes to Faygo, request shipments. And damn the $50 shipping cost. "It's funny because we're a family soda, and the Juggalos are a family too, and in that way it kind of fits," Bartlett said. "I'm very happy to see this particular group and their fans have such a good time with our brand. And that they're experiencing the fun and flavor of Faygo in their own way."

But no sponsorship.

Juggalos don't need no stinkin' sponsorship.

12

Suing the Government and Hacking Off Nipples

Maybe fifty years from now when a Juggalo is president, they'll get the Feds to say, "We were wrong."
—JOHN HILLIARD III, HELLS ANGELS LAWYER, SOUTH CAROLINA

No matter how the story is framed, however, there is an intangible moth-to-light fascination where Juggalo culture is concerned.
—*FORBES* MAGAZINE

It's always back to the trailer. Juggalos and trailer parks have been synonymous in the great Juggalo mythology since the start. Trailer trash is still a common sentiment among some types, a down–the-nose look at someone who enjoys a different lifestyle.

So when it was time to gather legal gripes, why not make everyone feel at home?

In August 2012 the Gathering was swinging, and the gates hadn't even opened. It was the first time the thousands of Juggalos got together since being deemed a dangerous national gang, and the cops got in the spirit with that in mind.

Sheriff's deputies in Hardin County, Illinois, came together with the Illinois state police and swooped down on the Juggalos as they waited in line, both standing and in cars, to get in the gates at Cave-in-Rock, the campground that had been home to the festival since 2007.

Law enforcement agents were tired of this annual funfest. It was year six for the Juggalos to converge on the park, and they needed to maximize the cash. They had very few incidents, and most everything that ran afoul of the law was handled on the spot—tickets for minor traffic offenses, some drug possession, a deadbeat dad. It was like shooting fish in a barrel, and they did it with vigorous intensity.

But this was an actual gang the cops were dealing with now, so they could take some liberties. They made fifteen arrests before the gates even opened.

Then Bill Dail had an idea: let's hire some of the cops to work traffic control. Pay 'em, in the tradition of the old-fashioned mobster, pay-for-protection approach.

It worked. The cops pulled back. The gates opened. Juggalos smoked weed openly and without cop interference. The drug bridge was open for business.

And the press was there for the first time, en masse. There were European camera crews, alty media reporters, photogs who had never heard of ICP before, and bloggers trying to pass themselves off as journalists. One author, carrying some book advance money with him, was there. Even, God save us, someone from the most tight-fisted of all corporate news groups, Gannett.

Somehow a wise reporter from the Gannett-owned *Detroit Free Press* had wrangled some expense money and made his way from Detroit to the Gathering, delivering news to the hometown readers about a festival two locals had built through a cultural empire.

It could have been a business-page cover or a front-pager. But it wasn't. These were Juggalos, after all. The reporter, music critic Brian McCollum, did a great job with what he had. The newspaper opted for surefire page-click bait with lots of photos—those crazy Juggalos sure are colorful, aren't they?

Everywhere, though, were stories from Juggalos, amidst the stoned revelry, about how this gang designation had fucked with them. New accounts flowed: the guy who lost his kids to a foster home because of his hatchetman tattoo, the Juggalo who was discharged from the US military for having a Psychopathic Records CD, the kid from Wisconsin who was prohibited from wearing Insane Clown Posse shirts to school but didn't have money for new clothes, so he kept getting suspended. There were even custody hearings that turned into arguments over which parent is the bigger Juggalo and therefore unfit to have a disputed child. The most rampant stories were about cop stops for no reason other than the hatchetman decorating the dirty back window of a battered Pontiac Grand Prix.

It seemed everyone had a story, and no doubt some were just keeping up with the other Juggalos. Who hasn't at some point been browbeat by a cop? It's way too easy to chalk it up to some form of law enforcement bias rather than just the notion that the cop field draws inordinately from power-hungry bullies.

Every Gathering features the Juggalo state of the union as delivered by Shaggy and J. It's among the numerous seminars that go down under a big tent, and when those guys are doing it, much of the Gathering comes to a halt. The emperors talk a lot of shit that is of great importance to their followers—new releases, tours, signings to Psychopathic, gripes. It's a laundry list that is inevitably ceremoniously scrawled on a piece of paper and pulled from J's pocket à la the envelopes of Carnac the Magnificent.

On Friday, August 10, J and Shaggy walked onto the stage in *Mighty Death Pop* jerseys—the album was four days from release—that featured a Joker-ish face. On each sleeve was a hatchetman patch.

But in contrast to the usual joviality, the ever-lovin' sense of fun that makes the Gathering what it is, the guys were . . . grim. The smiles were there, but something was missing. "This is really surreal to be standing here in front of y'all because me and Shaggy been waiting for this seminar for a long time—it's a very big seminar for us," J said. His reddish hair was cut short in a military crew, stiff on top of his sheared head. "We have something very big we want to share with everybody. I don't know if everybody's going to feel it's as big as we do, but for us, in our lives, it's pretty fucking big—I'm a little nervous." They talked for thirty minutes about routine stuff—then made history.

"The last thing we want to talk about is three letters," J said. "The F . . . B . . . I."

He held his right hand out and used it as a pointer downward on each letter: "Eff-Bee-Iii." Immediately the Juggalos went crazy. "Fuck the police," they started ranting.

"Yeah, fuck the police, indeed, but the FBI is beyond the fucking police," Shaggy told them.

"All right, check this out. This is real shit. This is REAL shit," J said. "Right fuckin' major news here in our world, and I hope you all feel us and understand what this means, what we're saying—I want you to understand the full gravity of what we're saying."

He steeled himself—he knew once he announced this, there was no turning back. Nothing could stop the move once he announced it on camera for thousands of Juggalos who jammed into the big top and flanked the outside listening.

"In October of last year the FBI named the Juggalos one of the top-ten gangs on the fucking FBI gang top-ten gang assessment list, right along with the Crips, the Bloods, the Aryan Nation, MS13—all kinds of fucking lethal, deadly, drug-selling, street-taking-over, hard-core street gangs."

He outlined how things were going down—the complaints they were hearing about, the shakedowns, the refusal of stores to carry hatchetgear, the added insurance venues were now required to take out as Psychopathic artists were no longer doing shows—they were holding gang rallies.

"They're telling Juggalos, without coming out and saying it, that if you listen to this music, you are going to be committing a crime in our eyes," J said. "That's fucking insane. Back in 1990, when N.W.A. came out with the song "Fuck Tha Police," they received a letter from the FBI. The record company and the band received a letter from the FBI, and the letter said, 'Watch it. We're watching you. Watch it, be careful.' And now here we are in 2012. We'll take the letter any fucking day compared to what they did to us—they officially made Juggalos a gang."

It's true: the letter written to N.W.A.'s management didn't do a thing. And unlike the N.W.A. case, there were no congressmen ready to come to the aid of the Juggalos as there were for N.W.A.

J told of a fan engagement in the spring in which Juggalos submitted questions through the Internet. "One of the questions was from a ninja who had a story about how he was fucked with," he said. "We hear all kinds of stories about people being fucked with. Ninjas don't put stickers in the back window of their car anymore because they get pulled over and fucked with. They can't even represent the family they love anymore. They can't even represent the music they love anymore because they get fucking pulled over and taken to jail for that shit.

"So that kid that asked that question and at the end of his story, he asked, 'What can you all do about it? Are you going to do anything about this?' And my reply at the time was, 'What the fuck can we do about it? It's the FBI.'

"And here's our announcement: no matter what it costs or what it takes, we are, as of right now, officially suing the FBI."

J and Shaggy stood and listened to the whoops and looked at the standing O, then the chant "FA-MI-LY! FA-MI-LY! FA-MI-LY!" It came out like a football cheer, like they were sitting in the stands of a stadium.

Away from the mic Shaggy looked at J. "Man, I got some goose pimples," he said.

As they spoke, a press release went out worldwide announcing the pending action. Nothing had been filed in a court yet. Instead, there was a lot of preparing to do.

Starting with the trailer.

Anyone with an encounter with law enforcement that was, in their opinion, predicated on them being a Juggalo was instructed to go to a trailer that was set up next to the seminar tent. In there lawyer Farris Haddad, an army of one for now, was handing out forms for the Juggalos to fill out, detailing their incursion the best they could with as much detail as they could muster.

If that was too much, there was a website, juggalosfightback.com, where Juggalos could file their grievances online.

After the announcement J and Shaggy sat on their tour bus. J started to cry. In a broken home life of abuse at the hands of a step-father and society-sanctioned emotional beat-downs, it was one of the most intense things J had ever experienced. As he had told everyone just minutes before: "There's never been a case like this anywhere in the history of music. The only reason that shit isn't all over the news and all over the topic of everybody's lips is because it happened to us. And everything about ICP and the Juggalos is a fucking joke to the mainstream world."

Being in ICP has made him a solid living—millions of albums sold, the love of a devoted legion of fans, comfortable lives for his friends and family.

The tours, in particular, were starting to make good money. Juggalos turned out for anything Psychopathic.

Their merch sales are also lucrative: the patent for hatchetgear spells out just a few of the items sold: "Clothing, namely, belts, under-wear, wristbands, socks, dresses, vests, gloves, hats, caps, jackets, pajamas, pants, scarves, shorts, shirts, visors, sweatshirts, sweat pants, sweat-jackets, sweaters, T-shirts and tank tops." Throw in action figures, lighters, backpacks, blankets, an energy drink, wrestling masks, baby clothing, jerseys, and knit hats. And then some.

The over-the-top hyperbole for all things Psychopathic, with its roots in the smack talk and exaggeration of professional wrestling, usually works on public reporting. Some of the Gatherings were reported to draw twenty thousand people a year, when about half that was more accurate. After an ABC newscast claimed Psychopathic made $10 million in annual income, that figure was repeated over and over until it became fact. There was another Internet site floating around that claimed Shaggy and J were each worth $15 million.

All of this gave ICP the idea that America truly was the land of the free. "I was always really happy with the government because I always thought, 'If we can get away with doing what we're doing, I'm happy with the government,'" J says. "We make this ruthless music with this really scary undertone sometimes, and we get to put it out and sell it. And as long as we take the right precautions in doing that professionally and we pay our taxes, we're allowed to do this. Me and my friend that I grew up together with. I get to see all the friends I had before all this, twentysomething years ago. I get to be with them every day. I get to work with my brother and get to work with Billy, one of my best friends from childhood. I get to work with Joey every day, and it's like a dream and I'm proud of it. I used to think, 'Man, if we can do this in this country, I got no complaints about our government.' I know we worked hard to do this—harder than all the other bands around us—and that's why we succeeded. So I was pretty happy with the government until now. Then I realize that you can't do that. 'Not you guys. You guys can't do that.' It's like saying we're doing something wrong. We aren't okay to do whatever we want to do. We got flagged for some fucking ridiculous shit. There are other artists talking as much crazy shit as we are on our albums, and why did we get flagged?"

Shaggy has no filters, it's clear, and his honesty is in spite of himself. He's had numerous incidents with the law, including some felonies and a protracted, messy child-support case dating back to 1997 that caused a court to issue a warrant for his arrest for being a no-show. He's been on probation, fined, and spent time in jail, including a stint that caused him to miss the LA sessions for *The Great Milenko.*

When he talks about what authority has meant in his life, there's some bitterness. So when he waxes about the FBI, his take is diffident. "I've never given a fuck about the government," he says. "Whatever. I hear every vote counts and all that, but I don't give a fuck. I got felonies. I don't think I can vote anyway, and I'm not registered. I don't care about who's in office. But this opened my eyes about how a government organization can just put their foot down and fuck up so many lives for no reason, if only they feel like doing it."

The FBI, which has named in its investigatory files everyone from Robin Gibb to the Monkees to KISS, had never been sued for its pursuit of an entertainer.

People sue the FBI, of course. It happened in connection with the Whitey Bulger case. Oklahoma millionaire Roger Wheeler was murdered in 1981 when, according to a federal lawsuit filed by his family, he was suspicious of Bulger's activities and contacted the FBI, which allegedly tipped off Bulger, who sent a hit man to call on Wheeler. Agents who feel they have been mistreated also sue the FBI, as do people who have been wrongfully accused or maligned.

Entertainers and artists don't sue the FBI, though.

"The FBI made an assumption based on ignorance," says Vanilla Ice, a longtime Juggalo. "Just because it's the FBI doesn't mean it understands what a Juggalo is."

He's watched the pop culture gestation of Juggalos and the raw treatment at the hands of the media and general public. He also knows how it feels. Ice was called the "Elvis of rap" by detractors when he hit big in 1990 with "Ice Ice Baby." His foes felt Ice was making millions by cashing in on black music made white and, therefore, more marketable. Although Ice is no legal scholar, his common sense works in a situation like this.

To move forward, Psychopathic and crew needed credible, aggrieved Juggalos to prove the real damage the FBI's designation had caused. So for three days Farris Haddad sat in a trailer talking to hundreds of Juggalos with gripes. It was a little surreal, watching these Juggalos in their hatchetgear scribbling away at a piece of paper on a clipboard as if they were applying for a job at Wendy's. Some were way off, and more than one of them asked, "Does this mean I can meet Violent J and Shaggy 2 Dope?" Others had stories of lost jobs and being told to leave malls or other public places. Many had tales that could not be independently verified, and still others, quite frankly, deserved what they got in the situations they described.

Juggalosfightback.com landed eight thousand complaints, some from far-flung places that had little place in the legal realm. Someone from Italy or Russia screaming of oppression means that there are some Juggalos who are pretty desperate for some attention.

But the real complaints came from cities. Albuquerque, New Mexico; Louisville, Kentucky; Las Vegas, Nevada; Pittsburgh, Pennsylvania; Jacksonville, Florida; Phoenix, Arizona—all had Juggalos with cop trouble. The biggest gripe was being placed into the gang database after getting pulled over, but there was much worse.

"We had one situation in Grand Junction, Colorado, where a guy got in a fight with his best friend, drunk, and stabbed him in the shoulder," Haddad says. "He got a felony assault charge. But the prosecutor filed a motion to enhance the charge to attempted murder because he was wearing an ICP T-shirt."

The judge in the case agreed. The Juggalo's lawyer was among those filing a complaint with Haddad.

And then there was the Hells Angels lawyer from South Carolina.

✛ ✛ ✛

John Hilliard III was in some shit. His clients were the Myrtle Beach Hells Angels club, and the Feds had netted 226 indictments through eleven raids that nailed thirty-four bikers in early 2012. He'd done Hells Angels cases before, but most of it was someone getting drunk and beating on his old lady, who gave it back as good as she got. But when the raid came his way, he had to do some adjusting in his legal approach.

"When I first started this case, it looked like a big, old fist fight," says Hilliard, who's been practicing in his home state of South Carolina since 1980. He's a wide, broad-shouldered guy in his late fifties with a hefty head of white hair. He had never heard of Juggalos until he began dealing with what he considered some seriously dubious Fed action regarding the Hell's Angels.

For years law enforcement in Myrtle Beach and the surrounding counties had been battling with the local Angels. It was a lot like chasing ghosts—today the thought elicited when spotting a bunch of guys on motorcycles is "look at all those accountants!" rather than abject fear.

But to the cops in South Carolina the Angels were still every bit the menace they were in the sixties, when media crucified them with the same lack of reason and dearth of evidence that the Juggalos were now getting belted with.

"They were really coming at us. They were trying to keep the main guys in jail and trying to take away their colors," Hilliard says. "They wanted to keep them from associating with each other and were successful doing that at first. It was all a big tug of war between the local governments and these gang units."

As he was winding through the case he started finding that the Feds were sticking on a secret list of terrorists anyone they felt was a remote threat—gang members, in fact, including some of those Angels he was defending.

"It was so stupid how they were classifying people in gangs as terrorists, then I realized that there were similarities in the classification—they were all groups committing crimes."

So the six drug cops in Philadelphia who were accused of shaking down drug dealers? Gang. A bunch of bankers working together to commit fraud. Gang.

"It dilutes the idea of what a gang is, with the way the cops are doing this."

Hilliard wanted to fight the gang designation that was being applied to his Angels. Along the way he read of the Juggalos and the gang assessment list and couldn't for the life of him figure out how the following of a band could be called a gang. He called Haddad.

"I wanted to join up with the guys in defense of Juggalos," Hilliard told him. "You guys are facing the same thing we are here, and maybe we can get some kind of national front, with national representation."

But the Psychopathic legal team shot down the idea. "I think they were of the position that they didn't need to drag others into the case. They felt better to be by themselves," Hilliard said.

The Psychopathic team consisted of the very able criminal defense lawyer Haddad and an entertainment lawyer named Howard Hertz.

On August 24, 2012, the legal team filed a Freedom of Information Act request with the FBI, seeking documentation of the allegations regarding Juggalos in the gang assessment report. FOIA is a national law that allows the public to seek records that are created with taxpayer money and involve public issues. In this case the team wanted to force the Feds to substantiate what it claimed regarding Juggalos.

The request was a matter of coming to the table late, to begin with. On August 11 a requester calling himself Rich Jones had already filed a FOIA with the FBI through open-records advocate website MuckRock, asking for "any and all responsive documents mentioning the Detroit, Michigan based hip-hop group the Insane Clown Posse, aka 'ICP', its members Joseph Bruce, aka 'Violent J, and Joseph Utsler, aka 'Shaggy 2 Dope', their classification as a street gang, any criminal activity carried out by 'members' of the 'gang' (known as the 'Juggalo Family'), their annual gathering, 'The Gathering of the Juggalos,' and any documents sent on behalf of the Insane Clown Posse directed to the FBI."

For legal purposes the request the ICP legal team had sent was a query. The looser the request, the longer it will take to fill and the more likely an agency is to kick it back to the requestor, creating more work and delay.

The Psychopathic request asked for, among other things, "all documents in support of the statement 'law enforcement officials in at least twenty-one states have identified criminal Juggalo sub-sets,'" and "all documents in support of the statement 'in January 2010, two suspected Juggalo associates were charged with beating and robbing an elderly homeless man.'" It would have taken twenty minutes online to find documentation of the incident, which happened in Corvallis, Washington.

As the Feds considered the request, Psychopathic began to feel some pressure from Juggalos, who were wondering if the whole FBI lawsuit thing was a publicity stunt aimed at ginning up attention to the label and ICP. How would anyone in either the Psychopathic camp or among the Juggalos know that putting together a federal action takes time?

So rather than wait for the FBI's response, Psychopathic's lawyers, on September 25, filed a lawsuit to force disclosure, a month after filing the FOIA request.

Although it served to placate ICP and its fans, it also sent a message to the Feds that the Juggalos were willing to push this issue.

The records were eventually delivered in a form so heavily redacted that no one could discern the genesis of federal gang declaration. The response would have come without the expensive lawsuit. This suing-the-Feds stuff had a pricey learning curve.

Every Halloween since 1994 Insane Clown Posse put on a show in Detroit that drew Juggalos from everywhere. It was a scaled-down

Gathering held at the local Fillmore Theater downtown for years, and in 2012 the idea was to change things up and deliver it at the Royal Oak Music Theater, a more intimate venue. They'd done it there before and it was cool. Just in case demand overreached the capacity, they kept the night before Halloween, October 30, open.

Justin Miller, the general manager of the Royal Oak Theater, had read of the gang assessment report. He didn't think much of it—after all ICP are local guys, and they'd always been a good draw for the theater and there was no gang activity in Detroit involving Juggalos.

But to be safe, he sent a note to the Royal Oak Police Department. The town's crime rate was very low; the whole place was known as a drinking and dining destination, and for the most part people behaved.

One of the reasons, some said, was that the town spent 66 percent of its budget on police, fire, and EMS. It was, for sure, a well-policed town.

And these Juggalos just wouldn't do.

"Thank you for informing us ahead of time that the Insane Clown Posse has decided to hold their Halloween concert at the Royal Oak Music Theater," Lieutenant Tom Goad of the department wrote back to Miller at the end of September. "I would like to take this opportunity to inform you that the Royal Oak Police Department is very concerned and would like you to consider cancelling this event.

"Our concern is based on the number of concerts, throughout the country, in which ICP followers have created significant problems for local police departments. . . . In 2011, the FBI's National Gang Threat Assessment listed Juggalos as an organized gang in their assessment of gangs located in Michigan . . . it is very likely that if this concert is held at the Royal Oak Music Theater, there will be police-related issue [sic] in and around the venue."

Goad told a local reporter that the department had never had any trouble with Juggalos before. He insisted it was a staffing issue, although that was never mentioned in his official memo to the venue.

"We're cut by 40 percent," Goad insisted to the reporter. A department analysis done a few months before showed they had scaled back 25 percent since 2006. Again, cops aren't always willing to tell the truth, and reporters aren't always willing to call them on it.

Miller caved. ICP moved the show back to the Fillmore.

The gang designation was working for the cops. More and more media reports connected Juggalos with crimes, and cops made sure to inform the media when a Juggalo was involved.

In Portsmouth, New Hampshire, cops investigating a robbery and assault found the accused had a hatchetman tattoo on his chest, which, the officer said in a public report, is indicative of an affiliation with the Juggalos. "I am aware that followers of this style of music . . . refer to themselves as 'Juggalos' and that the hatchet is a common logo," the investigating officer wrote in her arrest affidavit.

The sheriff's department in Allegany County, Maryland, decided that the county fair was ripe for Juggalo activity. Not that they had ever seen any trouble before. A few Juggalos had been at the fair last year, although they did not cause any problems, said Allegany county sheriff Craig Robertson. "They look like mimes. You don't think about those things until problems arise," Robertson said. "There's no issue, but we want to be proactive on it."

Robertson said the group's followers have caused problems at other venues. So county commissioners were asked to amend the county fair rules to limit masks and "identity-disguising face paint" from the fairgrounds. The new rule would not affect face painting by churches and charitable groups for children, but only cases in which identity would be completely obscured.

With the fervor of persecution running wild, there were more accounts of getting hassled, and the juggalosfightback.com website was working it. At the top of the web page it was designated as a "place for 'los and 'lettes to be heard."

"On behalf of the Juggalos," it said, "the Insane Clown Posse and Psychopathic Records are investigating a possible lawsuit against the

FBI or other governmental agencies that have violated the rights of Juggalos on the mistaken belief that they are 'gang members.'"

"If you or someone you know have suffered any negative consequence with a governmental representative, including law enforcement, border patrol, airline security, or other local, state or federal governmental agency or employee as a result of your status as a Juggalo, we want to know about it.

"We want to show our appreciation and support for our fans and we are prepared to assist you in learning about your legal rights and to fight for you in Court, if possible. Please take the time to fill out the questionnaire so we can keep apprised of this situation and assist you in getting the legal help that you deserve as a Juggalo."

A hot link took visitors to a questionnaire. It asked for name, address, phone, and then "Do you believe that your legal rights have been violated because of your status as a Juggalo?"

If the box for "yes" was checked—and presumably, that's why everyone was there—visitors were asked to "please describe in detail how you believe your rights have been impacted in the space below."

Meanwhile the cops were pissed off over the lawsuit against the FBI. Online, police chatrooms were alive with anti-Juggalo talk. Policemag.com posted a story about the pending lawsuit.

When the Insane Clown Posse was in my city for a concert, their Juggalo fans were threatening people and throwing beer bottles out of their windows. This is a gang and I'm glad the FBI is trying to control these thugs before it gets out of hand.
    —Tim

The "posse," ICP followers are well within the legal definition of "Gang." They are not a club, they are a gang. They clearly represent destruction and evilness. They are not volunteering at the local food shelf. They are committing crimes, and identifying them-selves. It's clear and simple. It is a fact, not an opinion.

—Zeb

As they became known as the Juggalos who sued the FBI, though, Adam Roberts cut his nipple off at the 2013 Gathering of the Juggalos. Roberts had done some pretty crazy Juggalo-styled shit before, like tattooing his entire face in a tribal pattern that makes Mike Tyson look like a pussy at the parlor.

Ten days before the Gathering, a couple of his "friends" back in Alton, Illinois, where Roberts was a factory rat in a nearby plant when he wasn't looting storage spaces, dared him to hack off a nip-ple. Sure, he said. On the spot, for the grand sum of $58.

Now it was the Gathering, and Adam's other friends wanted to buy his remaining nipple. "I was like, 'Welp, I'm going to try to auc-tion it off at the Gathering,'" he recalled. "I didn't know I could sell them." So Roberts announced the other nipple was going to the high-est bidder. His friend J. T., who cut the nipple off at a side stage at the Gathering, leaving what looked like the angry red burn of a large-ended cigar where that areola once was, bought it for $100. It was kept in a small plastic bag—clear, so anyone who wanted a look could help themselves.

But for outsiders this was one of those scary, crazy Juggalos sto-ries of the Gathering. "I've been getting mixed responses," Roberts told a reporter in the aftermath. "A lotta, 'What the fucks?'"

The 2013 Gathering, though, was mostly a placeholder, with low turnout in Cave-in-Rock, where everyone had overstayed their wel-come, including Psychopathic.

To top it all off, a kid died. Twenty-four-year-old Cory Collins made the thirty-mile trip from his home in Harrisburg, Illinois. His death was attributed to a drug overdose. He was not a Juggalo, but his death at the Gathering made national news.

So did the bouncing checks that Juggalo Gathering, Inc. cut to vendors and the Hardin County sheriff's department. Vendors chatting amongst themselves tallied $300,000 that Psychopathic collectively owed them. In late November Psychopathic spokesman Webber announced the Gathering was leaving Cave-in-Rock.

The local sheriff weighed in with a statement:

"With them being gone, it will take the worry and expense away from the county," Hardin County sheriff Jerry Fricker told the Associated Press. He couldn't put a dollar figure on the county's tab, though.

"I honestly don't have any idea."

The American Civil Liberties Union of Michigan was firmly connected to the pending lawsuit along with the Psychopathic legal team. "The first step is to get the Juggalos removed from the gang list," Michael Steinberg, the chapter director, said at the outset. But when he was asked about the individual state gang designations, he ignored the idea. "The first step is the FBI list," he said. "Then we can think about it."

Somewhat of an outlier joined Steinberg and his crew: a lawyer from one of Detroit's premier silk stocking law firms, Miller Canfield. Saura Sahu moved to Detroit in 2006 from Tarlow & Berk, a small boutique firm in Los Angeles. Tarlow & Berk handled every A-lister around, from Mel Gibson to Cameron Diaz. One of the few news hits Sahu ever had was a comment to the media about the wonderfulness of law partner Blair Berk.

Sahu was just a beginner when he joined Tarlow & Berk and was a beginner when he left; he had scant experience in a federal courtroom, but he was sharp and learning quickly. He had been part of a team defending a nursing home accused of falsifying Medicare reports, a case that was settled. Sahu was also on the defense side for Novartis Pharmaceutical in a case in which ex-employees accused Novartis of terminating two employees in violation of federal whistleblower law. The case also was settled. Then he represented a pension actuarial firm against a local union.

With that sort of dull-ass court action, no wonder Sahu was ready for the Juggalos. And here he was, preparing to handle a major civil rights case.

Sahu grew up in West Michigan, had never heard ICP until he took the case, and bought a copy of *Jugganauts*, a collection of songs. It didn't matter—he was part of a large firm that wanted a piece of something heavy.

"We'd been looking for a case to work on with the ACLU since I got back to Michigan," Sahu says. "It was hard to find such a case, but we started talking about the FBI here at the firm, and things fell into place. We're a very mainstream firm, and it's not every day we get to take something like this."

The plaintiffs had to be selected with a mind to how the Feds would challenge them. A staffer at Miller Canfield and two lawyers at the ACLU pitched in to help vet the complaining Juggalos. "To get the plaintiffs, we had to have people with clean records, and they had to be able to speak well," Haddad says.

Some Juggalos were interviewed for hours on the phone. They'd be told of the nature of the lawsuit and that it could be very uncomfortable taking on the FBI, which would be represented by the most powerful law enforcement agency in the country, the US Department of Justice. The defense had more money than anyone alive—that of the taxpayers.

"There were a lot of really interesting complaints that came into Psychopathic through the website in which we couldn't track down someone," Sahu says. "And then when we did, well, some people are better at expressing their story than others."

The team arrived at four individuals who would be the plaintiffs along with J and Shaggy. Robert Hellin, from Garner, Iowa, is enlisted military. Mark Parsons, from Michigan, Utah, or Nevada, depending on whom you believe, is a truck driver. Brandon Bradley is from Sacramento, California. And Scott Gandy is from Concord, North Carolina.

All claim that as Juggalos, they have suffered from being deemed gang members, which turned out to be tough to prove.

13

Religion: Juggaloism

Many people view Juggalos as nonconformists because of their musical tastes, their practice of painting their faces to look like clowns, and the distinctive Juggalo symbols—including the "hatchetman" logo—that they often display on their clothing, jewelry, body art and bumper stickers. Yet when Juggalos come together at concerts or their annual week-long gathering every summer, they know that they are in a community where all people are equal and where they will be accepted and respected for who they are.

—2:14-CV-10071 *PARSONS ET AL. V. UNITED STATES DEPARTMENT OF JUSTICE ET AL.*

Robert Hellin's dog tags list his name, social security number, rank, and religion.

That last: "Juggaloism."

Hellin grew up in Garner, Iowa, and by the time he was twenty he'd been in some scrapes with the law—the standard issue speeding tickets and other moving violations. Then he had an extortion charge dismissed. A third-degree harassment charge, also dismissed. Minor stuff. A smart guy, he enlisted in the Army in April 2008.

In his court pleading in the Juggalo case against the FBI, Hellin claimed that he was subjected to potential problems in the ranks because of his Juggalo beliefs. There may be some question to that, but there's plenty of reason to believe that he's a damn good soldier with a meritorious record. He's a search-and-rescue guy who has spent time in Iraq, Afghanistan, and South Korea. He can show you photos of him carrying the wounded on stretchers. That's a bad day in anyone's book, but it's part of Hellin's everyday reality.

He enlisted with his ICP tattoos blazing. With the FBI's gang report, though, the complaint claimed he worried about being sanctioned or even discharged from the military as a gang member.

Mark Parsons is also cut from a tough-guy cloth. He's a bail bondsman, like a Juggalo version of Dog the Bounty Hunter. Parsons also owns a trucking company he named the Juggalo Express.

Parsons, though, registered Juggalo Express as a business in July 2012 in the state of Utah, seven months after the FBI report.

In July 2013 Parsons was training a new driver using his truck, and drove into a weigh station outside Knoxville, Tennessee. A state trooper stopped the truck, presumably for a random safety inspection. "You a Juggalo?" the trooper asked Parsons when the two met at the side of the truck.

It was, according to Parsons, the start of a lengthy inquiry based only on the hatchetman that adorned the side of his truck. In fact, he says, the cop even said as much, adding that he was already aware that the FBI had determined Juggalos to be a gang. "Do you have any hatchets, axes, or other instruments like that in the truck?" the cop asked Parsons. For an hour this went on, and a search turned up nothing. After that, Parsons was told he was free to go, but he felt anything but free.

Parsons's credibility can be challenged if the case ever got into the weeds, and details mattered because of the date on which he registered his company as the Juggalo Express—naming a company after what the Feds considered a gang. Imagine naming your new cannabis dispensary "Smoke by MS-13."

Scott Gandy was seriously interested in enlisting in the military. He grew up around Concord, North Carolina, outside of Charlotte. Gandy is a Juggalo and smart enough to know there is a better future in the military than there is hanging around a car track, which is the best-known export in the region of NASCAR. When he went to the recruitment center he was asked, improbably, about tattoos. Sure, he said. He showed a nice fat ICP tat on his chest.

"That's a gang symbol," the recruiter told him. No military for you. He ended up working for a printing tech company, which had no worries about his Juggalo status. But he still dreamed of a military career.

In his complaint Gandy claimed the recruiter told him he would have to remove or permanently cover the tattoo. So he did. It took $800 and some pretty harsh pain—to tattoo over something, you have to go deep in the skin—but in the end he was rejected anyway. And what it comes down to is a fish. The damn tattoo now looks like a fish, so he is a fan of marine creatures rather than ICP. And he didn't get into the service anyway.

"Although the Army has not publicly released the materials it uses to identify criminal 'gangs' and their members, upon information and belief, the Army deems the Juggalos to be a criminal gang and bases that assessment on the DOJ's Juggalo gang designation," the legal complaint against the FBI reads.

Brandon Bradley has a trail of trouble with cops and his life as a Juggalo. He discovered ICP in 2002 when he was eight years old. His neighbor played *The Great Milenko* for him. It transcended music for him; it was what he'd always wanted to hear but couldn't find. When *The Wraith: Shangri La* came out that fall, he picked that up.

"I was a Juggalo all my life, but in 2009 I knew it," Bradley says. When he was fifteen he got his first ICP tattoo, a homemade logo on his ankle.

The cops started hassling him in 2011. Being a teenager, he was doing a lot of walking. Twice in 2012 and once in 2013 he was stopped for being a Juggalo identified by a jacket or T-shirt he would be wearing. He submitted his tales of harassment through the online portal and waited. He had no idea what the ACLU was, and he knew nothing about the law. He just knew he was getting hit pretty hard by the local cops, who kept telling him he was in a gang, which was news to him.

When he got a call from Farris Haddad, the Juggalo lawyer, it was a surprise. "I was glad to get called because I really wanted to help," Bradley says. He was getting paranoid, and it wasn't helping that he already got a case of the anxious once in a while. "I was thinking about the cops every day," he says.

So when he agreed to be part of the lawsuit he was sent a lengthy release form, "which was the most I've ever read in my life."

His parents were supportive, which, given the stories of parents going batshit on Juggalo kids, is refreshing. "They think it's awesome what I am doing," Bradley says. "I'm standing up for something."

Bradley flew into Detroit on January 7, 2014, to be part of the formal filing of the lawsuit. Sahu picked him up at the airport and checked him into the Holiday Inn downtown. He and Haddad talked with Bradley for a while and prepared him for what would be a damn big next day.

he ACLU headquarters on Woodward Avenue sits on a stretch of freshly rehabbed Detroit. It's a part of the avenue that says "comeback," and there's a lot to that. The city's bankruptcy in 2013, like the riots in 1967 and the recession in 2009 that took the city's unemployment rate to a hitherto unimaginable 27 percent, is behind them, and of course everything is going to be better.

The Michigan ACLU has taken a lot of important cases over the years, sometimes issues that seem minimal from a distance—challenging a law that allowed police officers to administer alcohol breath tests to minors—to large cases, including the turning back of random drug testing for welfare recipients. Both Fourth Amendment cases were battles worth fighting, and the ACLU's chapter in Michigan has shown a fearless streak over the years, not getting bogged down in politics as many of their chapters in other states have.

Taking on the Juggalo case is a good hit, publicity wise, of course. At the same time, these *are* Juggalos, and this is ICP, and they *are* collectively unwelcome at most parties other than their own. So that morning a dozen local media outlet reps attended the press conference to announce the lawsuit filing. Bradley was joined at a table facing the crowd by two of his fellow plaintiffs J and Shaggy, painted in their Stein's face paint for the occasion.

"This morning the ACLU filed a federal lawsuit against the Department of Justice and against the FBI challenging the designation of a musical fan base as a criminal gang," ACLU Michigan legal director Michael Steinberg said, starting the proceedings. He spoke in a formal, clipped tone, and it was hard to get past his dark suit, white shirt, and white dotted black tie and into the spirit of fucking up The Man.

So it was kind of weird, like hearing your mom say "fuck," when he tried to explain Juggalos. "The Juggalos are the music fans of the Detroit"—pause—"duo, Insane Clown Posse." That was as good as it was going to get.

The lawsuit filed that morning alleged that the FBI made an "unwarranted and unlawful decision" to classify fans of the band as criminal gang members, leading to their harassment by law enforcement and causing them "significant harm."

"Among the supporters of almost any group—whether it be a band, sports team, university, political organization or religion—there will be some people who violate the law," the complaint begins. "Inevitably, some will do so while sporting the group's logos or symbols. However, it is wrong to designate the entire group of supporters as a criminal gang based on the acts of a few. Unfortunately that is exactly what happened here."

The most succinct argument made is that the gang designation infringes on Juggalos' First Amendment freedoms. The freedom of expression, speech, and activity amendment is mentioned ten times in the complaint.

Noting that the First Amendment "protects individuals' right to associate for purposes of engaging in the forms of expression that the Amendment protects," the complaint explains, "Juggalos associate together for the primary purposes of listening to and appreciating the music of ICP and other Psychopathic Records artists, sharing ideas about that music and expressing their support of or interest in the ideas that ICP expresses through its music, expressing their affiliation with ICP and the artists on its record label, and expressing their affiliation with other Juggalos and their identification with Juggaloism as a philosophy, a set of values, a moral code, and a way of life."

Sub out any number of bands—Phish, the Grateful Dead, Fugazi, Social Distortion, Justin goddamn Bieber—and you'd have a lot of the same sentiments and disputable truths in there. Even if a couple of the plaintiffs would be on shaky ground if explored, the complaint was a strong statement.

When the lawyers were done, J restated a lot of what he said at the Gathering in 2012, when he announced the lawsuit. "We know our music is controversial. We know that it's explicit," he told the press throng. "But we don't cram our music, and we don't cram our style down anybody's throats."

Shaggy stood up and explained that "there's no question—we see it all over America when we tour—attendance is down, our merchandise is down, everything we sell is down because it's labeled as gang apparel."

Bradley was clearly the star, a humble kid in a red sweater over a white shirt, collar buttoned almost to the top, and a gold hatchetman medallion dangling from his neck. He looked like a choirboy.

"I'm not gonna change anything about the way I live my life," he told reporters after the conference. "I live a very honest lifestyle."

He was asked what he did for a living. "I work as a caregiver at a senior care home," he said.

He kept his cool even as he was pressed about being a Juggalo and if the gang designation was leading him to change. "I'm not doing anything wrong. There's nothing to change. I just like Insane Clown Posse's music. I can relate to it."

Bradley flew back to Sacramento, glad to be out of the spotlight. Although he had practiced his public speaking in his hotel room when he arrived in Detroit, he was unprepared for the lights and cameras. But he was also greeted with a package of goodies from J and Shaggy—it was Bradley's birthday, and he got a box full of Psychopathic gear. It was some consolation. But he still recalls the fear of declaring he was part of a lawsuit against the FBI.

"That press conference was really the last thing I wanted to do," he says. "I never wanted to speak in front of people."

In the eyes of some onlookers, the lawsuit looked self-serving, and for good reason: in addition to preventing Juggalos from undue harassment, the action sought to mitigate damage to the business of Psychopathic. Having the gang designation was bad for commerce, no doubt.

At the same time, it's not as if they were all sitting in the warehouse, counting stacks of bills.

Over the years ICP had done food drives and charity events. They'd require that people attending their shows bring a canned food item—no yams or other crap like that . . . only the good stuff, like ravioli—and performed benefits.

In 2000 they produced a CD, *Jacob's World*, that was free to people attending their shows if they brought five cans of food to donate. Juggalos who brought ten cans got two CDs.

There wasn't a peep in the local news in early 2012 when *Maxim* magazine contacted Psychopathic and made an offer: we'll give you $848, a limo, and expense cash for a night on the town with ICP. All they asked for is photo and story rights.

So ICP matched the $848, and sent out word to twenty-five select Juggalos that there would be a private party—but you have to bring a Snuggie and a couple of two-liter bottles of Faygo. They also loaded up a party bus with strippers.

The first stop: the HOPE Hospitality and Warming Center in downtown Pontiac. ICP delivered a free show for the Juggalos and about thirty residents of the homeless shelter that sits in one of the worst areas of one of the worst stretches north of Detroit. Instead of Faygo, it rained confetti.

"They didn't tell us where we were going or what we were doing," says one of the Juggalos who got the invite. She hit Walmart for a Snuggie and was on her way. Once they got to Psychopathic headquarters, all attendees had to agree to halt communication with the outside world.

"No one was allowed to get on their phone. No social media was allowed when we were doing this," she says.

On the way out of the selter, after loading the gear and cleaning up the graffiti, someone from Psychopathic found a small donation box at the shelter, located near the entrance. Several hundred dollars of that *Maxim* money found its way in there.

The show was the first of what would be called Juggalo Day, an annual free concert that required anyone attending to bring something for the less fortunate.

"I came up on charity, food stamps, welfare—whatever they call it today," J said later. "We got the food from the hunger barrel. Other people contributed to that. And here I am, this rapper living the dream, or at least I'm living my dream. More or less when I do things like that I'm looking for points with God. When I am judged, I want to be known as someone who did more good on this Earth than bad."

Without a press release.

"We don't care about that," J says.

"Any time we do something for charity, it gets no press," Shaggy adds. "Why should it? There's no controversy in doing good. Gang members sells newspapers and gets viewers."

Glass dildos in velvet bags, vagina tighteners, and Kid Rock. Now that gets press.

Andrea Pellegrini came to Psychopathic as a publicist in July 2009, five months after passing the Michigan bar exam. It was an odd turn for her, and it certainly couldn't pay what getting a job in her field would have. But the state was mired in one more economic downturn that, for a change, the country was sharing.

Pellegrini was the contact point for the media, and she began to issue the standard "no comment" to reporters who began to call Psychopathic about Juggalos' various misdeeds around the United States.

She was fired in November 2012, and soon turned up working as a lawyer at Detroit Legal Services, representing people trying to get on Social Security disability.

In her bio on the social service agency's website, Pellegrini reported that she joined Psychopathic because she "was feeling a desire to engage in a more personable job, and always loved music." During her time at Psychopathic "she was able to gain experience in entertainment law, as well as work on her already developing networking skills."

In September 2013 Pellegrini fired off a lawsuit against Psychopathic, alleging that she was harassed almost continually during her time, a tenure that was a "roller coaster of abuse." She singled out CEO Bill Dail and Dan Diamond, a DJ with Psychopathic, as her chief tormentors but also rolled in J's girlfriend, Michelle, who later became his wife, and a few other staffers, although the defendants were J, Shaggy, Psychopathic, and Dail.

The eighty-six counts made for some sordid reading. To begin with, she contended that Diamond told her he had a fat cock and he wanted to fuck her. She claimed that one day she came to work, and Diamond presented her with a glass dildo in a velvet bag after finding out that she was newly single. Diamond had also, she alleged, bought "vagina tighteners" for two other female staffers at Psychopathic that day.

Diamond was a local DJ who was always hustling for work and landed at Psychopathic through the band's producer, Mike E. Clark. When he arrived at Psychopathic, there was already a Diamond working there—Legz Diamond, aka guitarist Rich Murrell. To avoid confusion, Dan was dubbed Dirty Dan for his proclivity for salacious interests, as he also served at times as the MC at various adult entertainment events around the United States. And, as a perk, he received whatever the swag of the vent was—like said glass dildo.

Given Pellegrini's accusations, though, the nickname was apocryphal.

Diamond worked the Gatherings, hyping the crowd and MCing a couple of events, and also helped out with videos around headquarters.

Bill Dail was relatively kinder, according to the lawsuit—he yelled at her, called her a bitch, and ignored her when she told him others in the company were mistreating her.

Pellegrini made the place sound like a porno set in which sexually aggressive, foul-mouthed, untamed savages ran rampant.

Then there was the 2012 Gathering, portrayed in a bolded subtitle in the lawsuit as "a living hell." Among the travails, her lodging was changed, she had to use a different trailer from the year before, and she had to use the public bathrooms, where there were "strange men." At one point she was ordered to obtain automatic weapons for a video shoot, firearms, she said, that were "illegal."

Pellegrini said she spent almost four years subjected to "constant and pervasive harassment" and was "mocked, belittled, and the subject of sexual advances from top level persons at ICP's label, Psychopathic Records." Among her injuries: "fright, shock, horror, outrage and indignity."

Kid Rock felt something close to a couple of those sentiments when Pellegrini's lawyer issued a subpoena on him for the glass dildo. Diamond allegedly claimed in a deposition that he gave the toy to Rock after Pellegrini turned him down.

The music website *Stereogum* came up with a killer headline for the occasion:

Kid Rock Subpoenaed to Produce Glass Dildo as Evidence in Insane Clown Posse Lawsuit

You could pretty much stop reading there. But Rock didn't get the joke. He fired a letter to Pellegrini's legal team and posted it on his website.

Dear Jim Rasor and Jon Marko,

I'm told that you have issued a subpoena for a "glass dildo" that was supposedly given to me. No idea what you're talking about, and I definitely don't have it. I've never heard of, seen, or met any people involved in this case. . . . Say you were people who aren't a blight on our planet—wouldn't you be pissed off that your name,

for days on end, was being mentioned in the press when EVERY-
ONE involved knew you weren't involved in any way? Welcome to
my side of this story.

No dildo. Psychopathic settled the lawsuit with Pellegrini in a
sealed agreement. Pellegrini is not talking.

14

The Military Tribe of Contorted Belief

What is this Faygo? Is this code for drugs?
—US NAVY OFFICER, READING INTERCEPTED E-MAIL BETWEEN MILITARY
JUGGALOS

Once you enlist in the military, there's an implication of lawfulness. It connects to the recruits as well as the lifers, an unspoken agreement that, for the most part, rules are there to be followed. If you're going to be part of this military thing, at least adhere to the pretense of walking straight. The least of the worries in the ranks of the armed forces is a Juggalo uprising. There are military Juggalo Facebook pages, T-shirts reading "Support Military Juggalos," and thousands of enlisted Juggalos.

The claims of the litigants in the lawsuit against the FBI regarding their military status—Robert Hellin, already enlisted, and Scott Parsons, a hopeful recruit—run contrary to the reality. Their experiences of hard times related to the gang designation were no doubt valid.

And it's easy to see where it came from.

Among the trove of material available from law enforcement on the Juggalos is a 2010 report from the Denver Police Department that features a photo of Jason Faanes, a minister and Juggalo who served in the US Navy:

> 35 year old Jason Faanes (AKA Rev. Last Rite) of VA Beach, Virginia claims that his church is the first Juggalo faith system to be recognized by the federal government. Faanes is also actively serving in the US Navy. All of his information can be found easily on his MySpace page.

There's something alarming about a guy wearing a preacher's collar swearing like a sailor, but that's Jason Faanes. Add in the Joker's Card stickers on the back of his red Kia Rio, the ninja cartoon on the console, and the hatchetman pendant around his neck, and Faanes is a confusing package. It becomes even more vexing when you notice one of his other cars, a Ford Focus, has a hatchetman decal on the back and an excerpt from the Juggalo Creed—which Faanes wrote—on the hood.

The creed is:

> I am a Juggalo. I am an individual guided by Light. I know who I am and who I want to be. I recognize that the path to Shangri-La requires an open mind. I shall not judge. I am part of a Family. I shall Love my Family as I would my blood. I shall do my Family no harm as I know what is done to others shall surely be done to me. I shall strive to honor my Family and not disgrace their name. I am a Ninja. I have no Fear. I do not Fear the unknown for I embrace the wonders of the world around me and the differences in others. I shall meet adversity head on for I am a Survivor. Nothing can stop my Shine. I am Human. I recognize my flaws. I shall strive to change the things I can control and seek strength for the things I cannot. I shall cherish

the teachings of my ancestors and the Family who have fallen before me. I have Love. With Love there is Unity and Strength. Love does not hurt, nor does it seek to destroy. I too, shall not hurt or seek to destroy. With Love in my Heart, Love for my Family, and Love for the Carnival, I shall find my path to Shangri-La.

Faanes is now a retired Navy guy—formal title "Cryptologist First Class Petty Officer"—who spent many of his twenty years in the service teaching sailors how to ID radar signals. The enemy is a crafty bastard and there's no reason that a Juggalo priest standing around five-foot-seven, built like a fireplug with a crew cut and a Jersey accent should not be able to police the skies around our military installations.

Faanes lives on a middle-class street in the northern suburbs of Austin, Texas. Most of his days deal with handling his six children and serving as the minister of the Fellowship of Juggalos. That includes a weekly sermon that he tapes and puts online.

When Faanes retired, the ceremony was held in a low-ceilinged basement room on the USS *George H. W. Bush*. A four-member color detail—two with flags and two with guns—was composed of Juggalos.

Faanes gave the invocation.

"Almighty God, we ask that you be with us today as we witness a transition from one life on to the next. We ask that you reaffirm our commitment to our country, our Navy and our tradition, and, most importantly, our family."

Heads were bowed, the thirty or so service members solemn in listening to the guest of honor worship.

"In your name we pray, amen. Blessed be, 'whoop whoop.'"

Then Andrew Walton, the operations officer of the ship, took to the lectern. He looked at Faanes: "All right, you beat me to it: 'whoop whoop.'"

And from the group of sholdiers in attendance came the reply: "whoop whoop."

This is how seriously the military was taking this gang thing.

Even when Faanes was getting his National Security Agency clearance, his Juggalo status was known—the military knew he had a blue hatchetman tattoo on the inside of his left forearm, as he did nothing to hide it.

In short, a man who was a gang member was passing national security clearance.

Faanes found out about the FBI gang designation on the day it broke, and he walked into the morning meeting at Fort Meade, Maryland. "They were going over the usual FBI reports, and there it was," Faanes recalls. "And there I was, sitting there. And they knew I was a Juggalo."

"Is this a joke?" he asked.

"No, this is real. We just got it," came the reply from the commander.

And they all laughed.

Faanes came from military. His dad was a hospital corpsman in Vietnam, stationed on the USS *Sanctuary*. After he retired he gave Faanes his lighter and told him, "This lighter has lit a lot of men's last cigarettes."

Faanes took it from there. He enlisted in 1994 at age nineteen with a world of not much behind him. He was into *Dungeons and Dragons* from an early age. His first music purchase was a Twisted Sister cassette, and he rocked a mullet in those days growing up in New Jersey. He was married the first time early on in his military stint, and after five years he learned about ICP and what Juggalos were all about.

"I was listening to Metallica, Megadeth. I was dealing with some abuse I had when I was young. I was living on a ship, and I was angry."

But when his brother gave him a copy of ICP's *The Amazing Jeckel Brothers*, the comedy and the anger fit him perfectly, like finding a message he didn't even know he was looking for. It didn't take long to pick up *Ringmaster*, *The Great Milenko*, and *Riddlebox*. He played them on the ship, the USS *Detroit*, docked in Earl, New Jersey. He felt that being a Juggalo was a calling.

It was a quick turn, but his wife laid it on the line when he told her of his Juggaloism: "You can't be a freak because you're my husband."

She became his ex-wife shortly after that.

Faanes turned to his spiritual side.

Faanes knew from religion. He was brought up Catholic by a Mexican mother and an Irish father. And now he founded the Fellowship of the Juggalos. The message in ICP—buried deeply, he had to admit—was salvation and an eventual arrival at a better life. He felt there was a message of faith in there. Maybe no one else did, but he did. And he wanted to spread it inside the military and out.

It didn't hurt that by the early 2000s, as the United States began its war against militant Islam, great pains were being taken to assure all branches of the government that freedom of religion was paramount. So a fellowship for Juggalos, well, that should be okay.

Faanes went to his only Gathering in 2005, driving twelve hours from Norfolk, Virginia, to Garrettsville, Ohio. Four of them went, all military.

He wore his collar, and people thought he was being ironic, which is a gesture that is hard earned in the Juggalo world. "I'd do a lap around the groups and look at the boobies, did a couple of baptisms," Faanes says. One of his party, a girl they called Big-Titted Kitty, or BTK, handed out flyers for the Juggalo church in Norfolk.

Finally, near the end Faanes was sitting down, watching the people flow. He was wearing shorts, a hatchetman hat, and his collar. A teenager was watching this phenomenon, this man of the cloth in his midst. He was already tripping balls. A guy who was dressed as a priest at a Gathering of the Juggalos must be holding onto something good.

"Hey, listen, do you have any acid?" he said to Faanes.

"Seriously? You ask a priest if he's got any acid?" Faanes replied. "No, it's not a costume. And no, I have no acid."

Faanes began to meet other Juggalos in the military and created an e-mail distribution list for his service, which he held each Sunday. It was for everyone but focused on Juggalos.

The code given to the USS *George H. W. Bush* was CVN77, a simple naval designation. Faanes, therefore, calls his e-mail list CVN77 Juggalos, composed of the few dozen men and women on the ship who were Juggalos or simply were interested in being part of the group.

He sent a mass e-mail one morning in January 2014 to the list: "I wish you a day of Faygo and titties but anyone who pulls out a tittie, they're going to Captain's Mast." It was a joke—Captain's Mast was the punishment for minor infractions aboard a ship.

But he made a classic mass e-mail screw up: instead of just going to the CVN77 Juggalos, it went past that and into everyone's inbox, including the ship's commander, who had no idea what this meant but that it sounded like trouble.

"What the fuck is this?!" came back the reply from the commander.

The intelligence office called Faanes immediately.

"I want to talk to the master chief, now!" referring to a rank of leadership just below the commander, who is the top dog.

Faanes was called into a meeting with his superiors.

"What is this Faygo? Is this code for drugs?"

And that's where it went. Faanes took an hour to explain Juggalodom to a room full of career bureaucrats. It was a hostile audience, to be sure.

"These ICP, these aren't good guys," one officer said. He'd done some online research. The room listened. "These guys are having sex with dead bodies."

"If they were having sex with dead bodies, don't you think they'd be in jail?" Faanes said.

The officer, a crusty guy in his fifties who muttered a lot during the rest of the meeting, left unsatisfied.

Of the Juggalos Faanes had on his email list—and the military quickly developed and analyzed those recipients—some got pulled aside.

"Was he trying to have sex with you?" the brass asked the females. Two of them knew the game: they just mentioned that Juggalos meant religion to them, and the brass backed off.

"After all that, they were all trying to ID the Juggalos on the ship," Faanes says. "I retired in September. I was afraid they would take my retirement away if I stayed and they kept on doing this crazy probe."

Doubtful. Juggalos are now bouncing all over the military.

One evening, as the sun set on Camp Fallujah in Iraq, a few guys walked out to the red and yellow sign at the entrance to the Marine base. It was one of the most photographed spots on the base, and the sign, simply reading "Camp Fallujah" at the top and underneath a Marine logo, was the only landmark. The sign was bolstered by a thick concrete barrier, about six feet tall.

Someone pulled out a hatchetman flag, jumped on the top of the barrier. A photo was snapped. Indeed, Juggalos had infected the military. And even the upper brass didn't care. There were bigger things to worry about.

15

Policing the Rabble

If Beethoven can uplift the human spirit, then the Insane Clown Posse can lower it.
—JACK THOMPSON, CULTURAL VIGILANTE AND
DISBARRED FLORIDA LAWYER
FORMERLY FOR THE AMERICAN FAMILY ASSOCIATION

At **the end of** a dirt road, just past the railroad tracks, is where Danielle Keene, her husband, Dave, and infant daughter, Olive, live.

In the heat of a Michigan summer Danielle is chasing mosquitoes and cradling a brown bottle of Coors Light. So is Dave. Olive is sitting that one out, content to sprawl quietly in a crib in the living room, not far from the wood-burning stove that helps heat the small wooden frame farmhouse in the dead of the relentless Fowlerville, Michigan, winter.

In the summer no one needs air conditioning, as Michigan never gets hot, and Danielle and Dave can listen to the traffic on Interstate

96 whizzing by through the open windows. It's been home for fifteen years.

Dave works for Total Security Solutions, a small private company that manufactures and installs bullet-proof glass any place you need it. In Detroit, an hour to the east, any party store that hopes to see its employees alive has it. The same goes for banks. Dave, a short, balding stocky guy with some dark facial scruff and a goatee, teaches martial arts.

Danielle is a pretty, boisterous, big-boned girl with a gravelly voice who just attended her twentieth high school reunion in Farmington Hills. She pushes paper for a state contractor, poring over disability claims.

And they are serious Juggalo veterans. They even went to Woodstock, which takes on a whole new sheen these days. Not the 1969 hippie festival at which everyone was so high that it made sense to put Jimi Hendrix on at 9 a.m. No, having been to Woodstock today means the 1999 version, where the patrons beat the shit out of each other, assaulted some of the females on the site, ripped down some of the wood platforms and walls, then used them to help torch the place.

"Oh yeah, we went. But never got to see ICP," Dave says, like the festival was just another day at the park. "It took forever to get from one part of the site to another, and there were five hundred thousand people, so, well, we just started trying to get there and just couldn't."

Woodstock may have been a bust, but Danielle and Dave can reminisce for hours about the Gatherings they've hit. Those are bastions of civility compared to Woodstock '99.

In 2007 it was a muddy swamp at Cave-in-Rock two days after they got back from their honeymoon in Lake Tahoe. At another, they came back to their tent—they always camp—and there, face down on their air mattress, was a passed out, drunken Juggalo. "It was like Goldilocks," Dave says.

The guy awoke when they arrived and jumped up. "I didn't steal nothing," he said. He waited to make sure they believed him, then wobbled off.

Because stealing is something that is met with Juggalo ire.

"They used to have these little cages they would be put in," Danielle recalls. Their captors would feed them protein bars and water and extra humiliation. "They had to sit out for a while," she says. "And you never saw the same person in there twice."

The cages ended. But a couple of years ago the Keenes were around to see a thief among the Juggalos get some Juggalo justice. A guy was caught pilfering drugs, food, booze, and clothes out of tents. People were talking about things getting nabbed, and the good news was that they found their stuff—in the trunk of the kid's beat-up red Pontiac Grand Am.

He was spared. The car was not. It was bashed into a shell—its windows smashed out, door kicked in, run over by a monster truck, which just happened to be handy. This was, after all, a Gathering.

The wreckage was loaded onto a flatbed, which also happened to be around, and paraded through the Cave-in-Rock campground.

"Fuck the thieves," the Juggalos chanted as they walked alongside the flatbed.

"This is a march against thievery and general bad-vibedness," one Juggalo explained to one of the many folks capturing the episode on video.

The thief was punched around a bit and split soon after they went to work on the car. The only problem is that it turned out the car was stolen. Oops.

Danielle and Dave were not part of the wrecking crew, but Danielle has been down since the midnineties, when she was in high school. Her parents listened to Huey Lewis and Bob Seger, two sure seeds of rebellion. She was into Dre and Metallica and the digital rap metal that was sweeping the world when a friend played her *Carnival of Carnage* on cassette.

"It was love at first sound," she said.

Danielle plastered her car with hatchetman and ICP stickers. She was an "out" Juggalo as quick as she could be, as there is little self-consciousness to her. Later she got a vanity license plate for her car that reads "Wkdclwn."

"I tried 'ju66alo,' but it got rejected by the state," she says. "They sent me a letter saying it was offensive."

Danielle went to Hallowicked first, then began hitting any ICP show she could. Along the way she met Dave, who was way into metal. "I'd seen ICP posters everywhere when I grew up in Royal Oak," he says. But he grew up in a strict home, with a June Cleaver mom where Megadeth was pushing the moral envelope. One of his two older sisters got him into punk rock on the down low. Juggalos were far out, even for most punks, though.

When he got together with Danielle in 1996, Juggalos were part of the package. It took some time.

They went to their first Gathering in 2004, and Dave had an epiphany.

He'd been to Ozzfests, the aforementioned Woodstock, and other mega-aggro festivals. Testosterone ruled these places, and fights over minor disagreements were common. You could get a beat-down for looking at someone the wrong way.

At his first Gathering, Dave and Danielle were walking back to their campsite from a wrestling event, and Dave, a little groggy from a day of beer drinking, stumbled into and onto a very large, very cut gentleman who had put together an outfit of sartorial splendor for the evening. His choice of color was gleaming white, which was the color Dave turned when he realized he had stepped on the size-fifteen white-sneakered foot of a guy who resembled a statue of Dwayne "The Rock" Johnson.

"He grabbed me," Dave says. "And I was sure he was going to pound me."

Which is what would happen at most any other large confluence of drunk people. Instead the guy held Dave upright and looked at him with a smile.

"You okay?' he asked.

Dave nodded, muttering, "I'm sorry."

"No, man, it's cool, I just want to make sure you're all right," the guy said and gave him a little hug.

"I thought, 'Oh my God. I'm a Juggalo,'" Dave says.

On the walls of the farmhouse, along with the usual tributes to traditional family, is a photo of Dave, face painted, for a photo layout in *Murder Dog* magazine. Upstairs, they have devoted a room to their musical fandom, that includes not just Psychopathic events but also a wide sweep of shows, concerts, and meet-ups. To such fans, some kind of contact goes a long way, a connection that somehow binds or confirms or justifies this fealty to someone's work.

Psychopathic has had cookouts and softball games in the area—although Shaggy and J are lousy ballplayers, Danielle notes—and it's not impossible to see any of the Psychopathic crew at the local Best Buy.

"Juggalos are invited to things like wrestling shows," Danielle says. "MTV was shooting something on that one time, and ICP invited the Juggalos to come to the shoot, and J came out to the parking lot just to talk with us and take pictures," she says.

"I've followed them for years but never met Metallica or Slayer," adds Dave. "But ICP are so accessible."

He and Danielle love all things Phil Anselmo, former front man for Pantera. When he came through town with a side project, Down, they paid $150 to hit the band's meet-and-greet, which entailed watching sound check and some face time.

"What's that you have, this pendant?" Down guitarist Kirk Windstein asked Danielle as she stood talking with Anselmo. "We see it everywhere."

Before she could answer, Anselmo helped himself.

"It's ICP and it sucks," he said. "The Insane Clown Pussies."

And when Dave, Danielle, and Anselmo posed for a picture, he turned his thumbs down, emphasizing his disdain for anything connected to ICP.

Danielle kept the picture. She's not such an Anselmo fan anymore.

When the FBI came through with its gang announcement, making Danielle and Dave part of the overall conspiracy, they both shined it. Being in Michigan, there were plenty of cops who grew up hearing ICP and knowing Juggalos. A few were even fans themselves, and some have had their pictures taken with painted Juggalos. So even while Danielle read the tales of persecution and intimidation in other states, she felt mostly insulated from such things.

But there's always been a cop problem in Ohio. The speed traps are a state institution.

In July 2014, five months pregnant, she and Dave packed up their blue Jeep Compass and headed to Thornville, Ohio, for the Gathering. Her condition wasn't even a consideration—they were going.

The only thing that would be out of the norm was her alcohol consumption, which would be cut to zero. But that was a small part of the overall good time. They were closing in on the festival site on Interstate 70 East.

"I was driving, and I pass these two cops sitting in the emergency median," Danielle says. She wasn't speeding, but one of the troopers waited a count, pulled out, and began following. It took a couple of miles before he lit them up.

"You crossed the white line," the cop said. "Can you get out of the car, please?"

He patted her down, all one-and-and-half of her. They pulled Dave out of the passenger seat and checked him over.

The officer asked Danielle to come back and have a seat in the front of his cruiser. He asked where she was going and where they were coming from. The Gathering, she said, coming from Michigan.

Then the cop shocked her: "Tell me where the weed is."

He had searched her purse and found what he thought were blunt wraps, legally sold. But they were glow sticks. The cop didn't even know the difference. Then she realized the reason they were pulled over in the first place: he had seen the large white hatchetman sticker on the car.

"I'm five months pregnant. I'm sober," she explained patiently. Didn't matter. He put her through a sobriety test, the "look at my pen" and "walk a straight line" thing.

She was straight.

"You better tell me the truth, because a canine unit just pulled up," the cop said.

"I have nothing," she told him.

The dog got out and did two walks around. By now Dave was standing, watching. They asked him for the smoke as well. "We have none," he said. Then they put him in the car's backseat.

The cops, dejected, gave it one more whirl. As the dog got around to the trunk, the canine unit cop snapped his fingers and, like magic, the dog jumped on the trunk.

"Okay, he had a hit," he said.

The cops tossed the Jeep and turned up nothing except for a week of food and water and some ICP and Psychopathic wear.

"So what does that sticker mean?" the cop asked Daniele as they wrapped things up.

"It's just a band from Detroit," she said.

"The hatchetmen?" he asked. How would he know to call it that?

They had to let them go—no weed, no warrants.

They jumped back in the car and hit a rest area a mile down to cool out from the encounter. He checked the marker—twenty miles from the Gathering.

As they got back on the highway they saw another car pulled over. It also had a hatchetman sticker.

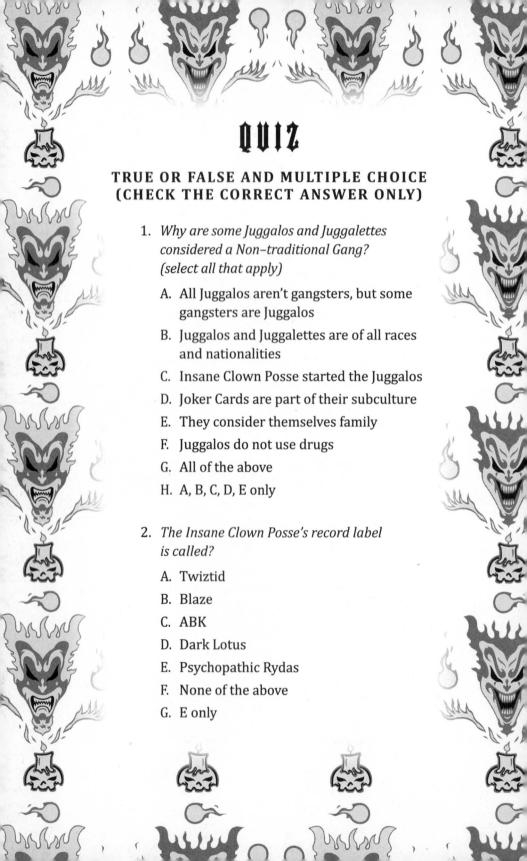

QUIZ

TRUE OR FALSE AND MULTIPLE CHOICE
(CHECK THE CORRECT ANSWER ONLY)

1. *Why are some Juggalos and Juggalettes considered a Non-traditional Gang? (select all that apply)*

   A. All Juggalos aren't gangsters, but some gangsters are Juggalos

   B. Juggalos and Juggalettes are of all races and nationalities

   C. Insane Clown Posse started the Juggalos

   D. Joker Cards are part of their subculture

   E. They consider themselves family

   F. Juggalos do not use drugs

   G. All of the above

   H. A, B, C, D, E only

2. *The Insane Clown Posse's record label is called?*

   A. Twiztid

   B. Blaze

   C. ABK

   D. Dark Lotus

   E. Psychopathic Rydas

   F. None of the above

   G. E only

3. The Psychopathic record label was started by?

   A. The Juggalos

   B. RCA

   C. Death Row

   D. ICP

   E. Disney

4. Basic Juggalo and Juggalette identifiers (select all that apply):

   A. Hatchet gear

   B   wicked clown (WC or WK hand sign)

   C. Faygo soda obsession

   D. Related tattoos

   E. All of the above

5. Is the hatchetman symbol on the back window of a vehicle probable cause to stop?

   A. Yes

   B. No

6. Have Juggalos been contacted in states other than Nevada?

   A. Yes

   B. No

7. Does ICP own Juggalo Championship Wrestling (JCW)?

   A. Yes

   B. No

8. What is Shangri-La to a Juggalo?

   A. Hell

   B. A hatchet

   C. Sex

   D. Heaven

   E. A Juggalette

9. Indicate key phrases that are affiliated with the Juggalos (select all that apply):

   A. Down with the Clown

   B. Runnin' with the Hatchet

   C. Juggalo Family

   D. Magic Magic Ninja What

   E. Whoop Whoop Juggalos

   F. All of the above

10. What is known as the Juggalo's Day?

    A. Christmas

    B. 17th of February

    C. Fourth of July

    D. Thanksgiving

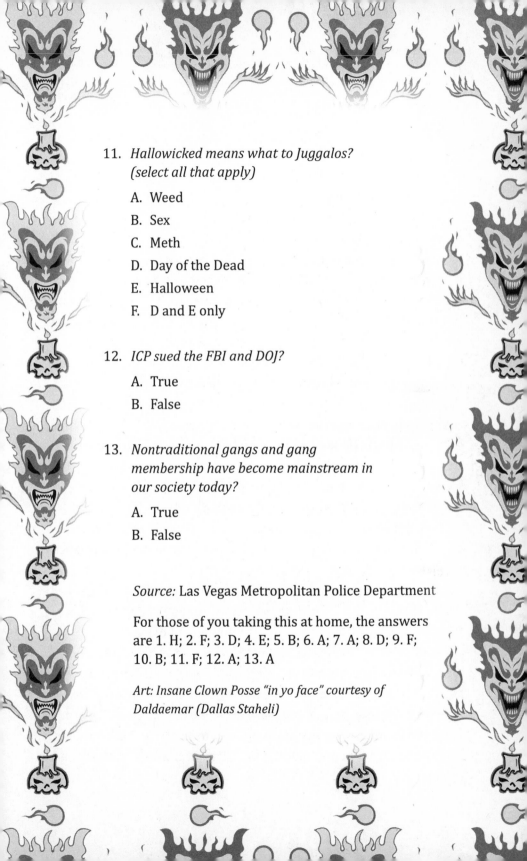

11. *Hallowicked means what to Juggalos?*
    (select all that apply)

    A. Weed
    B. Sex
    C. Meth
    D. Day of the Dead
    E. Halloween
    F. D and E only

12. *ICP sued the FBI and DOJ?*

    A. True
    B. False

13. *Nontraditional gangs and gang*
    membership have become mainstream in
    our society today?

    A. True
    B. False

Source: Las Vegas Metropolitan Police Department

For those of you taking this at home, the answers
are 1. H; 2. F; 3. D; 4. E; 5. B; 6. A; 7. A; 8. D; 9. F;
10. B; 11. F; 12. A; 13. A

Art: Insane Clown Posse "in yo face" courtesy of
Daldaemar (Dallas Staheli)

If you just sat through a day of Bernard Plaskett's class on Juggalo gangs, you must score ten or more to pass.

Plaskett, a gang squad detective for the Las Vegas Metropolitan Police Department, totes a frayed copy of Violent J's 2003 memoir, *Behind the Paint*, whenever he delivers a seminar on the dangers of the Insane Clown Posse.

Although, he says, gently patting the book's cover, "I know they've evolved past this knucklehead stuff."

The book was initially written with a cowriter in what the publishing industry would find an acceptable fashion—no street patois, no rambling, and no flavor. But it just didn't work, J thought, so he hit in his own style, which turns out to be a good read for Juggalos but not ready for prime time in the uptight literary world.

For Plaskett, the six-hundred-page book is a roadmap to the delinquency fostered and foisted by J and Shaggy.

But to be clear: Plaskett is one down motherfucker, a law-and-order renaissance man. He's an Air Force veteran, retired from active duty since 1992. He tested for the department when he got out and worked in the county corrections unit for a bit, then began a seven-year climb to the Gang Crimes Unit. His dad was NYPD, and Plaskett knew from gangs as he grew up in New York City.

"When I was coming up in seventies, it was the Warriors, the Savage Skulls, and the Golden Guineas," he says. "I went to school, played ball with them. So it was always around."

He's sitting in an interview room on the ground floor of the Las Vegas Metropolitan Police Department's building, 373,000-square-foot complex, a tribute to fancy law enforcement digs.

Anyone who's watched *The First 48 Hours* knows this is not a place to be for any reason ever. On this day we got the big room, with couches, stuffed chairs, and a wooden coffee table with a box of Kleenex on it because this is a place for some major tears. These are places you want to stay out of, along with hospitals and courtrooms, in order to live a happy life. It's the place of murder and loss and prison.

Plaskett is a slender wire, and you know that if he grabbed you, it would be wise to sit still and not fight it. He has a slight mustache and a good bit of gray in his high-and-tight. But he looks tough. How tough?

A couple of years back, Plaskett and his wife were out meeting some friends on the Strip and picking up their car at the Excalibur valet when a guy jumped in front of him and into the car.

"Get out, now," Plaskett told the guy. Everyone else was stunned, watching. But Plaskett didn't even waver. "I mean, now."

The guy was starting to put the car into drive, and Plaskett identified himself as a cop. The guy closed the door and dropped his hands, out of view—a gun? Plaskett pulled his service weapon and fired a single round through the door. Hit in the wrist, the guy jumped out and ran for the hotel doors. He was taken into custody and treated for a gunshot wound, while Plaskett and his wife got their car back.

Juggalos have always been in his sightline. He says he was running across Juggalos in the military ranks as he stayed active in the Air Force reserves as a crime and gangs instructor after his retirement. "Coming from New York, I was into the rap era—Grandmaster Flash, Melle Mel, and all these guys," Plaskett says. "Kool Herc and the Herculoids. Back in the day I was influenced heavily by a lot of those guys. I got myself doing some raps back in the day, and I always had a liking to that music. When I was coming up it wasn't like it is now, where the gangster rap has gone to a new level. When I was coming up it was about bragging about yourself, you know."

And he starts spitting some rhymes, right there, presumably with the eye-in-the-sky video cameras rolling.

"My name is a boney b, come from a place called a NYC," he delivers in a smooth flow.

"So back then it was all about you—know what I mean?" Then he's back to the mic.

"I'm six-foot-one and as boney as can be, but all the fly ladies just a flock around me."

But, he says, the Juggalos and many of the other rappers have evolved to a violent strain. "If you knew the Juggalos I've interviewed at the juvenile center, they get their marching orders from ICP," Plaskett says. "Even though I know and you know ICP is not telling them to go out there and commit the crimes, they read the book." He taps again on the dog-eared copy of *Behind the Paint*.

"Violent J pretty much says this is a real depiction of our life growing up."

Since 2008 Plaskett has given an eight-hour course on the dangers of Juggalos to any agency that will have it. The first slide gives the cops the *Reefer Madness*-styled lowdown on their lesson, printed here exactly as it was written:

Instructional Goal:
To familiarize students with the Non-Traditional, highly organized Juggalo Gang and their evolution since the early 1990's.

Instructional Objectives/Learning Outcomes:
Upon successfully completing the course the student will;

    A. Explain the Non-Traditional make-up of the Juggalo Gang.

    B. Describe the Juggalo's Faith.

    C. Familiarize students on the Juggalo Family Creed.

    D. Recognize the reason for the large number of Juggalos World Wide and Nationally.

    E. Recognize who the Juggalettes are, and understand their role in the Gang.

    F. Demonstrate Juggalo Hand Signs.

    G. Describe how to identify a Juggalo or Juggalette.

    H. Recognize the Juggalo's weapons of choice.

    I. List numerous events involving Juggalo's and Juggalettes across the Nation.

    J. Identify and understand Juggalo Graffiti.

    K. List of Juggalo Merchandise, and the Enterprises they are involved with.

L.   State the importance of the Juggalo's and Juggelette's Symbol's or Tattoo's.

M.   Explain how to recognize the Military Ninja.

Plaskett has given this to the West Coast Gang Conference, a huge audience. He's regaled audiences of judges, prosecutors, cops, and anyone else who is interested in tales of the fearsome Juggalos.

His assertions are bold, and he pages through the PowerPoint slides that include photos, lots of eye-catching photos of Juggalos in full paint—drunk, stoned, the classic Juggalette with the handgun.

Plaskett pages through pictures of J and Shaggy sans paint, J's son, JJ, and J's wife, Sugar Slam. ("I talk about how she raises money for causes," Plaskett says. "I'm here to show the good side of them as well.")

The show moves to isolated shots of Juggalos tattoos, from the homemade to high art done in luxe inking parlors, pics of drug vendors at the Gathering, Juggalo graffiti, more Juggalos with weapons, photos of the Psychopathic roster of bands, including Twiztid, and ABK, and the various Juggalo websites.

"I get most of my research from the Internet," Plaskett says.

Plaskett goes into the field as well. He's seen ICP a couple of times and also caught Twiztid. He sees the kids at the shows with the T-shirts reading, "I'm a Juggalo, not a gang member," and wonders. He's convinced that they are simply following orders, that ICP simply snap their fingers, and every Juggalo steps to.

"There was a flyer sent to all the Juggalo websites at the time. They wanted people to wear those T-shirts," he says.

Las Vegas police used to have a database with seven hundred Juggalo gang bangers in it, but "ICP came down with those marching orders a couple years ago—if the police contact you, don't tell them nothing, don't cooperate."

As a result, the list now numbers five hundred, he says, because only those who admit to being a Juggalo are in there, he assures.

"I'm a proponent of making clear that all Juggalos are not gangsters," he says. "I am more a fan of the music but not of what I see or a kid who goes out under the Juggalo caveat and kills. That's where the Juggalo name gets a bad rap. The Juggalos committing the crimes are not the fan base. I know its small smidgen. God forbid the 2 million Juggalos starting committing crimes—that would be a mess for law enforcement."

He's got a starting point for clearing the Juggalo name: have ICP stop calling its fan base by that name. "If ICP really wants to clean it up, just let Juggalos be Juggalos and the rest of the people that are decent be ICP fans," Plaskett says. "But it's hard for them to do that because they created the Juggalos, and they don't want to let that go."

One thing Plaskett wants everyone to know is that his workshop is not a hit piece on Juggalos or ICP. To prove it, he points to the fact that his copresenter is Lisa Kieger, a fellow officer from the department and, to be clear, a Juggalo. "She's the Yin to my Yang," he offers.

That's a stretch, as you can try to temper the message all you want, but it's not going to make a dent in a preconception.

"**O**h, yes, in 2012 Bernard came by my desk and said Juggalos are a gang and he wanted me to talk to his class," says Lisa Kieger. She's a fortysomething woman who went with a friend to an ICP/Twiztid show in Vegas in the late nineties and not only saw them with a friend but also went to meet them on the bus after the show.

"Are you twenty-one?" ICP manager Alex Abbiss asked them as they approached the bus. "And if you are, do you have a car?"

Yes, they were, and yes they did, so they were appointed to take the guys around to a couple of casinos, and they all ended up at the Crazy Horse Too, a strip joint off Las Vegas Boulevard.

"We thought we'd just drop them off, but they had us come with them."

They all sat at the back and talked not about the girls at the city's premier titty bar but songs and strategy. "From then on, any time they came through town, they called me," she says. She traveled with them a bit, then the Twiztid camp started calling her, and pretty soon she was friendly with much of the Psychopathic crew.

By 2006 Kieger was working at the Las Vegas Police Department and was focused on other things, including a new marriage in which she and her new husband pooled their kids for a total of six. On her desk at work were trinkets of her Juggalo world—bobble heads, laminates—much in the same way a Yankees fan uses one of those obnoxious mini-helmets to hold paper clips in his cubicle.

She went to an ICP show in late 2009 and while there she got embroiled in a little argument. She showed her police ID, and when she came into to work the next day her captain called her into the office. It wasn't about the fracas; it was about Juggalos, which were by then being talked about as a local gang.

"These are my friends," she told him. "They aren't a gang."

She boxed up her Psychopathic gear anyway. But no one forgot her Juggalo connection, and when Plaskett was doing his Juggalo seminars, he thought of her. "He came up and he wanted me to go to one of the seminars to see how good the intel they had was," says Kieger, who is no snitch.

So she went, and the first thing she realized was that they were profiling.

Plaskett, going through his PowerPoint, showed a hatchetman decal on a car and asked, "If you see this, can you pull the car over?"

As the quiz states, no, you cannot.

These were cops, though, and as anyone knows, you can think of any reason to pull over anyone if you think the person inside that car might be doing something wrong.

"If the decal is obstructing the back window, you could," piped up one Constitutionalist in the room.

"No, but make sure they come to a complete stop at a stop sign," said another.

For Kieger, it was too much.

"Listen, you're going to get someone hurt," she said.

But instead of walking away, she did everyone a solid—she said she would teach half of the class, the education part where officers can learn, ideally, that Juggalos are a music fan base above all.

But when the local news came calling—inevitably, as Juggalos are a sure ratings draw—it was Plaskett who went on camera to tell of the scourge of Juggalo gangsters.

Lisa was not invited.

16

Defending Revolution

Even the most primitive of societies have an innate respect for the insane.
—MICKEY ROURKE IN *RUMBLEFISH*

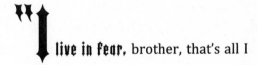**I live in fear,** brother, that's all I can say. I live in fear."

Violent J sits in a plush, high-backed leather chair in the control room of the Lotus Pod, the studio at Psychopathic Records, the sunny summer day filling the outside and a million-dollar recording room ready for action behind the glass to his left. Out in front sits his black Chevrolet Suburban, the extended version with chrome wheels and a silver hatchetman on the left rear of the tailgate. In the console of the SUV is a bag of Halls Mentho-Lyptus, honey-lemon flavor, to soothe his cords. Across from him sits his best friend of thirty years,

Shaggy. They have sold millions of records and are adored by tens of thousands of music fans.

I live in fear, brother, that's all I can say. I live in fear.

Such ambition is often driven by fear, which is a commodity peddled by everyone, from the media corporations to movie producers, who, speaking of fear, are becoming one and the same.

Fear extends past our self-interests and onto others. It sells books and packs theaters. Then there's the personal version. Fearing the death of a loved one, the loss of income.

There's also the fear of someone out to get you, familiarly known as paranoia. That's the sweaty mix of trepidation and paralyzing caution that stops a lot of otherwise ambitious people in their tracks.

The strain of fear hawked by entertainers is supposed to be rooted in the fantastic. Stephen King scares the shit out of people with his tales of "It could happen here." Whole sections of bookstores are devoted to horror.

J and Shaggy kick out fear as the transmission of the ICP oeuvre.

In turn, fear dogs both of them.

"Anything bad happening to my kids, I fear that," Shaggy says. "Putting out a record and having the Juggalos hate it—I really fear that."

"I fear death, having a stroke, being crippled," J adds. "I fear jail. I fear fuckin' one day driving down a street and hitting a little kid darting out in front of the car."

What about fear of rejection, a favorite among those favorites that destroy self-esteem and ruin dreams? And, worse, what about someone trying to stop you from even staying in the game, like the federal government?

"Oh, yeah, we live in rejection," J says. "CDs don't sell anymore, and that right there is rejection. The times have changed against us. We used to have a big staff here, and we can't afford them

anymore—that's real rejection. We were the masters of street promotion, and that's not working anymore. We're just not as skilled as
we were, not up to date. People say, like, 'Oh yeah, I remember ICP.
You guys still doing shows and putting records out?' That hurts.
These forms of rejection aren't our fault, but to me it's rejection
when the world changes, and all of a sudden you're old school and
your company is outdated and it's not set up for today."

There's one more thing that induces fear: "The FBI thing is scary
to me. I've never looked at the actual report, but I'd be scared to see
their reasoning."

He was at home one night after the FBI announcement, watching
Investigation Discovery on TV. The series *Web of Lies* came on and
featured the Farmville murders, a heinous quadruple homicide in
which a kid named Richard McCroskey caved in the heads of the victims. Turns out, McCroskey listened to ICP. Imagine sitting in your
living room and that comes on.

"It had nothing to do with the band, but there it was," J says. "I
would hate to see the information that the FBI has gathered in saying
why we're a gang. That shit might scare me to death."

That's a heavy dose of fear to carry around in what, by all appearances, should be the safe world of an entertainer and artist.

By the time of the first court hearing, the Feds were ready to settle.
The case was unwinnable, and the loud outrage combined with a
legally lethal complaint had them cowering like bullies under baseball bats.

In June 2014, as the first major hearing approached, the ACLU
sent out a press release inviting Juggalos down to the federal courthouse on Lafayette in Detroit to check out the latest round of legal
salvos from their lawyers.

What if the Juggalos decided to have their own little Gathering in
the chambers of the Honorable Judge Robert H. Cleland? Room 707
was prepared for the occasional defendant going rogue. But the face

paint alone would be enough for the judge to call the whole thing off until order was restored.

The hearing was fairly pro forma with a dash of drama—this was a point at which the judge could toss the case. The DOJ had filed a motion to dismiss, stating that the defendants had failed to show damages and that they lacked standing, that the only damages that could be inflicted were from a knavish cop in Wrong Place, Maryland, or some other like-wise unfortunate town.

After all, the gang assessment report never singled out anyone. Was Violent J ever called a gang member in the report? Of course not. Shaggy may have his own legal concerns, but the FBI never called him a gang member.

The settlement notion was known only to the lawyers on both sides. Clerks hear about talks, then murmur about things that then get passed along to the lawyers, and the next thing you know, we're on the unprecedented brink of the DOJ pondering just what it would mean to reverse itself.

The idea of putting Amy Powell on the case to represent the Feds was enough to make anyone wonder just what the hell was going on. Were things this serious?

Powell is a heavy hitter, a smart trial attorney who's earned her flight bars and then some via her time arguing in front of the top judges in the nation. A New Yorker, she's been with the DOJ since 2005 and has battled everyone from the First Amendment Coalition and the ACLU to various environmental groups seeking to overturn massive regulations.

Powell is a tiny ball of Beltway intelligentsia. Her brown hair hangs to her shoulders in disarray, tucked behind her ears in an Eddie Vedder do, framing a tiny face that held a bewildered expression.

She is strictly A-list in the halls of the DOJ when it comes to representing agencies in regional courtrooms around the United States. Her legal brawn is such that, although ICP had a gaggle of legal minds in its corner, Powell took the defense table alone in June 2014, presenting in a wrinkled navy-blue sweater/skirt combo and bare legs in need of sun extending into brown loafers. She is the everywoman you see on the DC Metro, hurrying with an umbrella and newspapers tucked under one arm, briefcase in the other.

Powell had won more cases than she'd lost. She represented the various civil divisions of the US government, forcing her to know a wide variety of specialties. And she moved into whatever jurisdiction she was needed, sometimes big-footing the locals.

And in Detroit those were some heavy locals who were chasing the bad guys. The Detroit FBI had been expanded post-9/11 due to the large Arab population in the region—there was still an element of the local population who feared Detroit would be the hatching nest for the next major attack on US soil.

But they don't have the time to take on the Juggalos or to defend the FBI's move to name them as a gang. They had real crimes to chase. Powell was the one who could keep the situation in hand, for sure. She filed several requests to delay the case as she prepared a response to the Juggalo complaint. She had bigger things brewing, and Juggalos were clearly not at the top of the list.

The day before the arguments, a Sunday, Saura Sahu, the lawyer on the Juggalo team who would present arguments the next day, sat in a large booth at the Great Lakes Restaurant in Fowlerville, Michigan, and delivered his arguments to me. A waitress may have caught a few words, but she wasn't interested in any Juggalo trouble. For Sahu it was a dry run, something lawyers commonly do before a big show.

He delivered a recitation of how the gang designation violated the federal Administrative Procedure Act, an attack on a seventy-year-old statute that goes after the fashion in which the government regulates us. It's a familiar punching bag when the federal government is accused of overstepping. A private party, like the Juggalos, can challenge an action taken by a federal agency, like the FBI, when it feels the agency has abused its power.

A party with some solid resources and a bad attitude could do some real damage in a court, something most law enforcement agencies aren't ready for when it comes to something as lowly as a street gang.

In this case, the FBI is accused of making a wrong conclusion. Juggalos as gang members? Naw . . .

As the presentation ended, Sahu noted he was not a listener of ICP, but he didn't need to be to represent the interests of everyone connected to his clients. "The music serves its fan base very well," Sahu said, picking at some leftover fries on his plate. "I grew up watching horror movies, and it's that same kind of thing. It can be funny; it can be used to express anger. That's what it's supposed to do."

He looked every bit like the smoothie lawyer slumming it—the two-day growth of beard, the motorcycle in the parking lot. He was the voice of the Juggalos. It was a far step from being part of a team representing Mel Gibson, as he had during his days in Los Angeles.

When we finished, Sahu hopped on his motorcycle and headed home. The next day would be the biggest presentation of his life, as he represented what many believed was the most misunderstood group of music fans ever. Others, though, were sure Juggalos deserved the worst and were glad to see even the Feds going after them.

The Theodore Levin US Courthouse on Lafayette in downtown Detroit is ten stories of Art Deco beauty that opened in 1934. Above the entrance are sculpted eagles, and inside, the floors are marble and the courtrooms are old school but incredibly clean and modern.

No Juggalos turned out to Judge Cleland's courtroom. In the gallery were small groups of law students, interns, and junior members of Miller Canfield. Even the media stayed away, save for an Associated Press reporter.

It's as if a First Amendment affront was not even news, which is at least half true in a city as beaten down and weathered as Detroit.

Or maybe the fact that the Constitution isn't so important to locals is the reason for the lack of interest.

Powell followed the script her brief laid out. She maintained that that the FBI designation "does not conclude that all Juggalos are members of a gang."

"There is no general right of protection to a social association" relating to gangs, she said. She argued that the FBI did not label all Juggalos as members of a criminal gang, only a "subset" of them.

The most recent FBI gang report doesn't mention Juggalos, she noted. The report she referenced came out in 2013, and there is nary a word of Juggalos. Therefore, the 2011 report is dated, she said. "It's increasingly unlikely to be used by any state or local agency as a source for any particular action."

She pushed on, saying that the gang designation imposes no penalty nor does it revoke any benefits. And the tattoos, bling, and T-shirts the gang report makes note of? She compared it to the Oakland Raiders jerseys some gangs used to favor. "Law enforcement can use that in gang identification, just as it can tattoos," Powell said.

She talked for fifteen minutes. It was her best stuff, and the judge was already with her.

Judge Cleland noted that other agencies—not the FBI—had made the injuries cited in parts of the complaint—the same argument Powell just made. "That's your problem here," the judge told Sahu as he stood to begin his argument.

Sahu fired back with the First Amendment argument, citing case after case to bolster the Juggalo cause. The rules the FBI created were guidelines to interpretation, he said, rules that should help rather than trample rights.

"They're supposed to have an impact on state and local law enforcement, and they do, and usually it's a really good one," Sahu said. "It's just that this time they went too far here. . . . To call someone a gang member or gang-related is to call that person a criminal. . . . These guys are standing up against what happened to them, but they are also standing up for millions of music fans. They're doing what we really admire . . . these guys are standing up for not only the things that have happened to them, but to a million other fans."

It was truly a stabbing of the First Amendment, he added. The paint, the hatchetman T-shirts, the tattoos are all declarations of love for a culture to which they belong with no criminal intent.

"The government went too far here," Sahu said of the gang classification. "Those are First Amendment–protected symbols."

Sahu was standing up for a million Juggalos as well as million other music fans who have appreciated the "fuck you" of irreverence over the years since Elvis pissed everyone off. The Sex Pistols, Alice Cooper, Marilyn Manson, Guns N' Roses, Black Sabbath—this is what rock 'n' roll was made to do: to intimidate those who didn't understand and outrage those who thought they did.

Here were pounds of pot smoke, gallons of whiskey and wine, ounces of coke, and a million tabs of acid being defended by a thirty-five-year-old man named Saura in a brown suit in a beige room with a sick green carpet.

After the hearing Powell watched lawyers for ICP do a media standup across the street, standing on the courthouse steps. The hearing was her first visit to Detroit in her life. For lunch she hit a classic, the Lafayette Coney Island, just four hundred feet from the courthouse.

We conversed about the city of Detroit. "I was expecting this to be a bombed-out ruin of a place," she said. "But it's not at all. It's got beautiful buildings."

She was leaving later, in for a day and out again. She noted that the DOJ office in Detroit was one of the department's finest, trying—and winning—numerous terrorist-related cases.

We talked a bit more, and I told her I had heard there were talks of a settlement in the case, which would be an amazing legal feat for ICP. In essence, it could be an "I fucked up" admission by the Feds that would be cause for celebration for First Amendment fans everywhere.

But these are secretive deals. No one on either side talks about them for fear of halting the whole thing.

"We're always interested in talking," she said.

"So what would something like that entail in this case?" I asked.

"I can't talk about the details," she said, inadvertently confirming that, indeed, a settlement was already being discussed.

I asked her why, if this case had no merit, ICP would fire off such legal action.

"It's good for the brand," she said, smiling. "Sticking it to the man."

In July 2014 Judge Cleland dismissed the lawsuit ICP and the four Juggalos filed against the FBI. Cleland agreed with the DOJ contention that the report is just a report and bears no responsibility for how local cops use it.

The report "does not recommend any particular course of action for local law enforcement to follow, and instead operates as a descriptive, rather than prescriptive, assessment of nationwide gang trends," the judge said in his ruling. An appeal was filed immediately.

Whether or not we can defeat the FBI, that's one thing, but it's important that people know we are fighting it," J told me a couple of months after Cleland's decision. "We cannot just stand back and say, 'Yes, that's correct: the Juggalos are a gang.' It's like being called the bad guy out of everybody at the party. All the people making records and everybody in the record industry, like a big, fat finger pointing down from the gods saying 'Fuck you, you know, you shouldn't be here, your fans aren't fans, they're a gang and that makes you gang leaders or some kinda shit.' It's scary to me. It's not scary during the day when I'm with my boys and talking about fighting it. But when I'm home, chilling with my family, it's so big to have the government say something like that about us to me."

17

There's a Day for Juggalos?

One Juggalo is worth fifty regular fans.
—VIOLENT J

Without the plastic wrap there
would be no Juggalo Day at Masonic Auditorium in Detroit.

The music space is part of the Detroit Masonic Temple, the largest such temple in the world and one more tribute to the neo-goth architectural influence in Detroit. More importantly it's been a landing spot for some of the best music in the world starting in the forties.

Duke Ellington jammed there, as did Miles Davis, Charlie Parker, Louis Armstrong, and on into Bob Dylan in 1964 and 1965 and then the Jimi Hendrix Experience played Masonic in 1968 (who, a local critic wrote, "played a horribly mediocre performance"). Springsteen played there on the way up, opening for the Guess Who. The Rolling Stones jammed the forty-four-hundred-seat auditorium on their 1978 *Some Girls* tour. Lou Reed danced in amphetamized ecstasy on the stage in 1975, and Queen opened with "Bohemian Rhapsody" there the next year. The Clash played its first Detroit show there and sucked. And if the music doesn't get you, H. G. Wells delivered a lecture there in 1937.

And now ICP would join the ranks of the accepted.

Juggalo Day is Insane Clown Posse's annual tribute to its fans, a cheap show every February since 2012. It landed in the Cass Corridor on its fourth year. Drop a couple of cans of food for the Gleaners Community Food Bank at the door, and you're in. No lima beans or yams allowed.

"Fuck that—bring the good stuff: SpaghettiOs, you know, Chef Boyardee, something like that," J urged. There are no lima beans as far as the eye can see among the huge piles of canned goods that are slowly stacking up in the entry way of the hall.

On the day of the show stage crew removed ten rows of floor seats and wrapped the whole front and side monitors, stacks, amps, and wiring in plastic.

By the end of the night they would become Faygo soaked and possibly ruined without the wrap. Decades of rock 'n' roll in this place, historic bursts of antisocial noise and attitude, and no one had before considered the possibilities of a sea of soda.

The auditorium has soft red velvet seats and red carpeting set off by gold framework and two enormous chandeliers weighing one and a half tons each. Check the Venetian Goth décor and the huge stage drapes in purple. This is no outdoor pasture, like the venues for the Gathering, where social development is miles away and the rules of life are suspended.

No, this is a free show for Juggalos held in the confines of the 135 square miles that is Detroit. Civilization is at a minimum here, for sure. The Masonic, though, is a serious culture icon. For a batch of booze-loving, weed-whiffing Juggalos, it is an incongruous match, to be sure.

The place also contains several smaller halls, two ballrooms, a bowling alley, a swimming pool, and a private restaurant. Plopping four thousand Juggalos down for some gratis horrorcore in the dead of winter is an excellent way to break up the short, gray days and keep the eyes forward to the next Gathering.

This is no place for a gang meeting, but there you go. Somehow they got permission, and in keeping with the finest of rock 'n' roll tradition, the corridor leading to the various production offices smells like weed, the smell of collegiality, and work getting done on its own terms. What's a little different is that as soon as Juggalos begin filing in, the security guards put on their yellow ponchos. Ushers are not provided such protection.

"Hell, I'm going down the ramp before any of that starts," one usher says. For now he watches Juggalos fire up joints and checks out the occasional titty popping.

By 8 p.m. J and Shaggy are in a boxy, linoleum-floored room just off the main hallway, behind a solid polished oak door, preparing to meet Juggalos, who paid $100 for the privilege.

It's tense in there for unknown reasons, but J wants some towels, and he needs towels—NOW. Ten of them, body sized. The fluorescent overheads make their paint look whiter than usual, fresher, like it just hit the side of the barn. He likes the venue to be sure; he was married in this very building in August 2013, in fact, which gives the place some good vibes for him.

Still, there are a lot of nerves going around.

Shaggy is in a better mood. He's talking about his family. He's got Ronan, who was born two weeks before. And then the twins, Isaac and Cyrus, who are eighteen years old. He's worried about Cyrus, who is in Virginia at military training after enlisting in the Army a year before. He's learning to defuse bombs.

"He's in denial. He thinks he's going to Germany or something," Shaggy says, bouncing a bit on the balls of his feet. His head is dangerously close to knocking out a tile in the drop ceiling and raining asbestos all over the whole room, and every time his toes go up, the head gets closer. "But I tell him he's going where the bombs are— there's stuff going on."

J is still quiet, looking down, clutching a black magic marker, waiting for the doors to open. Shaggy is unfazed by the drama.

So did Cyrus have any trouble getting into the military with his dad being a gang member?

"Nah. He doesn't even have any tattoos," Shaggy says. "Not because I restricted them."

When his sons turned sixteen he offered to buy them both tattoos as a gift. "But just know anything you get when you're sixteen you're gonna hate down the line," he told them. "By your midtwenties this tattoo is piece of shit. But you got it when you were sixteen—what do you expect? And be careful what you get."

So both of them opted out, and Cyrus entered the military, attached to the Juggalos only by lineage.

By the time the door opens and Chop, assistant to ICP, escorts the first visitors in, J's mood has lightened. Or at least he's fronting well.

Some fans have their kids with them; others want special photos, like the couple who take what they call a prom picture, as she is wearing a formal gown.

Two guys come in drinking on twenty-four-ounce PBRs. One of them mentions that his mom grew up near Ferndale. The other is standing straight up, frozen in awe except for the beer pulls during an encounter that takes all of sixty seconds. He shakes his celebrity stupor near the end of the visit. "For real, this is a real big pleasure," he manages, before walking out. Some fans want just a quick photo; others want to talk. Either of which are fine with the guys.

Every Juggalo is happy to be there, even in the cold, bunker-like room that features three sinks and a rotary phone on the wall.

"Hey, look at that incredibly fresh jersey," J says, greeting a couple. She's got a *Great Milenko* garment that looks homemade but she nailed it, with the colors perfect. A lot of Juggalos make their own gear, appropriating the hatchetman or a record cover and creating something unique.

"We got married in ICP jerseys," the woman says.

Near the end of the hour-long greets Kyle Hutchins is rolled in, sitting deeply in the wheelchair that is his home. Kyle is thirty years old but looks like a fourteen-year-old who sprouted a mild mustache.

At the age of eight he developed ankylosing spondylitis, which is a disease that causes the vertebrae to fuse, a painful and debilitating malady that there is little help for. He had a hip replacement at the age of twenty-four but still walks unsteadily with a cane when he has the energy to get out of his chair. Every day he has to take four heavy-duty pills, and every six weeks he takes a four-hour IV to ease the condition. Since 2012 he's put on ICP videos during the IV to take him away from the ordeal.

"That's when I first heard them. I was on the Internet and listening to music from Detroit, and I did more research. I just fell in love with what they did, and after a little while I started to understand the message behind the violence of the music."

He studies Juggalos—his family—as he lives a life in which everyone has to take him anywhere he needs or wants to go.

"I get down and have a lot of pain. I've never had a girlfriend, and I get depressed," he says. "These shows keep me going. It's the light in my life."

This isn't the first time he's met ICP—he met them at the Hallo-wicked meet-and-greet a few months before. Every time is fresh for him. After all, he says later, he feels as close to the two guys in ICP as he does to some of his blood family. "I get an IV, and you guys help me get through it," Kyle tells them, looking up from his chair. He holds out a joint, which is burning between his fingers. He has a medical marijuana license, he tells them.

"I also have edibles," Kyle says, an invitation to share.

"I know it may sound hard to believe, but I like anything edible," J says, pointing to his ever-broadening girth.

✝ ✝ ✝

Try as they might, the Juggalos cannot fill Masonic. The ones who do crowd in smoke cigarettes like there was never a ban in place and blaze through weed like it was Colorado. They absolutely devastate the bar, the particular favorite being the cheap stuff. It's freezing in the auditorium, but the guys' shirts come off, and the pit is blazing with them.

Backstage the crew fights with the heavy woolen curtains. Few places ICP play are as regal and ornate or come with as many possibilities as this fabled venue. And that includes a thousand pounds of curtain that can't just be moved back and forth repeatedly.

Since Thursday the Faygo has been kept warm on the truck via portable heaters, as cold Faygo doesn't bubble and foam nearly as wildly as warm Faygo does.

It arrives at the loading dock, and a crew jumps out of the truck. Psychopathic boss and production manager Bill Dail has embossed dark-blue work jumpsuits with "Faygo" on the back for the guys hauling the crates of soda from the truck and into the backstage as if they were employees of the brand; instead, they're paid help for the evening for Psychopathic.

"Billy gets these guys to help us, and I don't know where, but they're always pretty good," says one stage manager. "He pulls them in every city when we're on the road too."

He pauses at that one.

"I wonder where he gets them."

(Billy: "I just keep a crew of people I know in every city and call them up when I need them. They always want to work because I pay them well.")

At one point, while one of the opening acts plays, J walks out from the production area and stands behind a crate, watching the crowd in the front. He wears a black and red hatchetman jersey with leather trim and red sweatbands on his wrist like he's Pete Rose and it's 1970. No one says a word to him. He's got a second to himself before Chop comes up and shouts into his ear. There's another crisis. He leaves.

ICP hit stage last, and it's one more blur of Faygo, with two-liters reaching the very back of the venue, fired one-handed by J and Shaggy. Plastic can only do so much protecting, and chairs are drenched.

Onstage the crew works in an orchestrated synchronicity. Dressed in clown suits and masks, they maneuver props in and out of place, two giant Faygo bottles, a Faygo cannon. They twirl hatchetman banners on cue and restock the huge silver barrels that hold the two-liters. They come out with red buckets filled with Faygo and splash the audience. All in front of a huge "ICP" spelled out by thousands of tiny white light bulbs with two glowing hatchetmen flanking the letters, also in white bulbs.

For weeks this show has gone through dress rehearsals back at Psychopathic HQ on the sound stage at the back of the warehouse. A hometown show like this, being done without the momentum and tightness that touring brings, takes more preparation. And in keeping with that, the production can be more elaborate.

The place goes off, and it's one more Juggalo night for the ages.

A lot of bands do a lot of cool things for their fans, but few put on a free show at a major venue while soliciting food for the poor and lazy. Of course free concerts are a staple of rock history. Every summer free concerts by huge acts dot the boroughs of New York City, from Wolf Eyes to Lyle Lovett.

It's something else to get your fans to come to an urban wasteland, a place in which one enterprisingly wise Juggalette from Philadelphia bought a house for $500 for the sole purpose of having a home base for Detroit-based Juggalo events in which to generously house out-of-towners.

After the whole thing was over, two semi-trailers pulled up to take out the canned goods. It took an hour to load them both up.

"I've never seen so much Chef Boyardee in my life," said one of the handlers, with blue plumes coming out of his mouth as he spoke. The lights outside Masonic glowed yellow in the 10 degrees. You could still smell the Faygo root beer in the air, carried from the sweaty floor of the auditorium and outside, as the clothes of the soaked Juggalos quickly froze solid.

The Juggalo Day postmortem was done starting at 9 p.m. five nights later in a fifteen-by-fifteen square-foot room in an upstairs room at Psychopathic HQ. The place is overflowing with extension cords, and wires drop out of the ceiling, snaking along the floor to . . . somewhere, presumably.

The occasion is the Psychopathic Radio show, which is kind of like *Wayne's World* for Juggalos, broadcast on both web video and audio. It's hosted by Rob Bruce and Rudy Hill and includes a rotation of others, including Natalie, a Juggalette who won the Miss Juggalette contest a couple of years back and drives 150 miles one way in the dead of winter to sit in at the studio table and occasionally weigh in. She's there this evening, in fact, sitting proudly in her black hatchet-man jersey.

The show, though, revolves around Rob and Rudy, longtime homies waxing about anything from wrestling to favorite television shows to Juggalos news.

Rudy claims he is still pulling slivers of glass out of his back after his wrestling match—wrestling as Rude Boy, of course—with Necro-butcher the previous weekend at the Juggalo Championship Wrestling exhibition.

"We had to give it 110 percent because it was Juggalo Day," he says. Everyone is ebullient over the Juggalo Day extravaganza, which also featured the two ICP movies, *Big Money Rustlas* and *Big Money Hustlas*, shown in the Jack White Theater, a fifteen-hundred-person-capacity side room so named after White paid off the bulk of a back tax bill laid on the theater in 2013.

"Just driving up to the theater, to see this prestigious theater that allowed us to take over," Hill says. He's like a little boy who got the keys to the car. Allowed us to take over. Hell yeah, and we didn't even wreck the place. "There's wasn't a bunch of damages. There wasn't a bunch of graffiti."

The self-congratulations flew. A couple of listeners called in. Dead Body Dan wanted to know how the parking was going to be at the Gathering in July, and a guy from Oklahoma wants to send a video in for airplay consideration.

Near the end of the show Farris Haddad, the Juggalo lawyer, drops in to talk about the FBI case. The two sides had been exchanging filings, and things were headed for the US Court of Appeals for the Sixth Circuit in Cincinnati.

Two days earlier the Juggalos filed a twenty-eight-page brief. This one aimed right at the damages done not so much to reputation but in fact to the violations of the First Amendment in the Fed's actions.

> The real issue is whether the DOJ is violating and unconstitutionally burdening Plaintiffs' personal rights by adhering to a vague and excessive gang label that targets them. . . . The impact of the DOJ's gang designation is nothing short of defamatory, and it has an objectively foreseeable chilling effect on Juggalos' constitutionally protected expressive and associational activities. It brands them as criminals and subjects them to unjustified government action. Contrary to the DOJ's suggestion, the effects are not speculative or impersonal.
> —plaintiff's filing, February 24, 2015

"We're the only gang that does charities," Haddad tells listeners.

He goes back to update new Juggalos to the FBI lawsuit, recalling the ten thousand people who came forward both in person and through the various web portals to complain about being harassed after the gang designation.

Haddad, a defense lawyer, recalls the freshly released convict whose parole officer checked his Facebook page to see who his charge was consorting with and found among his friends a Juggalette. "He was sent back to prison for associating with gang members," Haddad says.

Everyone guffaws. By now J-Webb, the Psychopathic flack, is there, and Dean the webmaster and Kuma the video producer are also sitting about in case anything goes awry with the technology, which continues to flow through wires masked with duct tape and maybe some spit.

Rob wonders aloud why no one in the arts community was coming forward to at least lend some spiritual support. One would think that in a field that relies so heavily on protected speech, someone would be pissed off enough to speak out against the FBI and the ill-advised designation of a fan base.

But no one puts anything on their website, and "artists, they have a mic," he says.

"You don't have to like us or love us to be a part of this because eventually, if it gets out of hand, it's going to affect you and what you do as well," Rudy adds.

"I don't know why that is," Rob says. "Maybe they're afraid they'll be put under the scope? If you think this is bullshit, you gotta join us in the fight."

Rappers like Lil Wayne, Snoop Dogg, and The Game have actually stated their gang affiliation—blue and red flaggin'—with no repercussions.

And there they were, dangling, dropping some cash to fight for the right . . . to be Juggalos.

Haddad promised the Juggalos that victory over the FBI was right around the corner. It was, he said "100 percent" a sure thing.

But even at this stage, was it already a win?

The FBI changed the name of the report, from the National Gang Threat Assessment to the National Gang Report in 2013. There was no reason given for the switch, at least publicly,

Juggalos did not make the 2013 report, and the 2015 edition also ignored the Juggalos, although there is no evidence that anything had changed in terms of Juggalo conduct.

It was serious enough to report in 2011, but the Feds seem to want everyone to believe that the Juggalo problem, such as it was and is, has fixed itself.

18

Lucille Ball, John Lennon, and the Juggalos

See those Juggalos sitting over there? Ten percent of them are gang members. They aren't really in gangs like the cops know, but they have some kind of game, some kind of thing going on that someone could call gang related. Another ten percent are just losers. They'll try to hustle you, get something over on you. And the other eighty percent are okay. They do it all right and make a living and are truly decent.

—BOB ADAMS, WHO HEADS THE SCRUB CARE UNIT AT
EVERY GATHERING OF THE JUGGALOS,
HANDING OUT FREE WATER AND HOT DOGS TO JUGGALOS

You're basically seeking almost a name-clearing process, aren't you? For the organization?

—US JUSTICE, SIXTH CIRCUIT COURT OF APPEAL,
TO ATTORNEY FOR THE JUGGALOS IN LAWSUIT VS. FBI

Bob Adams is sitting in the shade of one of many single-hitch trailers that have come to the Gathering to hand out free supplies to Juggalos who may have spent their last buck to get to the festival grounds.

There's a guy with a purple and orange mohawk, a black Twiztid T-shirt, and black jeans sitting in a lawn chair just outside the seminar tent, waiting for the state-of-the-Juggalo address from ICP. He is a routinely rough-looking character, brawny with well-worn tattoos flowing from his short-sleeve tee, a thick, black beard with flecks of gray. He's one of those people who may be thirty or in his fifties, and either way there's been some potholes along the way and a few people are missing teeth from those bumps.

"To look at that guy, you'd think he's some kind of meth-dealing crackhead," Adams says. "And that's what he was ten years ago. Not anymore. He has his own business and he loves his old lady."

The "old lady," a plump Juggalette with a shock of hennaed red hair that glows in the afternoon sun, is wrapping a bright yellow bandana around his head to protect it from the sun.

When the FBI came out with its gang report declaring Juggalos a part of a gang, Adams, a fortysomething who works as a social services worker for the state of Missouri, came into work and sat down in his supervisor's office. "Hey, I'm a Juggalo, and if this is going to be some kind of problem, let's get this done now." he told her.

There was no problem, she said. Even state bureaucrats could see the silliness.

Adams speaks in dramatic declarations and vignettes. He is lean and intense, with dark brown hair and a consistent four-day scruff of beard. He wears jeans and a plain T-shirt—no logos—and a walkie-talkie in his hip. Adams came back from serving in the Navy during Desert Storm with a new family, no job, and shitloads of pissed-off fury. He got in fights with both friends and foes. "I was a dipshit," he says.

He scared his family and he loved fantasy expressions, from Star Wars to Rob Zombie. Someone passed him a thrice-dubbed cassette of ICP's *Carnival of Carnage*, and it changed his life.

"It was like a part of my soul had something musical plugged into it," he says. "It had metal, which I loved, it had rap, which I also loved, and it had this twisted sense with a lot of white elephant topics."

Between working two jobs, raising a family, and being a Hurricane Katrina evacuee, he kept picking up ICP releases. Pretty soon his friends starting calling him a Juggalo.

"What's that?" Adams asked. He was directed online, and it was then he realized he was one of them.

While he was moving and shaking to make ends meet, Adams got himself an MBA and a master's in psychology. In 2013 he assembled the Scrub Care Unit after hearing that kids were showing up at the Gathering with just a ticket and the clothes on their back. The Scrub Care Unit took donations from other Juggalos, and next thing you know they were handing out water like it's the first stop at the Badwater Marathon.

And that's where it lands him every summer now. He talks to everyone, a nervous inquisitor, and remembers their stories.

"Look at those two kids," Adams says. He'd met them and talked with them a couple of times in the last day or so. They had no cash. "Now, can you tell me what they are all about?"

Both are in their twenties, and it's pretty simple: they work at McDonald's, live in a small town, and neither owns a functional car. "Close, but there's one more thing," he says. "They both will sell any drug they can get their hands on. They have to hustle."

There's violence, there's theft, and there are some bogus drugs at the Gathering. But the instances of such are so rare that everyone hears about it quickly.

Why?

"Because it's family, and that's not how you treat family," Adams says.

It's also why there are an inordinate number of people whom life has dealt some tough blows. There are people like Sherry Huddleston, forty-seven years old, wearing a Twiztid T-shirt and working in a McDonald's in West Virginia. She finds the "outcast music" and the Juggalos welcome at her station in life.

And there is Travis Mercer, who was eighteen months old in 1993 when he was severely burned in a fire at a rented duplex in Davenport, Iowa. His three-year-old brother, Bradley, was killed in the blaze, which was sparked by a smoke detector in their upstairs bedroom. Travis suffered second- and third-degree burns over half his body, head and face included.

Twenty-two years later, Mercer stood outside the seminar tent in disbelief at his good fortune. The scar tissue forms a sort of mask on his face around his mouth, and his burns are evident in the bright sunlight. He's got a sleeveless shirt on, showing off some crisped, off-brown-colored skin that runs from the top of his wrist on his right arm toward his shoulder. On his Facebook page he wears the same type of shirt. In photos with his family. Now, he says, he has two families. "I'm coming back here every year," he says. It's his first Gathering. "These people have never met me before, and they are already my friends. Everyone is just so good to me."

He'd been into Psychopathic bands since he was fifteen, when a friend played it for him, "and it just hit me right away." No one here gives a fuck about his burns, he says. They treat him like anyone else.

He's with a buddy, Michael Meinharet, whose backpack was taken from their tent the night before. Inside was a hat that he had thrown up on.

"So bad on them," he says, with a smile.

But also inside was a Dark Carnival logo flag from the VIP package he had purchased. He had it autographed by Boondox, and it was to be a gift for his eight-year-old son.

His wife found out about the theft and posted on Facebook, asking for its return. A week later the flag showed up. There was no return address.

The 2015 Gathering is tame as hell. Sure, you have Gathering Gummies coming out of Oregon for $15 a pop, and there's more weed smoking here than in prior years, giving everything a cloudy ganja sheen. People are happy, content in Juggaloland. There's no drama, and for once the focus is purely on the bands and the sideshows.

Most of these folks are now recalling memories, like your parents do when they get together with long-lost relatives. Home movies are now those little things people share on their cell phone. It takes Chuckie Ross back to the days when he was a virgin, and he's glad to tell you about it.

At the 2005 Gathering of the Juggalos in Nelson Ledges Quarry Park in Garrettsville, Ohio, Ross lost his virginity at sixteen. The lucky girl—well, who knows? But the fact that he scored kept Chuck, a muscled kid with close cropped hair, some stubble, a mouth, and an attitude, coming back to the Gathering for seven of the next nine years. He's a member of the Reno Rydas, one of dozens of Juggalo groups that gather ever summer. They hang out shingles on their campsites with area codes, names, and symbols that inevitably include the hatchetman.

So it's summer, and "it's the time I get to see my family," says Ross, who works as a cable guy in Reno, Nevada. "Think about it. How many times do you actually see your best friend? Never often enough. For me this is how life should be—planning a time to see my best friends. I know that every year I get to see them for four days straight."

He found ICP in 1999, when he was ten years old. "But I didn't become a Juggalo until I found the message, in 2002."

And when he says family, he means family—he's conceived two kids at Gatherings after being deflowered.

He took a bus from Reno to Columbus, Ohio, with the mother of his last one. Tay Murphrey and Chuck Ross are the parents of Echo Lotus Ross. The bus took four days, "and it got weird at night on that thing,'" Murphrey says.

They got into Columbus, carrying their camping gear, and hailed a cab. They had the cabbie stop at Walmart for supplies on the way out to Legend Valley. The fare was $130 for the thirty-three-mile ride.

Ross braved a line to get in that is long even by concert standards. You had to wait six hours or more to enter the hallowed grounds, even if you bought a ticket in advance.

In fact, thousands of Juggalos, most of them clutching tickets, stood in the mud, fresh from an overnight downpour, in a withering summer sun, waiting to get their wrist bands, which proves they have that ticket.

Although that sounds like a bit of circular logic meshed with physical hell with a dose of overall frustration—yes, it is—there's something odd about the situation: there's no fighting.

Juggalos, including the Scrub Care Unit, passed out water to each other. Sure, they do it Juggalo style: full sixteen-ounce bottles thrown into the masses, and if you aren't watching, you might catch one to the head. But at least it's wet and you can slake your thirst with it. And apply it to the bump on your nog.

But even though it's hot, everyone just keeps muttering shit about family.

"Yeah, that's exactly what we are—one big dysfunctional family," explains a muscled guy who looks like a *Living Colour* outtake, only with a slim patch of purple and yellow hair atop his otherwise shaved head. He says his one-word name is Freekshow, and you had to believe him because it's stenciled across the back of his red, short-sleeved bowler shirt that reached below his knees. This is his tenth Gathering since 2001, and this time he drove from his home in Tacoma, Washington, where he claims to be in the field of preventative medicine. "For us, we have the Gathering, which is like Woodstock meets Sodom and Gomorrah. And this is something, today, that we get through together."

The conversations run from drugs to . . . drugs. A guy is talking about last year's Gathering, when a "hippie girl" offered him a snort of something powdered and yellow. After he indulged, she bid him farewell and advised him to "be safe." It was an odd warning, he thought. Until he spent the evening huddled in his sleeping bag with some serious terrors and a heartbeat that wouldn't stop. "I guess I should have known better," he says. "The guy who sold me four hits of acid the day before didn't tell me to be safe."

Oh, they gripe. Once the line reaches the sight line of the single portable trailer and the three people who were—slowly—handing out the admission bracelets, it's on.

"I've never been in a line this long—not even at Walmart," barks a chunky gentleman into a portable megaphone, the kind you can buy at Walmart. "It's like being at the DMV—three people, a thousand waiting."

Although bunches of those in line were veterans of the Gathering, some with ten or more under their belts, Sahara Stewart, from Madison, Indiana, was hitting her first. "I'm not sure it's worth this," Stewart muses. She's one of the most unfortunate—a fair-skinned patron turning several shades of pink, her first memento of life as a follower of Psychopathic Records, the label operated by Insane Clown Posse, which presents the four-day festival.

She'll get used to it.

At least 60 percent of the people who attend the 2015 Gathering are repeaters. The media presence is down and overall attendance is up because, as almost everyone notes, there are a lot of new faces.

The crowd is larger too—the largest in five years, well up from last year's forty-five hundred. That's because ICP, through courage, longevity, and skill, is finally getting a bit of love from the world. More people at the four-day Gathering, some solid record sales, and an even-handed interview with *Rolling Stone*. It seems like even the Internal Revenue Service keeps the Gathering of the Juggalos on its calendar.

On July 15, exactly one week before day one of the Gathering, the Internal Revenue Service filed a court order to force Shaggy to turn over documents related to $162,417 in back taxes allegedly owed for 2011 and 2012. And on the same day, the US Attorney's Office filed an order to force Psychopathic Records to turn over financial records. The IRS is investigating the label's tax liability for 2012 and 2013.

The timing was curious, at the least.

"Clearly, [the IRS] is trying to get some publicity," Jerry Abraham, a former IRS agent, told the *Detroit News*.

Really, imagine, after all this, that one federal agency is piggybacking on the Juggalos to get some press while the FBI tries to defend itself from allegations that it is abridging the Constitution.

That came in June 2015. The two sides argued their fifteen minutes in front of the Sixth Circuit Court of Appeals in Cincinnati.

They came in after one more year of law enforcement propaganda regarding Juggalos, showing that the gang designation was still leading to mislabeling. A piece on PoliceOne.com that ran a few weeks after the judge in Detroit had dismissed the case was titled, "Three Things Cops Need to Know About Juggalos."

> Law enforcement professionals should be aware that this group routinely attracts members who come from difficult lives filled with trauma, parental neglect and, in many cases, serious mental disorders.
>
> This combination makes them easily manipulated by their leadership of radical organizations such as the Juggalos who have for the past several decades used these groups as recruiting centers.

The courtroom of the Sixth Circuit is carpeted in a floral red that could easily find itself in favor on a Juggalo's T-shirt. The walls are wood paneled, and at the back of the room are large portraits of justices from the past.

In 2012 the Sixth Circuit became the federal justice system's most reversed appeals court, meaning that its rulings were the ones most frequently overruled by the US Supreme Court, being given nasty legal smackdowns. Still, a victory in the conservatively tilted tribunal would be a giant leap forward in the legal quest.

In a brief filed before the hearing the Juggalo legal team wrote that the Department of Justice still

> maintains a digital warehouse containing Juggalo data that—by Congressional design—plays a leading role in law enforcement's identification of gang members. The warehouse includes an encyclopedia of gang images and a database of materials cataloging distinctive First Amendment-protected Juggalo symbols such as the hatchetman logo and other ICP-related symbols and other information about these music fans. . . . Within these materials, the DOJ does not provide any way for law enforcement to distinguish the vast majority of law-abiding Juggalos from the purported "subsets" of gang members. Now, the DOJ suggests only a circular definition that the good Juggalos are the ones who don't commit gang-related crimes.

Saura Sahu's opening on Thursday, June 18, was dead on: "Every once in a while, in all of the amazing and laudable work that the Department of Justice does, from time to time they stray and they target partisan entertainers and their fans," he said. "Happened to Lucille Ball, happened to John Lennon, happened to newscaster Mike Wallace. Happened to the Grateful Dead, happened to KISS fans in the late seventies and early eighties, that threatening group. And now it's happening to the music band the Insane Clown Posse and their fans, the Juggalos. The Department of Justice's hybrid gang rule burdens the rights of over a million people, in the Department of Justice's own words, based on the actions of a few."

The justices frequently stopped Sahu to ask their own questions, forcing him to depart from his organized presentation. In general, his best work is done within a defined framework. But this played to another strength—he can wing it.

He was asked whether any Juggalos were, in fact, involved in activity described by the FBI, primarily violent crimes.

"No, just like any million police officers or any million church members, we don't dispute that some absolutely minor fraction of that group of people has done bad things," Sahu said.

He urged the court to examine the method under which the FBI classified the Juggalos and how it affected the First Amendment right of freedom of expression. "We're not challenging the finding that maybe eight people someplace in Idaho are acting as criminal street gang and bearing the name Juggalo for reasons that are out of our control," Sahu said. "We are disputing things about the process that the DOJ has undergone to announce to the world that Juggalos are, in some broad fashion, a gang."

Arguing for the Department of Justice and the FBI, Amy Powell was replaced by Lindsey Powell for the Feds (no relation). She, like her predecessor, argued that the gang designation caused no harm to Juggalos. The claim aroused the court.

"You believe there's absolutely no harm, but, not to be facetious, but could you pass the FBI background check and be in your job if you were a member of the Juggalos?" US District Judge Edmund Sargus asked Powell.

It was the first time a federal judge ever uttered the word "Juggalos" in a context that could be construed as positive.

"Aah, I have no reason to think that I, I could not your honor," Powell stammered.

✝ ✝ ✝

Titus Martell stood in the doorway of a Dollar Tree in Heath, Ohio, with a simple question. "You have Faygo?" he asked the manager, who happened to be walking by the door when he came in.

Martell, thirty, is a burly, bearded man with multicolored hair and a bit of a stare. Around his neck dangles a tangle of charms and trinkets, not the least in importance is the treasured hatchetman amulet.

"No, we don't carry it," came the answer. "Giant Eagle does."

Jennifer, the cashier, scoffed under her breath. "Why would anyone want Faygo?" she muttered. "It costs sixty cents a two-liter."

Because Faygo peels paint in the right doses and flies off the stage in cannons during an ICP set? That's a hard one to explain to a Dollar Tree cashier in Ohio.

Martell traveled sixteen hundred miles from Billings, Montana, in a van with a half-dozen others, give or take a few who were dropped off to visit friends or relatives along the way. And now he needed some Faygo in a little town down the road a piece from Legend Valley.

"Nothing but diet, except for ginger ale," came the report from the Giant Eagle.

That's no good for the Jungallo Juice. Faygo's Ohana Punch is a key ingredient. "It's a mix of Captain Morgan Black Flag, fruit, Everclear," Martell explained, "and Ohana Punch."

When Psychopathic announced that Martell and thousands like him would be coming back in 2015 for another Gathering, there was no resistance. Local hotels even asked them to come back.

Rose Mary Elson, who manages the Shell station and convenience store next to Legend Valley, made a pre-Gathering hoarding of Faygo from a distributor in Columbus, which stacked over six feet high in a colorful mountain of plastic bottles. She doesn't even carry it the rest of the year. "I sold more Faygo than I did beer last year," said Elson. The Gathering days last year tripled her daily sales, even compared to other events.

Inside the gates the usual festival antics went down, although the guys have kept their nipples on, unlike 2013, when Adam Roberts had one of his removed.

Techno band Flosstradamus defied some of its fans when it agreed to play the Gathering in 2015. After it announced the deal in May on Instagram, some claimed to call it quits on Flosstradamus.

"Well, its been cool being a fan . . . but I think this is the end," one posted.

"goodbye flosstradamus you officially suck now," wrote another.

"career suicide . . . " said one more.

Others just used the post as another reason to hate.

"give me 3 reasons why it's not a cult," posted one.

It was one more instance of any artist's connection to ICP being powerfully disparaged, as it was when Jack White produced an ICP single for his Third Man label. One way-too-serious White fan went ahead and summed it all up in a post on Stereogum: "this is the biggest setback to human civilization since Hitler," followed by someone else's idea that "I'm pretty sure that Jack is fucking with us."

In the case of Flosstradamus, the band responded with its own post:

> Our mission statement is to bring our sound and vision to every corner of the world. Whether its at Coachella or the Gathering we are going to turn the fuck up because honestly . . . we dont give a fuck.

In the opening minutes of the set DJ J2K, aka Josh Young, caught a rock with his face. It was a shot under the left eye, and blood flowed for the whole set.

As Flosstradamus ended, Young addressed the crowd and noted that they handled the shit they got for signing on, but "when we started this set some asshole hit me in the face with a rock," he said. "Fuck that motherfucker. Everyone else is cool."

The packed pit went crazy for him.

Young then exhorted the crowd to make the peace sign and fly it high. That's how he left everyone. The crowd knowing that one of their own—once again—had, as Juggalos put it, "fucked up." This time, however, the Juggalos didn't earn the everlasting scorn of the one who bore the brunt of that act.

But for years now they have had to shoulder many people's sweeping judgment because some among them, who share the same taste for music, considered outside the average, have committed crimes.

People could get dubbed gang members for something like that these days.

EPILOGUE: WRAP

I feel the rumblings of the Juggalo March on DC, that's all I'm saying. We're waiting for the right time, but it's coming like a fuckin' dark storm.

—JUMPSTEADY, AKA ROB BRUCE,
PSYCHOPATHIC HONCHO, FEBRUARY 2015

If this was political, it'd be a real threat. They'd shut it down.

—ICE T, ON THE GATHERING

The idea of a Juggalo march on Washington is so enticing, it's hard to imagine. There are plenty of marches, protests, demonstrations, and rallies along the Washington Mall every year. For $120—check, credit card, or money order—you ask the National Mall and Memorial Parks division of the National Parks Service to review your application, and you should be in.

The thought of even thousands of Juggalos—let alone tens of thousands—emerging from the DC Metro and doing their thing on those hallowed grounds strikes some fear into some hearts, no doubt. But if the case against the FBI is turned back at the appellate court level, the last place to try is the US Supreme Court, and "we'll go as far as we have to take it," Shaggy says.

If that were the case, consider the march a done deal. "If we go to the Supreme fucking Court, Psychopathic Records is gonna organize a march on Washington," J told hundreds of Juggalos under the blue and white canvas big top at the 2015 Gathering during the annual ICP seminar. "And it's gonna end with a jelly-candied free concert at the end of the night."

The crowd went nuts with the whoops, even the three hundred people who stood outside the tent in the sun. To sound Washingtonian, J was speaking in the line-pause-line cadence of a Hillary Trump, coming down hard on every third word.

"If we march on Washington, who's coming?"

Wild cheers.

"Who's gonna make the road trip?"

Hands waving, more cheers.

"That's what the fuck we're talking about."

And the concert. The Faygo would be tricky, for sure. But to follow in the path of the Beach Boys, one of J's all-time favorites, would be something. They'd also be trailing Bob Dylan, the Flaming Lips, Metallica, Britney Spears—the show would be something that even the khaki-and-loafered Beltway pundits could not resist writing about.

The best part might be the wait on the courthouse steps, where Juggalos could gather while the suits inside discuss whether the Feds did take a leap over the Constitution when they dragged the Juggalos into the whole gang mess.

And what if the application to match were denied? Few have been. The Boy Scouts, the Ku Klux Klan, a batch of rabbis, and the Black Panthers have all been allowed to take to the mall. More recently, though, things have changed, as they might if the presence of opposing groups might get ugly.

A batch of bikers was denied a license to gather in 2013. The 2 Million Bikers to DC team applied as a counter to the Million Muslim

March. They presented themselves as concerned Americans who just happened to ride motorcycles and wanted to get together on the exact same day, September 11, as this group of Muslims.

It is unlikely that the Juggalos would be denied. Who knows what would happen if they were?

✦ ✦ ✦

Text message to me, September 17, 2015, 11:03 a.m.: "We won the appeal!"

It came from Farris Haddad, Juggalo lawyer and part of the team representing the Juggalos against the FBI.

Twelve minutes later Psychopathic flack J-Webb texted: "We won the appeal today. I have no specific info, but we won that bitch. Call Farris later."

It was true. The Sixth Circuit Court of Appeals in Cincinnati agreed with the Juggalos and reversed the prior court decision to dismiss the case. They had suffered, and they had enough standing to move the case forward against the FBI. The case would go back to the original court and be heard again, only this time with the dictates of the higher court in place.

Saura Sahu called a little later. He was in heaven, and reasonably so. Victory does that. "It's just an amazing thing that this court agreed with us, what we have said all along, that there were damages suffered as a consequence of this wrongful designation," Sahu said. He sounded like he was rehearsing sound bites. But his jubilance was refreshing. Even on a good day he's a closed-down, suspicious guy.

The opinion was an inadvertent talking-points memo for Insane Clown Posse and its hope to exonerate the Juggalos. "The group is well known for elaborate live performances and has enjoyed substantial commercial success," the justices noted.

It went on to talk about the report: "From its publication through at least the time of the filing of the Complaint in this case, the 2011 NGIC Report has been available to the general public on the NGIC website."

The ruling outlined the damages incurred by Parsons, Hellin, Bradley, and Gandy as well as ICP, citing the canceled Hallowicked show in Royal Oak in 2012. In arriving at its conclusion, the justices cited numerous cases involving different parties, including the National Rifle Association, the Adult Video Association, Amnesty International—even the Citizens United case gets a name check.

The court noted that the damages ICP presented were, in fact, real and that the gang designation certainly did have a "chilling effect" on the band's activities. Taking that a step further, it found that "the Juggalos' allegations that their First Amendment rights are being chilled are accompanied by allegations of concrete reputational injuries resulting in allegedly improper stops, detentions, interrogations, searches, denial of employment, and interference with contractual relations. Stigmatization also constitutes an injury in fact for standing purposes. . . . The Juggalos' allegations link the 2011 . . . report to their injuries by stating that the law enforcement officials themselves acknowledged that the DOJ gang designation had caused them to take the actions in question."

The case was ordered back to the courtroom of Judge Robert Cleland.

Not a single justice dissented. If the courtroom was the Gathering and the FBI were sitting there, a tribe of Juggalos would start the chant: "You fucked up."

Because ya know everything icp does from now on is either for money or just plain stale.

U all realize these dudes are old enough to be ur grandfather. And living pretty comfortably on ur money. But it's "family" tho. Lmao

Dude those albums we're trash how bad are the outtakes? Please just sell Psychopathic to Twiztid and retire. Being a juggalo now is a fucking joke.

—Various comments from around Facebook, 2015

It's the beginning of the end of a defining chapter of Juggalos and the Insane Clown Posse. The courtroom is the last place anyone would have thought the crossroads would be for the Juggalos, unless maybe it were a criminal or traffic court.

Psychopathic has spent tens of thousands of dollars in legal fees, and that's taking into account the generous work of the ACLU and some of the other counselors working on behalf of the Juggalos.

Juggalos are now used in Internet headers as click-bait, and you can sell any publication on a Juggalo story. It is the start of the mainstreaming of the Juggalos.

On a sunny spring afternoon the boys sit around the first floor of Psychopathic headquarters, watching a video on a laptop. There's Shaggy, J and a couple of warehouse guys in the studio control room while others filter in and out of the studio, up and down the stairs. The place is jamming with busy.

It smells like weed, and sitting in the middle of it all, J looks blown out. He's been working crazy hours, finishing a double-package LP, *The Marvelous Missing Link* (Lost) and *The Marvelous Missing Link* (*Found*). Really, he looks wacked, with his eyes red and his face drawn. Even his tats look tired. How long can you hang on like that, when the work becomes a physical burden?

The conversation turns to the future and what would happen if the world defied the odds and began to embrace Juggalos. "Now you can hear the name ICP dropped by Stephen Colbert," J says.

"But if we sold more records, the only thing that would happen is that we would have cooler videos, cooler stage sets, and have money to do cooler things on tour. But nothing would change the sound of the music. That is number one."

It's an old story but a little easier to believe when you think about the outsider, pariah status ICP has had to manage. Sure, it's given them spoils. Moms got cars and houses, kids got college paid for before they even hit ten years old, and friends got lifetime jobs.

But how can you be sure the music, which is what Juggalos care most about, can stay pure?

"I may not be what I was fifteen years ago, physically," J says. "We as people may not live up to people's expectations, but ICP, when you close your eyes and listen, that is number one. There will be no pop producer coming in and telling us how to make music and, 'Can you do more of this?' and 'What everyone wants is more dubstep because that's what everybody is listening to now.' It's just not going to happen.

"But good things happen for us. Cool articles have come out in papers that are big, and there is something of a change of heart. People are like 'These guys have been around a long time—I'm going to look into them.'"

He's concerned about aging only to the degree that it affects what he and Shaggy can deliver. He's fought with his weight since the late nineties. He's seen a shrink, taken a number of anxiety meds, and gobbled Nyquil by the case over the years just to get some sleep.

Shaggy, for his part, developed a serious drinking problem that he's battled over the years, including some stints in rehab.

"Age is something that is harder inside," J says. "I'd like to be in better shape. My wife tells me I should shut up about it, and I probably do worry about it more than I should. I say something like they're probably thinking, 'Look how old he is,' and she'll tell me to shut up. Or I think they're probably thinking 'Your voice don't sound the same.' But it's nothing like a thought of 'Should I quit?' or 'Am I useless?' We know we're still hot. We move over one hundred thousand units, and to do that in 2014, that shit's good. But we're just never going to stop. I know we're going to be one of those bands that's going to be old as fuck. A lot of bands hate each other, and they have to take years off to get away from each other. But me and Shaggy love each other."

They did two seasons of a show, *Insane Clown Posse Theater*, on Fuse network. Of course, Juggalos loved it and ratings were decent, but they weren't good enough to keep it moving. It was their first real entry into what could be called network TV, such as it is. Fuse was sold to another network, and ICP theater was never canceled, but a third season remains to be seen.

It wasn't the first time ICP brushed up against the mainstream. When VH1 came calling about a possible reality show, one of the first things the producers asked about was strife between the two.

"We said there was none, and that was the end of the show," Shaggy says.

"**Well, the music** has changed," says Ma Bruce. She's musing on her son's band like a critic and spiritual adviser at the same time. "Like the sixth Joker's Card, *The Wraith*, had a message, and anyone real close knew that was about going to hell, and I was worried about Joe's soul."

She told him that one day.

"Kids that don't have a mom or a dad or have other problems. They're listening, and maybe this is the only thing they listen to, and that's where you get into trouble," she said to her son, sounding eerily like any number of so-called Juggalo gang experts. "They don't know the fantasy parts. And when you are pointing out the ills of the world without offering a solution, kids take this to heart. There is accountability for everything when you make music like this."

Today she acknowledges, "There are kids who actually think Joe is a wicked clown."

This can't be all that easy for a woman who sent her kids to church and made sure God was in their house. "He told me, 'Mom, there's going to be an end to the Joker's Cards, and we're going to reveal that this is a message from God. First, you have to get them to listen.' It took a long time, but all the Joker's Cards point in that direction."

When the money started to flow, her son bought her and her husband a Town & Country van. "It had the cool doors that open automatically on the side," Linda says. "He bought us a house, and when we got older we moved into a condo and I told him, 'That money you gave us is still here,' because we paid cash for the condo off the house."

Linda's not crazy about the violence that has gotten so much of the attention, but she's still astounded at the success her son has achieved. "I take no credit at all for that," she says. "There are songs on every album that are violence for the sake of violence, but then again there are songs where I think, 'He's a genius.' And I can't get over that my son did that."

She still recalls when she realized he and his boyhood pal Joey were bigger than just a local hit. "It was when my dad knew," she says. "I went to see my dad, and he was always hanging out with these guys who would work on cars, and one of the guy's sons came to visit him one summer. He was there, and my dad mentioned ICP, and this kid went nuts. 'You mean you're the grandfather of ICP?' So my dad was telling me that this kid lives down south and knows who Joe is."

At every Gathering there is a moment when the virgins are called to the front of the seminar tent.

Their virginity pertains to their first time at the Gathering, and there is no ceremony, no prize, and no special accommodation except for accepting whoops all around.

These are the newcomers to Juggalodom. Like Beau Lewis, who will, in the next couple of years, be called to the front and fussed over for half a second. He's nineteen, from Kent, Washington, and has been into ICP since he was eleven years old and in the sixth grade. A group of kids were messing around in class on a computer and hacked through the firewall that keeps them from hitting sites that might unduly influence the youth of tomorrow. He loved it.

Lewis has ten Psychopathic shirts, which were a chore to accumulate. His mom, after hearing Juggalos were a gang, refused to allow him to have any merch and tossed out anything she found. He moved out.

When ICP came to Silverdale, an hour from Lewis, for an in-store autograph session, Lewis was among those in the line that snaked around the block. "We got there at noon, and it started at seven," Lewis says.

It was his first time meeting ICP, and he sat at the front of that line for seven hours. When it came his turn, and there were J and Shaggy in the paint, he was struck dumb. "I opened my mouth to talk and I couldn't speak," he says. "I was hyperventilating. My heart was beating like crazy. It was surreal. It was like they were real people. They helped me through it."

What he got out: "I was little when I started listening, was bullied as a kid and didn't respect myself and took to heart what people would say about me. But when I started listening to ICP, hearing not to give a fuck about what anyone thinks about you, it gave me self-confidence. And I want to thank you for inspiring me to do better for myself."

He's the next generation of Juggalo, much like the first. Starting young, they don't have a lot going: Lewis is unemployed, a credit shy of his high school diploma—"I had a hard patch"—and lives in a room with his girlfriend with her aunt and uncle. She has a job at Old Navy.

They are the future of something, but no one can tell what right now.

ACKNOWLEDGMENTS

Thanks to Farris Haddad, the Juggalo lawyer; Rich Tupica, social media brainiac; and Scottie D at Faygoluvers.net.

Thanks also to the folks at Psychopathic. It's a small indy label with a big heart, as has been the legend of labels that choose not to get in bed with the industry. J-Webb for his good ideas and his support, George Vlahakis, Hazin, Jason Shaltz, Mike E. Clark, and Joel Fragomeni/Upchuck the Clown. Also to Bernard Plaskett, the Las Vegas gang detective who was cool enough to sit down and talk about Juggalos and defend his view when all others refused.

Additional thanks to Ben Schafer at Da Capo, David Patterson, Small Mouse, Boyd and Julie, Brian Bowe, the Fix, and The Big Black Dog.

NOTES

The reporting for Juggalo includes interviews done over three years, some conducted formally in a sit down or arranged phone contact and others done on location or in otherwise crowded circumstances. All interviews were recorded either by note or tape, and in some cases, both. Several interviews were done on background/off-the-record with sensitive sources who did not want their name used in this book.

CHAPTER 2

17   *Juggalos are ICP's insanely devoted*: James Grainger, review of "I Am Sorry to Think I Have Raised a Timid Son by Kent Russell," *The Star* (Toronto), April 4, 2015, http://www.thestar.com /entertainment/books/2015/04/04/i-am-sorry-to-think-i-have -raised-a-timid-son-by-kent-russell-review.html.

CHAPTER 3

43   **The *Telegraph* in Nashua published a post:** Andrew Wolfe, "'Horrorcore'" Rap Fans Increasingly Inspired to Violence," *Telegraph*, October 16, 2009, www.nashuatelegraph.com/news /386727-196/horrorcore-rap-fans-increasingly-inspired-to -violence.html.

48   **To them, "a longhair was a longhair.":** Frank Kusch, *Battleground Chicago: The Police and the 1968 Democratic National Convention* (Westport, CT: Praeger, 2004), p. 49.

CHAPTER 5

73   **"My childhood was without a doubt the greatest time of my life.":** Violent J interview, date unknown, Angelfire Juggalo site http://www.angelfire.com/oh2/juggalos/alonewviolentj1.html.

CHAPTER 6

95   **"The Hollywood Records guys didn't know about rock and roll":** Mark Yarm, *Everybody Loves Our Town: An Oral History of Grunge* (New York: Crown Archetype, 2011).

CHAPTER 7

108   **"There was a guy named Link Wray":** Iggy Pop on *The Colbert Report*, Comedy Central, April 29, 2013.

113   **Several months later a six-person jury:** Mike Clary, "Jurors Acquit 2 Live Crew in Obscenity Case," *Los Angeles Times*, October 21, 1990, http://articles.latimes.com/1990-10-21/news/mn -4279_1_live-crew.

113   **Meanwhile a three-judge panel:** Chuck Phillips, "Appeals Court Voids Obscenity Ruling on 2 Live Crew Album," *Los Angeles Times*, May 8, 1992, http://articles.latimes.com/1992-05-08/news /mn-1911_1_live-crew.

CHAPTER 8

117   **"Even if the killers left notes in their bedrooms":** Associated Press, "Group Insane Clown Posse Plays Off Growing Criticism," *Lubbock Avalanche-Journal*, July 16, 1999, http://lubbockonline .com/stories/071699/ent_0716990096.shtml#.VsORDLQrLDc.

120   **"A hole was punched in Mr. Amphibian's hat":** "Posse's Fans Cost $54,000 in Local Services," *The Blade*, July 26, 2001, www .toledoblade.com/local/2001/07/26/Posse-s-fans-cost-54-000 -in-local-services.html.

122 "considerably ironic coming from supposed First Amendment martyrs.": Mike Rubin and Mark Dancey, letter to editor, *Spin*, April 1998, 33.

CHAPTER 9

134 **270 requests for $19 million in funding:** Midwest Atlantic Gang Resistance Education and Training (G.R.E.A.T.), "FY2009 G.R.E.A.T. Funding Update," Newsletter, Winter 2009, www .great-online.org/documents/PDF/Newsletters/MW/MWA _V4_I3.pdf.

134 **DARE is a cash cow:** Jonathan Riskind, "[D.A.R.E.'s] Program's Cost Soars Past $1 Billion with Little Accounting," *Center for Educational Research and Development*, June 30, 2002.

134 **kids are more likely to get high *after* going through DARE classes.:** Natalie Wolchover, "Was DARE Effective?" LiveScience. com, March 27, 2012, www.livescience.com/33795-effective.html.

136 **Walker told jurors that he read some of Fritts's journals:** *State of Tennessee v. Robert Edward Fritts*, Appeal from the Circuit Court for Anderson County (Tennessee), No. A7CR0219, Donald R. Elledge, Judge No. E2012-02233-CCA-R3-CD, filed February 10, 2014.

CHAPTER 12

190 **Oklahoma millionaire Roger Wheeler was murdered in 1981:** Bryan Robinson, "Families Sue Boston FBI for $600 Million," *ABC News*, May 14, 2001, http://abcnews.go.com/US/ story?id=93310.

197 **Online, police chatrooms were alive:** Comment from reader, "Insane Clown Posse Threatens to Sue FBI Over Juggalo Gang Label," Policemag.com, August 14, 2012, www.policemag.com /channel/gangs/news/2012/08/14/insane-clown-posse-threatens -to-sue-fbi-over-juggalo-gang-label.aspx.

198   **Ten days before the Gathering:** Sam Levin, "Photo: This Is the
Scariest Mugshot We've Seen in a Really Long Time," *Riverfront
Times*, March 8, 2013, www.riverfronttimes.com/newsblog
/2013/03/08/photo-this-is-the-scariest-mugshot-weve-seen
-in-a-really-long-time.

INDEX